THE FUNDAMENTAL PROBLEMS OF WESTERN METAPHYSICS

Xavier Zubiri

Translated by Joaquín Redondo

Translation Critically Revised by Thomas Fowler

This translation was made possible by a grant
from the Spanish Ministry of Culture

University Press of America,® Inc.
Lanham · Boulder · New York · Toronto · Plymouth, UK

**Copyright © 2010 by
University Press of America,® Inc.**
4501 Forbes Boulevard
Suite 200
Lanham, Maryland 20706
UPA Acquisitions Department (301) 459-3366

Estover Road
Plymouth PL6 7PY
United Kingdom

Library of Congress Control Number: 2009936082
ISBN: 978-0-7618-4877-6 (paperback : alk. paper)
eISBN: 978-0-7618-4879-0

Co-published by arrangement with
the Xavier Zubiri Foundation of North America

The Fundamental Problems of Western Metaphysics is a translation of *Los problemas fundamentales de la metafísica occidental*, published by Alianza Editorial/Fundación Xavier Zubiri, Madrid, 1994. This translation is published by agreement with the publisher and copyright holder of the Spanish original.

CONTENTS

TRANSLATORS' INTRODUCTION

This book introduces the profound reflections of Xavier Zubiri (1898-1983) on the history of philosophy to English-speaking audiences. As a philosopher who in many ways rethought all of philosophy and much of theology, Zubiri felt it necessary to be in continuous dialogue with earlier thinkers. The present work and others that he wrote dealing with the history of philosophy stem from that need, and show how seriously Zubiri took all philosophers and philosophical systems. The theme of the book is the transcendental in Western philosophy, and how a firm grasp of it reveals underlying unity in the philosophers considered, but also fundamental problems that Zubiri believes require a complete rethinking of certain basic notions and theories. Zubiri sketches this in the Conclusion; a thorough treatment may be found in his major work, *Sentient Intelligence*.

In this Translators' Introduction we shall not attempt to summarize the book; that is done briefly in the Editor's Introduction, and in any case Zubiri's own text speaks quite eloquently, so little in the way of summary is required. Nonetheless we may observe that in some respects the presentation (and the selection of philosophers) may seem strange to a culture steeped in the empiricist tradition, as is that of the Anglo-Saxon world. Hegel, for instance, is rarely taken seriously any longer in that world. Zubiri, however, shows how Hegel's thought is indeed part of a tradition with a unity that is key to a deep understanding of Western philosophy. Accordingly, we believe that many will find Zubiri's point of view, the depth of his analysis, and the breadth of his thought quite refreshing and insightful.

This is a very serious book that will require some effort on the part of the reader—effort that will be repaid in terms of new insights into philosophy and metaphysics. The book is *not* an introduction to metaphysics or philosophy, intended for beginners. Its audience is that group of people who have a serious interest in the history of philosophy and the fundamental problems that have driven it for two and a half millennia.

With respect to the translation itself, we have stayed close to the original Spanish text, while at the same time attempting to produce a readable English version. But as any student of philosophy is aware, there are hard limits to this task, especially in the case of a philosopher whose ideas are very radical and original, and who consequently must utilize many neologisms and employ words in an almost poetical fashion with respect to their meaning. To assist the reader, English neologisms have been kept to a minimum, and footnotes are used to explain terms and concepts that might not be immediately clear to those in the English-speaking world. Pleonasms (common in Spanish) have been removed, and in some cases repetitive sentences (of the type used for emphasis in oral presentations) have been deleted as such repetition sounds odd and can be confusing in printed English text. To facilitate reference back to the original Spanish edition, the pagination of that original is indicated by numbers in curly braces, e.g., {25}.

EDITOR'S INTRODUCTION

The present volume is the seminar *Los problemas fundamentales de la metafísica occidental* [The Fundamental Problems of Western Metaphysics], which Zubiri gave in twelve sessions during the academic year 1969-1970 at the *Sociedad de Estudios y Publicaciones*, Madrid. It belongs, therefore, to the period when Zubiri's thought had reached its maturity.

A few months earlier, in March of 1969, Zubiri had given a brief seminar in two sessions entitled *Estructura de la metafísica* [Structure of Metaphysics], which is a preparation for and complement to the one published here. That seminar consists of two parts: an historical first part, which presents in a very compressed way the same historical material covered in the present text, and a systematic second part, which presents in greater detail what will be covered in the last chapter of the present work.

The seminar we present here has several peculiarities. Although Zubiri held the chair of History of Philosophy from 1926 to 1942, the dominant tone and basic objective of his enterprise has a distinctive theoretical accent, something that is ever more patent in his mature works. It is true that in our time the great majority of "theoretical" philosophies are accompanied with {ii} developments and perspectives confronting earlier philosophies—at least some of the issues considered important—and Zubiri is no exception. In his theoretical works we find numerous historical references, but in that context very schematic references almost always appear as critical differences with respect to his own thought. In this sense, Zubiri's references tend to return over and over to a few authors, and they do so with such determination that it seems to suggest an interpretation of the history of philosophy different from the usual one. The present seminar could also be understood as the explicit presentation of those interpretations and therefore as an elaboration and ground of what in the theoretical works appear as schematic references.

With the title *Cinco lecciones de filosofía* [Five Philosophy Lectures], Zubiri had published another seminar in 1963. In it he analyzed several historical variations of the concept of "philosophy" in some important philosophers, such as Aristotle, Kant, Comte, Bergson, and Husserl (with some additions on Dilthey and Heidegger), a selection that Zubiri himself considered "absolutely arbitrary." That "arbitrariness" does not appear to concern the *importance* of the chosen authors, but rather the *incompleteness* of the selection, since in the last prologue (1980) that Zubiri wrote for that work he said, "An adequate exposition should cover many other thinkers. Actually, in one of my other seminars I have attempted to add four other authors to the five covered in this present work: St. Thomas, Descartes, Leibniz, and Hegel. Perhaps some day I may decide to publish these studies."

Zubiri clearly refers to the seminar that we now present, the continuity of which with the previous one is established {iii} by the author. This means that the present seminar has an expository level and in it Zubiri develops what he deems central in the thought of six authors whom he considers quite important at different stages of Western thought. The "techniques" of his exposition are common. Taking as a guide a central text of an author there is an effort to present the structural coherence of the author's thought. Here again we find the great expository qualities of Zubiri that unite both clarity and maximum rigor. Those qualities, which garnered so many readers for *Cinco lecciones de filosofía*, will continue to do so for this seminar, which however, deals with some very complex issues. Obviously, Zubiri's expositions can and should be contrasted with the contributions of historical criticism in each particular case.

But what is most remarkable in this seminar is the presence of another stratum, which no doubt is more original and will interest those who know Zubiri. The expositions mentioned are framed within a conceptualization, pointedly theoretical, of the basic substratum on which Western philosophy is nurtured. Such a substratum, not visible at first sight, is what surfaces in light of Zubiri's own philosophy. According to it, Western philosophy appears as a progressively accentuated deviation, which Zubiri calls the *entification of reality*, resting on a base where we can discover a progressive *logification of intelligence*, culminating in the total primacy of the "conceptive intelligence" in Hegel. The present seminar is the detailed development of this notion of the "entification" of reality with its consequent "logification" of intelligence, which together form the backdrop against which Zubiri expounds his mature philosophy.

With this we are able to understand not only the numerous and important critical observations about the authors presented, but also {iv} the fact that the seminar begins with a highly theoretical treatment. This is done in order to define "the fundamental problems of Western metaphysics" or perhaps it might be better to say "the problematic ground of Western metaphysics." For this reason, the seminar does not end with Hegel, the philosopher that carried this trend to its maximum; Zubiri adds an important "conclusion" outlining his doctrine of sentient intelligence, which tries to offer a positive correction to that basic deviation.

This last point is of great importance to those interested in Zubiri. We are presented with a broad outline of what later will be developed in his trilogy *Inteligencia sentiente* [Sentient Intelligence], and therefore is an important document concerning the development of this topic in Zubiri's work. To confirm this, one has only to compare the broad outline in this volume with the article *Notas sobre la inteligencia humana* [Notes on Human Intelligence], published in 1967-1968, which clearly shows a close relationship to the treatment given to the subject here. This allows us to document thoughout the entire course of Zubiri's philosophy how basic the issue of sentient intelligence is, and also permits us to document the progress of its elaboration, which only culminated with *Sentient Intelligence*, which incorporated many important precisions over points he had held prior to it.

As a whole, the present book makes two things clear. In the first place, it reveals the historical line that nurtured and inspired Zubiri's mature philosophy, endowing it with its full measure of radicalness, and filling in its numerous lacunae. In the second place, it shows the broad profile of Western thought—at least, such as Zubiri believes it to be—from the heights reached by his mature philosophy. Without doubt, this will contribute to clarify several points of the thought of the philosopher.

Although it does not appear that Zubiri had seriously thought {v} about publishing this material during his lifetime, he did carefully review the original transcript, which shows signs of having been revised throughout his lifetime. Not just stylistic corrections (this aspect appears to be somewhat ignored), but additions and changes were made to incorporate greater precision. There exists a reorganization of the whole seminar by means of a later detailed table of contents penned by Zubiri, which makes the work much more systematic. That reorganization is the one we have used for this edition.

My heartfelt thanks to Carmen Castro de Zubiri for her interest in the publication of this seminar, her valuable help in the reading of many additions, and the identification of some quotations. My thanks also to the *Fundación Xavier Zubiri*, Madrid, particularly to Asunción Medinaveitia, for the help she provided to me. Diego Gracia read and carefully corrected the first draft of the manuscript, contributing important improvements in every respect. J. Antonio Martínez Martínez reviewed the chapter on Descartes.

Antonio Pintor-Ramos

{11}

AUTHOR'S INTRODUCTION

On the following pages we are going to be dealing with *The Fundamental Problems of Western Metaphysics*.

The title may seem clear enough, but in reality the subject is rather obscure. Hence, to delimit the problem, it is useful to comment on the four terms involved: "problems," "fundamental," "metaphysics," and "Western." What do we understand by "Western"? What do we understand by "metaphysics"? What do we understand by "fundamental"? And what are those fundamental "problems" to which our reflections are going to be dedicated throughout this entire exposition?

I. *East and West*

To begin, what is *Western*? Western, for geographic reasons, obviously is the opposite of *Eastern*. And we may ask—quite reasonably—to what kind of "Eastern" are we referring when talking about Western metaphysics?

1) In the first place, of course, we refer to what is opposed to Eastern in the sense of the Asiatic east, primarily India. {12} We are not going to be concerned with Indian metaphysics for one fundamental reason: not any lack of interest in Indian thought, but because there is always some kind of equivocation when discussing "Indian metaphysics." Something analogous happens when books are written about the History of Religion. Reference is often made to the "mysteries" of Eleusis, to the Orphic "mysteries", and so forth; and writers tend to distort those mysteries by using the vocabulary of Christianity, for example. Then, it is quite easy to say that those mysteries included initiation, and that they had sacraments. Yes, of course, but only because we apply these concepts to the exposition of those religions; in that way, all religious seem the same, or as we say in Spanish, "at night all cats seem black".

For the same reason we must be very careful with the "Philosophy of India". Certainly, there are many ideas there—a very large number of them—that we could reasonably call "metaphysical." But, are they metaphysical for them? Did the Hindus have any kind of precise and rigorous concept, perhaps different from ours, of what we call "metaphysics"? We may reasonably wonder

about this. It is not the case—I repeat—that there few metaphysical ideas in the *Upanishads* themselves. If not the oldest—like the
Chandogya or the *Brihadâranyaka*—the more recent *Upanishads*
have a great number of ideas that for us would be metaphysical.
Needless to say, commentators on the *Vedanta*, like Shankara
and Ramanuja, have made many philosophical developments.
But is it rigorously and formally speaking what we call "metaphysical"? That would be worthy of a separate study.

If we are not going to be involved with Indian metaphysics it is
precisely for this reason, viz. that it would be a separate question,
subject to lengthy disquisitions. {13} We must avoid the conclusion that Indian metaphysics is what we understand by metaphysics, but just using Indian ideas. Unfortunately this type of
serious mistake is often made. I shall illustrate with an example
different from metaphysics. There is a famous book on the Theology of St. Paul;[1] reading its Table of Contents we can see it is a
Theology discourse. The book is simply concerned with the St.
Paul's *response* to the discourse, instead of addressing the question of what theology St. Paul actually had in mind, which is
clearly what we are most interested in.

2) Nevertheless, within Europe there is—or can be—a difference between Western and Eastern thought. Greece, in this respect, is the Eastern end of Europe. And "Western" is precisely
what happens in Europe after Greece.

But now the matter becomes more complex, with a completely
different dimension than the one we observed with respect to Indian thought. The fact is that Greece is not something that remains outside Western European thought—just the opposite.
Here complications begin. Greece does not remain outside Western European thought the way Europe remains outside India. Indeed, Greece continues to belong in one form or another to the
intrinsic cultural tradition of Western metaphysics, of the metaphysics of the European West. In what way?

A) Above all, as a point of departure.

We shall not argue the point usually made—and to my way of
thinking, not quite true—that metaphysics {14} began with Parmenides. Probably it began earlier with Anaximander, but let us
put this question aside. At any rate, Greek metaphysics is undeniably the point of departure for and the start of Western metaphysics. Nevertheless, matters are not quite so simple, because
the starting point, the point of departure, is something completely
extrinsic to the internal structure of a way of thinking.

B) The fact is that Greek thought belongs to Western thought
in a manner much more profound than just being the starting
point of some speculations that have continued for centuries.
Greece belongs to us in a more fundamental manner, because

even today it constitutes the very possibility of Western philosophy.

a) To be sure, the Greeks have passed away and no longer exist. In this sense, Greece belongs to a past that no longer is. But
where there is historical continuity, a curious phenomenon is observed. That which disappears does not fall into a vacuum, but
rather leaves those who follow in a special situation, one defined
by the possibilities bequeathed to them by what no longer exists,
and these possibilities handed down to posterity do constitute
and define the situation of the successors.

In this sense history is dis-realization in the sense that what
is past no longer exists. Nonetheless, what was a reality in the
past continues to be the primary possibility from which its successors emerge. And in this sense, Greece belongs to the internal
possibilities of Western philosophy.

b) The dialectic of these possibilities is very complex. Western
philosophy has internalized Greek thought. But, what has been
internalized? It is easy to assume {15} that there is just continuity: Anaximander, Parmenides, Plato, Aristotle, and the other
Greeks dealt with a series of issues, and these issues continue to
be discussed in the Western world. Viewed from the outside, this
is true in a relative sense—only relatively, but let us grant it for
the time being. In fact it is not internalization; the most that we
can say about it is that it is a mixture, a kind of cocktail of the
past and the present. It is not a true internalization: our reception
of Greek ideas consists in the fact that these ideas, the list of concepts that the Greek world has left us as intellectual possibilities,
will be used to resolve problems completely alien to the Greek
mentality.

Then the matter becomes much more complicated. Christianity—that which has definitely constituted Western Europe—
contributed more than just concrete ideas; with respect to philosophy, it contributed a new idea of the world and of man.

The problems that this new idea presents are precisely the
problems Western thinkers are going to try to resolve, or at least
to study, with the set of concepts received from the Greek world.
Greece is the intellectual *organon* through which the West understood its own problems. This is the origin of the radical ambivalence of Western philosophy. On the one hand, it has its own
situation. But on the other, its thinking is mostly Greek. The
Greeks in one form or another provided almost all of the concepts
comprising the cultural tradition of Western metaphysics. But
there are some exceptions. It is curious that the Greek world
never had the term or the corresponding notion of what a person
is. It is curious that the Greek world never had a concept or a
term that would correspond to what we {16} understand by "exis-

tence." Strange though it may be, the abstract of existence, *existentialitas*, appeared in the fourth century at the time of Marius Victorinus and the term was coined by him. So with a few exceptions, Western thought utilizes concepts received from the Greek world in order to deal with its own problems, problems that are completely alien to that world. This is the source of a problem, first with respect to Greece, and second with respect to discovering the essential modifications that Greek concepts have undergone in their new Western version.

II. *What is metaphysics?*

Having thus delimited the concept of Western metaphysics with respect to Asia and with respect to our own East, i.e., Greece, we have to explain what is understood by the second term: Western "metaphysics".

As I said with respect to the world of India, we have to distinguish between the "ideas" that the Hindus had—which appear to us metaphysical—and a strict and rigorous concept of what metaphysics is. Our "ideas" are in good measure Greek ideas, but our metaphysics has little to do with Greece.

So what do we understand by "metaphysics"?

1) Although this may appear to be an exaggeration—I shall explain forthwith—metaphysics is materially identical to what we understand by philosophy. And I stress the term "materially." It can be said that metaphysics is part of philosophy, in addition to logic, ethics, and the philosophy of nature. But all this too in the end is metaphysics; logic is the metaphysics of knowledge, just as ethics is the metaphysics of life, and philosophy of nature {17} is the metaphysics of nature. In this sense, metaphysics is not "part" of philosophy, but is materially identical to philosophy itself. The term and concept of "philosophy" were born in the "Socratic circle," and perhaps a little earlier in the Pythagorean world, to designate the attitude of men searching for supreme wisdom, i.e., for the ultimate and radical wisdom of life and things. This defines precisely what philosophy is.

2) But metaphysics—what metaphysics is—is something more. It is there to provide the precise characteristics of that radical ultimateness for which philosophy searches. That is why, although there is a material identity between metaphysics and philosophy there is no formal identity. In other words, metaphysics is the "real" definition of what philosophy is in general terms. Metaphysics is the "formal" definition of philosophy.

3) Of course, we now must proceed to explain what is meant by the term "metaphysics."

Metaphysics is the real and actual definition of what philosophy is; it must reveal to us what this radical ultimateness for which philosophy is aiming truly is. The term "metaphysics" has two components: *metá* and "physics."[2]

A) With respect to the first part of the term, *metá* means that metaphysics aims towards something that is "beyond," a radical ultimateness. And, if we wish to use a term that I am not going to justify now (because we are going to use it in a more or less general way), we shall say that *metá* means "to transcend," "to be beyond." This "beyond" is what metaphysics is searching for, what the beyond has of *metá*, of transcending. And now we must say in what this "beyond" consists.

In the first place, "beyond" may mean the following. When man encounters things and addresses {18} them, in a certain way they confront him; they come to meet him. There is this bottle, this glass; we are all here, etc. These are the things that are there. It is to them that we spontaneously refer, and they are what comes to meet us. In Latin, "coming to meet us" is *obviam ire*, they appear on our way. And precisely because of this, things, taken this way, constitute the domain of the "obvious." The obvious is not that which is understood without further ado, but what one encounters on the way towards something. The things that come to meet us on the way are the obvious ones. Therefore, to explain the term "beyond" consists in explaining the "obvious," the beyond for which, as we have seen, metaphysics reaches. What do we understand by the obvious? What is the obvious?

A) Based on what we have just said, the reply is relatively clear. What is obvious is the list of things man encounters, and to proceed beyond is to proceed to *other* things that are not obvious, i.e., that do not appear on our way, and do not come to meet us. There is no need here to think of great transcendent mysteries. Let us take an electron: no one has ever seen an electron, and besides, an electron, by its own physical nature—at least from what we know of it—is invisible. One does not encounter an electron. And, in this sense, to proceed beyond the obvious would mean to proceed beyond the things that man encounters and that come to meet him in his direct contact with reality. It would mean proceeding to *other* things that are not obvious, i.e., that do not come to meet us, and that man has searched for, e.g., in science or in other human activities. In this sense, "beyond" has a precise meaning, it is that which is *ultra*. Beyond would be the ultra-obvious, that which is there further than the obvious, that which refers to things that are not obvious in this sense. This is a perfectly acceptable meaning. {19}

B) Nevertheless, is this the meaning that defines the *metá* of metaphysics? No, because there is a much deeper meaning. There are things we do not perceive directly, not because they are *ultra*, beyond the things we encounter directly, but precisely the opposite: because they are something that is in every perception and in each thing. We do not perceive them precisely because they are constitutively inscribed in the obvious; we do not perceive them, not because they are *ultra*, but because they lack that minimum opacity necessary for human beings to encounter them. That lack of opacity is what the term *diaphanous* expresses. The diaphanous is not obvious, not because it is not in things, but because it is too obvious; so obvious that in its very diaphaneity we do not perceive it. We must stress this. To be beyond for metaphysics does not mean to go after things that may be *ultra*, but to go after the diaphanous, to that which because of its diaphaneity is inscribed in everything obvious that man encounters in his elemental acts. In this sense we say, as I shall explain presently, that the diaphanous is *transcendental*. It is transcendental not in the sense that it is something very important, but in the sense that it *transcends* in one form or another those things that are obvious, without however being outside of the obvious things. The radical difficulty of mataphysics rests precisely on the fact that it is the science of the diaphanous. Consequently, it rests on performing that difficult operation which the shocking vision of the diaphanous is. Therefore we shall have to explain first, what do we understand by "diaphaneity," and second, in what does the shock of this vision consist?

i) "Diaphaneity," on the one hand, means something like a glass through which we see the object on the other side. In this sense, "diaphanous" involves the moment of "*through this*," transparency. {20}

But it has a second moment: "through this" is not simply transparency, but rather the fact that in one form or another what is diaphanous not only *allows* us to see, but *makes it possible* to see whatever is there on the other side. It is not simply the case of a ray of light passing through without obstacles, but of actually making visualization of whatever is there on the other side possible. The glass not only presents no impediment to seeing what is on the other side, but just because of its diaphaneity makes it possible to see whatever is there.

In a third moment, the diaphanous is not only that through which we are able to see, not only what makes us see, but in one form or another it is that which *constitutes whatever is seen*. This may seem to be a paradox, but it is true. The diaphanous constitutes whatever is seen in the sense that it is a true moment of things. If things were not accessible to diaphaneity and if diaphaneity were not to put them precisely within our view, it would not be possible to see them. Because of this, the idea of the diaphanous is enormously complex. In that complexity rests one of the radical difficulties of every metaphysical thought. Metaphysics is the science of the most diaphanous, and yet, it is a difficult investigation. Why?

In view of the considerations I have just outlined, the term "diaphanous" has a primary meaning. "Diaphanous" would immediately suggest that which is "evident." Someone working on the demonstration of a mathematical theorem, which turns out to be quite simple, will say it is diaphanous, that it is evident.

Nevertheless, being evident is not diaphaneity. Diaphaneity is located beyond evidentness, making it possible. Evidentness is the fact that things make us see what they are. But this presupposes the moment of diaphaneity. It follows that *evidentia*—a term invented by Cicero to translate the Greek εναργής—points to something more fundamental, which is closer to the diaphanous. {21} One would think, then, that diaphaneity consists at least in *lucidity* or clear vision as the font of evidentness.

But this is not the whole story. Diaphaneity may indeed produce lucidity and be the font of evidentness. But this does not mean that metaphysics is something lucid, because in fact it is not lucid nor an instance of clear vision, but of something much more difficult, of having a *vision of clarity*. It is not lucidity or clear vision, but the *visibility of clarity*. This is just what constitutes the difficulty of metaphysics, i.e., the visibility of clarity as such. The diaphanous is, in this somewhat constitutive sense of things, the clarity itself which things have. In what kind of dimension? This we must discover.

This moment of clarity is transcendental in two dimensions. In the first place, it is beyond obvious things–not beyond as if going to "another thing," but precisely because it is something immersed in things and that permits us to see them. Precisely because of its diaphaneity it appears to us as imperceptible. It is transcendental in this dimension. But there is a second dimension, because the diaphaneity proper to one thing is not different from the diaphaneity proper to others. Therefore, what is diaphanous in one thing in its own way involves all the others. It is transcendental in this second way. Taken together, as transcendental in each thing and as involving all of them, the diaphanous is constitutively and formally transcendental. Δία-φάνεια, diaphaneity, is just *the transcendental*.[3]

Therefore, to reach for the diaphanous is what the progressive work of philosophy is, a progression towards the transcendental in the sense indicated. That is what metaphysics is. I mentioned above that metaphysics is the definition of philosophy. Now we say that the transcendental is the definition {22} of metaphysics. We have explored three concepts: philosophy, metaphysics and the transcendental; each defines the previous one and contains it securely.

ii) This vision of the diaphanous, this vision of the transcendental, is enormously shocking. It is the shock of clarity, the shock of perception and of the diaphanous. What kind of shock is it?

At this point—as in many pages of this volume—a certain ambivalence appears. The difficulty of pursuing the diaphanous is partly due to us, since we pursue things other than the diaphanous; but it is also in things themselves inasmuch as they all involve this dimension of diaphaneity. Aristotle told us that the difficulties of knowledge are partly in things and partly in us: "In the same manner as it is with bats' eyes with respect to the midday light, so it is with the intellect of our soul with respect to those things which are the most visible in the world."[4] Aristotle did not decisive importance to this observation, because he just wrote these lines and tells us nothing else; in the end, he was merely referring to the limitations of human intellection, which are abundantly clear. What is not so clear, sixteen centuries later, is what happened to this same text quoted by St. Bonaventure [1221-1274] and the mystics in general.

St. Bonaventure uses the text translated into Latin, "In the same manner as the eye of the bat behaves with respect to light, such is the behavior of the eye of our understanding with respect to what is most manifest in nature." It might seem {23} that St. Bonaventure is but repeating what Aristotle said. But the phrase does not end there. St. Bonaventure addresses reason, "Because, used to the obscurities of beings and sensible images [it never occurred to Aristotle to call these things "phantasms" or "obscurities"], when it sees the light of the true Supreme Being it seems as if nothing is seen, not understanding that this obscurity is the supreme illumination of our mind".[5] In other words, here St. Bonaventure is thinking of something else: he is thinking of God and his presence in the world. What he wants to tell us is that the light of God blinds us. Nevertheless, blindness is not that in which primarily and radically the vision of the diaphanous consists.

As we can see, this is an example of the cases in which the same concepts, placed in another context, acquire a completely different meaning. All mystics have referred to this idea that man finds himself blinded by that which is the supreme light of God, an idea completely alien to Aristotle's thought, despite their repetition of his text. As such, the *manifestissimae naturae*, the τή φύσει φανερῶτατα πάντον of Aristotle, is translated in light of the supreme being, in light of God. However, the shock we are referring to is not blindness in this sense, simply because metaphysics is not formally an investigation about God.

It is definitely a shocking vision, but why? In the first place, it is not something obvious, but still it is something that is in all things. And, in the second place, the shock consists precisely in trying to see the clarity, but without leaving the clarity itself. It is a kind of twisting back upon itself, {24} and here is where the difficulty resides. Metaphysics does not pretend to take us *out* of things, but to keep us *in* them to make us see the diaphanous, which is not obvious not because it is not in things, but because it is what is most obvious about them. Therefore, metaphysics as something *metá*, as something beyond the obvious in the sense I have just explained, is knowledge of the diaphanous.

There is nothing more diaphanous than metaphysics. So much so that the things metaphysics addresses appear to be nothing but platitudes not worth the time spent on them. But let us be careful that this presumed waste of time may not turn out to be the radical way to reconquer the diaphanous in its greater intimacy, or at least possess it intellectually in its greater intimacy. Metaphysics is the radical and ultimate vision of the diaphanous.

What is diaphanous might be thought of as something more or less implied or understood in all things. Though true, this is inadequate. It is implied or understood, but not because it is familiar or habitual, which is the meaning that these terms often have. That is not the case because here what is implied or understood is a moment of things themselves; they are what actually has this intrinsic moment of diaphaneity that pertains to them.[6]

Let us take an example. Aristotle thought that metaphysics was going to be about being (τὸ ὄν).[7] Let us ignore the fact that the translation may be deficient, because, in all its generality, ὄν is a neuter participle of the verb εἶναι, "to be," and simply means "that it is" not as a substantive, being, but simply "that it is." And the "that it is" is understood in many ways, as we shall see. Strictly speaking, {25} then, τὸ ὄν is not "being," but a simple "that it is". And in a very natural way one may think that actually what is diaphanous about things is "that they are." Therefore that which all things are, namely, "that they are" is what constitutes the supreme difficulty of metaphysics. This term was translated into Latin by the term *ens*, being, a term that does not exist in standard Latin because the verb "to be," the verb *esse* in Latin, does not have a present participle, at least in that form of *ens*.

Were it to have one, it would have to be *essens*. And actually, not in the form *essens*, but in the form *sens*, it appears in the compounds of the verb "to be" and is preserved even in English: *absent (ab-sens), present (prae-sens)*, etc. With a different linguistic formation, with "o", it appears in an ancient juridical term of Rome, the term *sonticus*. For example, *causa sontica* is a reason or an excuse that is valid, i.e., it is true. And in fact with this root, -*es it has become the term "truth," for example in the Indo-Iranian *sátya*.[8]

The preceding has been an example of what can be understood by "diaphanous." The diaphanous is something that is in all things; but if we do not perceive or do not think of this moment whereby things simply "are," it is because this is so diaphanous that instead we only think about *what* things are. However, this is nothing but an example and, as we shall see further on, a deceptive example.

So here we have more or less what metaphysics is as *metá*, at least with respect to the transcendental. Now we must discuss what the second part of the term means, i.e., we must explain what the "physical" is. {26}

C) Let us set aside historical disquisitions. Not everything that is diaphanous is the object of metaphysics. Why? Simply because metaphysics deals with an "ultimate" or "full" diaphaneity. In what does the ultimateness or fullness of diaphaneity consist? That is the question. Putting it now in a somewhat dogmatic way, it consists in here-and-now being beyond things "such as they are." The "such as they are" is the term that translates the term "physical", "things such as they are." At the proper time I shall justify not the translation, but the concept. And with respect to things such as they are, the diaphanous, in the previous example, is this "they are." That "they are" is precisely that which constitutes metaphysics. The ultimateness of things comprises ultimateness in the order of being beyond every suchness, beyond every particularity or individuality. Of course, one may ask, if we eliminate from consideration all that things are as such, as individuals, does anything remain? It seems nothing remains. That is precisely the difficulty with metaphysics: it seems nothing remains precisely because what remains is diaphanous. To cause it not to disappear is the shock in which metaphysics by its nature consists.

Metaphysics is a transcending, that is, a proceeding beyond things such as they are towards the diaphanous, without which we could not even begin to talk about things such as they are. What is that ultimate diaphaneity? I have only given one example.

To answer this question more fully is one of the tasks of this work.

That is also the aim with respect to the other term, *fundamental* or *ground*. What do we understand by "fundamental" in metaphysics? By "ground"?

III. *Ground of metaphysics*[9]

"Fundamentality" or "ground" can mean several things. In the first place, it is that which is most immediate. The fundamental is that which is most important, {27} what is most important to us. But the term "importance" has several meanings. One is that for me a certain particular thing may be more or less important; another, that the thing has considerable import for me, i.e., it takes me with it, so to speak. In this last sense, "import" does not involve the reference that for me it is important, but that the matter is one that "imports" me, "in-portare": reaches deeply into me and carries me with it. For this, two conditions must be present.

1) First we must specify what it is in things that carries us along with them. This is the moment we have previously called "diaphaneity." The intellective apprehension of this moment is the principle of metaphysics. "Principle" does not mean "beginning;" it also does not mean a first truth or a series of first truths from which others truths derive. "Principle" is purely and simply the diaphanous as such, insofar as it is that "from" which we have a vision of clarity. This moment of "from" (Gr. ὅθεν) is what, since Aristotle, has been called ἀρχή, principle. And in this sense, the principle "from" is just diaphaneity itself as principle of my intellective apprehension of things. It is a principle that is in each thing itself. It is the principle that is the principle of all knowing. Thus, for example, the notion of organism is the principle of all my anatomical and physiological knowledge. Therefore, in that sense the moment of diaphaneity of things is that from which we understand things intellectively. But this "from" is as problematic as diaphaneity itself. Is this a question of being or something else? Modern philosophy (beginning with Descartes) has tended to think that the diaphanous in this sense is truth rather than being. At the proper moment we shall discuss this inflexion of thought.

2) In addition, it is also necessary that the diaphanous, which {28} obviously *has import* for us, be accessible to human beings, otherwise it would not have *importance*; all of which involves a certain idea of human intelligence. The diaphanous alone is insufficient for there to be intellection and vision. Something elemental is necessary; e.g., we need eyes to see, and unfortunately this is often forgotten. Otherwise there would be no possibility of

diaphaneity or intellection of diaphaneity. In particular, we need an idea about what intelligence is.

Now, it might seem that this is a duality: on the one hand there is the idea of things, and on the other the idea of human intelligence. But this is not true, and is not true because between these two dimensions of the subject matter there is an essential unity. Indeed, diaphaneity forms the unity between intelligence and clarity. Intelligence has a certain sameness with things. This means that it is determined by and has its import through things themselves. Diaphaneity is a moment of things, that which is absolutely obvious, and therefore that from which intelligence is intelligent and has its proper intellection. Intelligence as something determined from things is in this sense "the same" with things, not because intelligence and things are the same, but because things are indifferent to any intelligence knowing them. However, is the converse true? Of course not. Intelligence without things could not have its intellective function. Intelligence is the "same" with things inasmuch as intellection is constituted "from" them. Intelligence has its intellectual function only inasmuch as it is actually borne along from things, i.e., from their diaphaneity. The intrinsic unity between intelligence and things is diaphaneity itself, transcendence itself. Inasmuch as things not only manifest their transcendence, but drag us toward it, {29} they constitute the world of intelligence and intellection. That being the case, what intelligence does is to submerge us deeper in things themselves at the moment of their ultimate diaphaneity. And this is what is fundamental in metaphysics, what grounds it.

The fundamental in metaphysics, its ground, does not consist in being a science with some pillars, one that has some explanations and some principles more or less properly expounded. Undoubtedly that is something important, something interesting, but it is always secondary. Regardless of what the structure of metaphysics may be, it is definitely determined by that which the metaphysical of things is, the diaphanous that has import for us and drags us with it. The metaphysical is the ultimate diaphaneity of things, of the real. And only drawn by that clarity can metaphysics be constituted as a science. Let us understand that it can be constituted simply as a possibility, because no one has ever demonstrated that all minds throughout history have had access to metaphysics. I said this—now we can see why—referring to Indian thought. Metaphysics only begins where man, knowingly or not knowingly, seeking it or not seeking it (probably seeking it) has hurled himself into the search for the diaphanous, precisely *qua* diaphanous.

One may ask, why does man decide to do this? There is no answer to this question. Despite the many historical speculations

about the origin of Greek philosophy, or of philosophical thought
from the Near East, the Far East, Egypt, Mesopotamia, etc., an
essential consideration has always been omitted, viz, the fact that
the Greeks had the "talent for this." It may appear irrational, but
if the Greeks had not had the talent {30} to direct themselves towards the diaphanous, *qua* diaphanous, there would have been
no metaphysics. It is not the same to have a great deal of rigorous
intellectual knowledge as to have, for example, science. As
mathematicians the Babylonians knew much more than the
Greeks; they practically invented algebra—something more or less
abstract about which the Greek had no idea. But the Greeks simply take two or three numbers and what they immediately set in
motion is the logos, doing a demonstration—something totally
alien to Mesopotamian thought. Every ἐπιστήμε, particularly the
metaphysical, is a possibility. The possibility of the diaphanous
as such is dawn of metaphysics. But we must understand, as we
said above, that we should not identify diaphaneity with evidentness; as we pointed out, the vision of the diaphanous is always
shocking.

That shock is the fourth point must explain: *the fundamental
"problem" of Western metaphysics.* What do we understand by
"problem"?

IV. *Problematic character of the ground of metaphysics*

We might think that metaphysics, which was more or less created by the Greeks, was received by the Western world in the
sense just explained. To be sure, it dealt with some problems different than those the Greek world dealt with, as we have seen in
the example of Aristotle and the bat. Therefore *metaphysics*, like
any other way of knowing, deals with certain *problems*, some
greater than others, and the *problems of Western metaphysics*
could be a compilation of these problems. {31}

However, this is not to what I refer with the title, because we
must not forget that behind the term "problem" lurks what we
have just said: we are dealing with a "problem" which is "fundamental.". Therefore, we do not actually refer to "problems" in the
plural, existing behind metaphysics, but rather to what is fundamental as a problem for metaphysics, not just as a science, but
also as the metaphysical in things.

Here is where we find a profound antinomy between ancient
thought—including in this case not only Greek, but also Medieval—and the modern world. On one hand there is the great accomplishment of the Greeks, with all its re-elaboration and trans-
formation at the hands of Christian and Medieval thinkers, and
that is metaphysics. On the other hand, Modern philosophy was

born with a different program; it was born from the perspective of the "I think," of thinking. It is fundamentally a theory of thought, of its intrinsic limits and of its intrinsic condition; metaphysics is something that remains outside, something that belongs to another way of seeing things. This development might seem to be a radical and fundamental break in the development of Western philosophical thought, and naturally, this situation can be remedied in many ways. One remedy—palliative actually—consists in taking the point of departure of the "I think," and trying to find out how we can manage to extract the necessity, the possibility and the structure of that which constitutes metaphysics. The term "fundamental" would then signify the critical foundation or ground of metaphysics. But as obvious as this may seem—here the term "obvious" appears—it is quite problematic, because it would consist in a relatively simple operation, that of reaching metaphysics, but reaching *that same thing* that we had before. It would be, purely and simply, a case of restoring {32} metaphysics upon bases called "critical." In this sense, the fundamental problem would consist in a critical rehabilitation of metaphysics, of that metaphysics that—as we have said—was annulled at the birth of Modern philosophy. But this is never the primary and fundamental.

This is because the metaphysical of things, in the first place, is not something that is simply *there*, to which there is no alternative but to accept it again, reject it, or simply develop it within its internal limits. Metaphysics and the metaphysical are not something that are just *there*; they have to be *done*, they have to be *created*. And therein lies the difficulty.

Not only does metaphysics have to be done and created, but the difficulty has two aspects. First, we must know what it is that has to be done. In other words, what is the problematic context of metaphysics? It is usually assumed that this has been completed already and confronting it there is nothing more needed than a critical reception—however "critical," but still a pure "reception." That is why I said that this is nothing but a palliative, and like all such, quite deficient. In the second place, it is necessary to be installed *within* metaphysics itself. That is why metaphysics continues to be an intrinsic difficulty, because a ground does not consist only in the content or the road that leads to metaphysics, but in the very character of the transcendental order. Therein lies the great difficulty. But in the transcendental order lies the ground of metaphysics, because the diaphaneity of the transcendental is what determines intelligence. Therefore, the very structure of that transcendental diaphaneity is what constitutes the supreme problematic moment of philosophy, of metaphysics. The difficulty, the problem of metaphysics, is nothing but the intellectual expression of the shock proper to the vision of the {33} diaphanous. The fundamental problem is the structure of diaphaneity, i.e., the very structure of the transcendental, not with respect to us, but in itself.

Unfortunately, even the "received" metaphysics has never stopped to consider this; just the opposite. It rested on "being" as the transcendental, with its five properties, deemed something finished, done. The usual encounter with this problem led to either acceptance or rejection of that assumption, instead of asking in what the transcendental itself consists, which is a subject full of thorny problems. If one runs through all possible types of metaphysics, or at least some of them—as we are going to do here—it is clear that there are several problems that have never been incorporated into metaphysics. However, these problems constitute the fundamental core of any metaphysics, both with respect to metaphysics in things, and to its intellective determination by human thought. This is not a question of subtleties.

Anticipating ideas, let us take an example, the first one that comes to mind. When the Greeks talk about being (τὸ ὄν), the "that is," they certainly have some precise ideas about it. For example, if we read Parmenides, he tells us that there is no other way to approach things except through the way of "it is": it is or it is not. We cannot admit that sometimes it may be one way and at other times another, because if it is, it is, and if it is not, it is not. That is why Parmenides tells us, τὸ ἐόν κεῖται, what is just here-and-now there, what lies before us. However, this text has elicited some very interesting interpretations, all of them quite peculiar. In our day we contemplate the third or fourth reinterpretation of the history of Greek philosophy from the perspective of the systematic philosopher who uses it. For Hegel, this is a kind of dialectic development of the idea; for others, {34} for example Heidegger, it is an investigation about "being" as distinct from "entity," something completely alien to the Greek world. Parmenides shows this in his *Poem* where he mentions that being is a sphere, and the title of the Poem is, Περὶ φύσεος, "On nature". Although the title may not belong to Parmenides, but to his editors, it clearly indicates the meaning that the Greeks gave to the *Poem*, namely that Parmenides tried to give us an idea of nature even though he denied that there is true generation and destruction. Be that as it may, Parmenides regards τὸ ἐόν, the entity, from the framework of motion. Things are born, develop and die after great vicissitudes; things, the stars, the cities, men, animals, etc., are in the process of generation and corruption. Parmenides does not say that there is no motion—as far as I can tell, Parmenides never said this—

but that this motion is never a real and effective motion of generation and corruption. Democritus sought to resolve the problem by
saying that things are conglomerates of atoms, but each atom en-
joys the characteristics of the sphere of Parmenides, since it is
perfectly indestructible.

The Greek world always saw the idea of being, the idea of diaphaneity, within the framework motion. And this is still clearer in
Aristotle.

Aristotle is not satisfied with just saying that "being" is something κείμενον, that is there, but that it is ὑπο-κείμενον, that it is
under-lying. Not only does it lie there, but it also under-lies; it is
just substance as permanent substratum. Aristotle knows—in
this sense he is quite against Parmenides—that there is true generation and corruption, but of what? There is true generation and
corruption of every individual human; but each individual human
is the synthesis of a prime matter {35} and the fundamental form
of the human species. Actually, though each individual may die,
neither its prime matter nor the human species as such dies; it
continues to be transmitted from individual to individual. There is
a permanence that, in this sense, is completely separated from
motion.

The Greek world essentially viewed the idea of ens, the idea of
ὄν, from the framework of motion. If we place ourselves in the
medieval world, we find something completely different. The first
thing a medieval man considers is why there are things rather
than nothing. It is curious that this question—not long ago Heidegger was still saying he could not believe people were not interested in it—is found within the framework of nothingness, which
is the framework of Creation. The idea of nothingness never
crossed the mind of a Greek. For the Greek mind, God, the θεός,
did not make the world, not even in Aristotle; the world is just
naturally there. On the other hand, for a medieval person the
world begins by reaching the point of having reality. Therefore,
the whole problem of being is inscribed within the problem of
nothing and nothingness.

This problem has held on tenaciously up to our own time. We
just mentioned Heidegger, who, when finishing his lecture entitled Was ist Metaphysik?—What is Metaphysics?—says "Ex nihilo
fit omne ens qua ens," i.e., from nothing every being qua being is
constituted not by creation but ultimately from nothing. We
should also remember the title of the book by Sartre, L'Etre et le
Néant—Being and Nothingness. The framework of nothingness
remains there as a framework, and within that framework that
which apparently is as obvious and diaphanous as being will be
interpreted.

This indicates that at least the transcendental order in itself involves an important problem. This transcendental order {36}—regardless of how transcendental it is—has in its very structure and in its transcendental core a serious problem concerning its framework. It also has many other problems that we shall have to investigate. There is also something that is not absolutely immediate and can lead us, not to an attitude of simple acceptance or rejection of metaphysics, but to just the opposite: to the attitude of manifesting the inner fabric of metaphysics.

The study of these problems can be done several ways. Here we are going to do it by approaching the metaphysics that have been developed and observe them in their historical unfolding. We do this not with the idea of presenting a summary of them, because this is devoid of any interest; after all, it is enough to take the books and read there what the philosophers themselves have said. Rather, our interest is to show that there are problems that underlie every metaphysics. In order to demonstrate this, more than a summary is necessary; it will be necessary to disentangle their internal structures and bring to the fore the diaphanous, that which is clear, that which constitutes the inner fabric of the transcendental order *qua* transcendental, in other words, "the" metaphysical itself.

* * *

To do this, in the next chapter we shall begin with what we have already suggested in this one, viz. a study of the Greeks and of Aristotle. From there we shall proceed to consider not all metaphysical systems, but five that I consider especially important.

- Medieval metaphysics, which we will center on St. Thomas. {37}
- Metaphysics in Descartes.
- Metaphysics in Leibniz.
- Metaphysics in Kant.
- Metaphysics in Hegel.

I am aware that this contradicts the idea that some have of modern philosophy, which is considered as a kind of rejection of the metaphysical order in favor of the *I*. We shall see whether this position can be maintained. At any rate, whatever truth may be in that statement, it belongs as an internal problem to the transcendental order itself, and is not something external, something useful for criticizing the ground of metaphysics one way or the other. The history of philosophy will be taken as that which reveals the internal structure, the inner core of transcendence as such.

These are exactly the fundamental problems of Western metaphysics with which we are going to be concerned.

---

1 Zubiri refers to Ferdinand Prat (1857-1938), *La théologie de Saint Paul*, I, Paris, 1908 (^{23}1942); II, Paris, 1912 (^{28}1941) (there is a translation in Spanish, Mexico, 1947). [There is also an English translation, *The Theology of St. Paul*, Burns, Oates and Washbourne, Ltd., London, 1926-1927, 2 vol.—trans.].

2 [Of course Zubiri knows quite well that the title *Metaphysics* comes from Andronicus of Rhodes' compilation of Aristotle's work, where it referred not to the *subject* of the essays we now know by this title, but to their *position* in his compilation: τὰ μετὰ τὰ φυσικά—"the things (that come) after the physics." In this section Zubiri is discussing the meaning the *metá* has taken on in Western thought, the meaning not of "after" but of "beyond."—trans.].

3 [Zubiri's term *transcendentalidad*, literally "transcendentalness," is here rendered as "the transcendental" to avoid a very awkward and strange-sounding English neologism.—trans.].

4 *Met* A 993b 9-11.

5 *Itinerarium mentis in Deum*, Ch. V, no. 4.

6 *Zubiri note:* "Clarify these concepts".

7 [In Spanish there are two words that can mean "being" in English. The verb *ser*, from the Latin *esse*, can be so translated, as can *ente*, from the Latin *ens*. A problem arises however because *ente* can also mean *entity*, though there is a separate Spanish word also with that meaning, *entidad*. However, the Spanish suffix *-idad* is used to transform an adjective or a concrete noun into an abstract noun, as English does with the suffix *-ness*. Thus, *mismo* = same becomes *mismidad* = sameness. Hence *entidad* can also mean *entitiness*. Zubiri generally prefers *ente* for *being*, though he sometimes uses *ser*. The English translation will depend on the context. The reader should bear this issue in mind throught the book.—trans.].

8 Cf. X. Zubiri, *Naturaleza, Historia, Dios* (Nature, History, God), 9th ed., Madrid, Alianza/Fundación X. Zubiri, 1987, pp. 38-39.

9 [The Spanish word *fundamentalidad* would translate as *fundamentality* in English. But we do not generally use this word, since *ground* (from the German *grund*) means more or less the same thing. Unfortunately this makes for some awkwardness in the translation, as Zubiri constantly uses the various forms of *fundamental* in his discussion. The reader should bear this in mind when reading the text.—trans.]

CHAPTER 1
ARISTOTLE'S FIRST PHILOSOPHY

In the Introduction we sought to clarify the type of issues with which we shall occupy ourselves concerning *the fundamental problems of Western metaphysics*. We said that the Eastern part of Europe—namely, Greece—underlies the whole of Western (i.e., European) philosophy, as its first flowering and historically earliest great effort. Since Greek philosophy forms part of the European tradition we must discuss the Greeks, at least briefly, to see just how their thought so deeply underlies all subsequent philosophy. It is Greek philosophy that has led to our own unique adventure, something that we shall try to define with more accuracy at the end of this chapter.

Greek philosophy, including Aristotle, is eminently concrete. It is necessary to stress this because in the course of the adventure that we shall be discussing, Greek philosophical ideas have been converted into abstract concepts that probably were quite remote from the mind of the Greeks, or at least were not formally part of their thought. It is necessary to mention this concreteness especially with regard to Plato and Aristotle. Heidegger often mentions that it is a case of trying to find {40} "what is happening at the bottom of that philosophy" (*Was im Grunde geshieht*). But these interpretations of what happens "at the bottom" of a philosophy are always quite perilous, because it generally seems as if they dispense us from saying what the Greeks really and actually thought.

In order to see in all its concretion just what these philosophers thought we must directly engage them and their works. There is a text in Aristotle where, after expounding what we shall be dealing with below, he says, "And indeed the question was raised of old and is raised now and always, and is always the subject of doubt (ἀπορία), viz. what being is (τί τὸ ὄν)" [1] (this is the usual translation, to which we shall return presently). Aristotle gives the impression that always—in ancient times, now and in the future—something is being sought. We must ask, then, what is Aristotle thinking about when he says that we have always been searching for something, and what is that something? In the second place, in what does that difficulty, that *aporía* consist, that great difficulty the Greeks handled so brilliantly? And in the third place, how does Aristotle—himself, personally—handle the difficulty? These are the three steps we shall follow.

§1

PHILOSOPHICAL SEARCH BEFORE ARISTOTLE: THE QUEST FOR THE ὄν

Let us consider, in the first place, what since earliest times philosophers were searching for. Of course, this refers to a relative antiquity; for us two centuries seem like a brief period. However, for the Greeks, who had a very poor memory of their own history, it seemed like a long time. So what is it that they were searching for?

It is true we do not have to limit ourselves to the Greek world. It will be sufficient to consider the East—Far and Near—and the cultures of this East and Egypt itself to become aware that thinkers, regardless of type, attempted in one way or another to discover the origin of the things surrounding us. Of course, this presupposed the fact that things are born at some time, last for a while, and finally, disappear or become corrupt. Perhaps some of them even resist this process. Nevertheless, a Greek philosopher would dismiss this as μύθος, which here does not necessarily mean "myth," but "story." Such stories tell us, indeed, how things are born. What a Greek searches for is something totally different, it is θεωρία, to see and understand, to contemplate that which is occurring at the origin. For the Greeks, the origin of things is not a question of history; it is a question of θεωρία.

This origin is always a kind of motion, taking that term in the Greek sense of κίνεσις, motion in which some things are being produced. And in this motion {42} things acquire something fundamental, something which properly belongs to them when we contemplate them and talk about them.

The first one who posed the question this way—at least from the best accounts we have—was Anaximander [c. 610-c. 546 BC]. In the only fragment from him that has been preserved, Anaximander tells us that "the beginning of all things is the ἄπειρον".[2] The important point here is that Anaximander faces a problem of ἀρχή, a problem of the "beginning" of things, a beginning that surely still retained in Anaximander's mind the multiple resonances that the term ἀρχή had in the Greek world.

'Αρχή means, on the one hand, precisely the *start*, the *beginning*. On the other hand, it meant the *archon*, i.e., the one who

commands. It also means the domination with which this beginning is dominating the whole universe.

Putting aside these historical references, what is important for
Anaximander is that things proceed from an ἀρχή, from a beginning. Of course, we shall limit ourselves to extracting the concepts relevant to the problem in which we are now interested, and
therefore it is beyond our scope to expound all the details of pre-
Socratic philosophy.

In the first place, the first relevant concept is that of ἀρχή, beginning. Inasmuch as from this beginning all things in the universe are produced and born; that beginning is φύσις, i.e., nature.

In the second place, and as we have just seen, Anaximander
tells us that this ἀρχή is ἄπειρον. This term has been translated
in many ways; actually it means the "indefinite," and in the hands
of Western philosophy sometimes ἄπειρον often has been understood {43} as an infinite—which is absurd since this idea never
crossed Anaximander's mind. The beginning is an ἄπειρον, an
indefinite. In what sense? Is it in the sense that this, from which
all things proceed, is a kind of formless, inexhaustible matter?
That is possible. Perhaps because this first ἀρχή is that from
which all things proceed, it is not any one of the things that proceed, but something different, something that remains indefinite.
Surely this was also part of Anaximander's thought. In any case,
that ἀρχή is ἄπειρον, something indefinite.

From this indefinite something, Anaximander tells us, the
things that are (γένεσις τοῖς οὖσι) are born, the things that actually *are*. However, by contraposition to this ἄπειρον, to this indefinite, there now appears a notion that is going to play a role in
the whole of Greek philosophy. Things are πέρας, πεπερασμένον:
they are something *finished* and *delimited*. The Greeks never
thought that the beginning of reality and of things *qua* real consisted in a reference to something beyond them. Things are in
themselves such as they are. For a Greek they are precisely
πέρας, something perfectly delimited with respect to the *in*definite,
which is their ἀρχή, their beginning.[3] It is evident that the problem of this delimitation is the great question posed after Anaximander's time because, in the end, movement or change—and
here the framework of change first appears—seems to be opposed
in some way to this being determined and delimited.[4] Change or
movement struggles with that constitutive delimitation present in
each thing.[5] {44}

Be that as it may, Anaximander sees the characteristics of
things as limited and delimited within the framework of change.
In conformity to it these things are engendered by an ἀρχή, a beginning.[6]

This, which may have seemed to Anaximander at least easy to say if not clear, is not in fact so simple. Not too long afterwards the great Heraclitus of Ephesus [c. 535-c. 475 BC] will completely deny the existence of an ἀρχή, a beginning of things.

What for Anaximander was an ἀρχή, that from which things proceed, for Heraclitus is something much simpler: some things proceed from others. And what we call the "totality of reality" is, as he put it, ἁρμονία, assembly, the assembly of all things some coming to be from others and perishing to give place to others. Here is where the term πέρας appears, not as a delimitation of things with respect to the indefinite beginning from which they proceed, but as a delimitation of some things with respect to others. The assembly of all of them thus constitutes the very structure of the real world.

This idea of the delimited is going to have a different fate in Parmenides [c. 515-c. 450 BC]. Parmenides sees with his own eyes the problem that others have seen. After all, the Greeks gave the poem of Parmenides the title Περί φύσεος, "On Nature", the same they did with earlier works. Now it matters very little whether the title belongs to Parmenides or not because the point is that the Greeks felt that the problem Parmenides was dealing with was the problem of φύσις. However, Parmenides {45} takes a stand against Heraclitus and Anaximander. Why and in what way?

He tells us that Anaximander's theory is true, that there is a beginning, which makes things to be. But here is the question: Does this way of being, on the basis of which things "are," admit a beginning? Because things either are or are not, and one must be true since there are no other ways to reach the truth. If we take real things, just *inasmuch as they are*, to be the result of a beginning, we embark on a false way. This is the third way of those he enumerates, the last two of which are false. The first is to declare that actually things are not—this is unthinkable, Parmenides says. And another, also false, is to say that at certain times things are one way and at other times another. (Let us be perfectly clear—and this is the key question—as far as I can tell, it never occurred to Parmenides to deny that things change in the world.)

How does Parmenides manage to reach a unitary conception of the universe? He tells us, "There are two ways, the way of being and the way of not being. And it is necessary for being to be, and for not being to not be." It seems as if some tremendous concepts are being elaborated, but the truth is that no Greek, historically speaking, had this impression. We shall see forthwith what Parmenides means when he declares that things "are."

He tells us, "There is no other way except this one for investigation," viz. to say, to think, to understand intellectively that things "are." And Parmenides adds a fragment that for many years has been considered independent of the one we have just quoted. However, as far as I can determine, Kranz[7] has overwhelmingly demonstrated that it is the ending to that fragment, and it reads, "Because actually knowing (νοεῖν) and being (εἶναι) are the same." {46}

It makes one think that this is an affirmation with enormous ramifications, similar to Hegel's phrase when he affirms that "everything rational is real and everything real is rational." The truth is that no Greek was ever that impressed after reading Parmenides' expression. Aristotle and Plato, who quote Parmenides' texts, never feel shaken by that kind of identity between knowing and being, even though Parmenides tells us at this point, τὸ γάρ, "because *in fact*" being and knowing are the same. This "in fact" indicates that this is a reason everyone is going to accept. There is no other way except the way of "is," and the way of "is-not" cannot be undertaken because, in fact, knowing and being are the same. Therefore, it is something that had to be obvious to the reader; and what is obvious for the reader is quite simple to discover. Knowing something is knowing that it is. Since for the Greeks equals are always known by equals, e.g., the eyes must have a luminous entity in order to see light, Parmenides tells us here that what is proper to knowing, its nature, is precisely to understand "being." Though not a formal identity between knowing and being, in any case there is something in Parmenides' affirmation that will be decisive and will thematically impact the thought of Plato and Aristotle. Regardless of the form it takes, we are dealing with a ταυτόν, with a "sameness" between knowing and being.

So here we have a completely new concept, quite different from earlier ones, a concept that will become extremely important. But everything depends on Parmenides telling us what he is talking about when he says "that which is" (τὸ εόν, as he says in his Ionic dialect). Parmenides adopts what Anaximander has already told us, viz. that things are perfectly delimited. What {47} he calls *being* is something perfectly limited, i.e., strict necessity; it is a *moira*, an implacable destiny the limited being has inside itself, in such fashion that it cannot multiply or change from itself.

Here we have again, but from another point of view, that idea of delimitation, the idea that being is perfectly delimited. As perfectly delimited, it is here-and-now (κεῖται), it is something underlying in the world. All that we see, viz. that things are born and perish, is therefore alien to what constitutes the internal sub-

stance of things, which consists purely and simply in being
(εἶναι). So much so, that this being does not admit any differentiation inside itself. How could it do so? How could it have any
differentiation? This would imply that inside being there is a moment of diversity, and therefore, of non-being. But that being is
ταυτόν, in itself it is always the same. It remains identical to itself
with no change at all. Precisely because of this, Parmenides considers it a sphere (σφαίρα). Reinhardt has assumed that this is a
symbol;[8] though for me it does not look like a symbol, rather more a reality. Parmenides thought that the entire universe a great
sphere with no other characteristic except "being."

However, this being, which is Parmenides' fundamental idea,
has no beginning, it is ἄναρχον. In contrast to Anaximander, Parmenides says that it has no beginning, it only "is", and does nothing except to be. It follows that this being, which has no beginning, is also not the beginning of things in Anaximander's sense.
If it were, it would have internal movement, and since every
movement, every change, involves a certain moment of non-being,
it could not be the full being, the one that is. Being does not have
{48} a beginning and also is not the beginning. Of what? It is the
beginning of what previous philosophers maintained: the beginning of generation and corruption of things. In other words, the
change or movement against which Parmenides argues is the
movement of nature, nature as movement, φύσις as generation
and corruption. That is what is not included in the being of Parmenides.

As I see it, this does not mean that Parmenides denied change
and movement. How could he possibly deny them? He says that
these are the opinions of mortals, to be sure; but in what do these
opinions of the mortals consist? They consist in mortals believing
and affirming that the variations we see, which for Parmenides
occur on the external surface of being without altering its identity
at all, affect the very characteristic of being, and that being is a
beginning or principle of nature. For Parmenides, being is something perfectly immutable; it is not nature in any sense whatever.

Perhaps someone might ask how we can conceive of a movement that preserves these characteristics of being. A century later
Democritus will tell us how.

So let us take Democritus' atoms. Each of these atoms has
the characteristics of Parmenides' sphere. It is born that way, it is
indestructible, and if it changes place, such change does not
mean a change in being. Nonetheless, despite what has often
been said, Parmenides had the brilliant idea that there can be a
knowledge of movement that is not necessarily the idea of an *ens
mobile*, i.e., of an entity or a being that in itself is moveable or

changeable. This is the crucial step, the step that consists in saying that yes, Parmenides is right; but that does not mean there are not many spheres (as he assumed), provided that each has the characteristics of his sphere. There is no *multiplicity in being*, but there can be a *multiplicity of beings*. This is what {49} the atoms of Democritus addressed, as did the roots of all things, as Empedocles thought in qualitative fashion.

Parmenides' philosophy led directly to the idea of the ultimate elements that constitute all things, the idea of στοιχεῖον. It seems that Democritus' idea about these elements, that non-being has as much reality as being, remained in philosophy up to Aristotle, and had a decisive importance at the hands of Plato. Let us be clear that Democritus is not talking about non-being in the abstract, but in a very concrete way. He understands by non-being the vacuum, the space in which the atoms move, and in this sense the function of space is to distinguish; i.e., in addition to making motion possible, it permits atoms to be distinguished from each other. Curiously, Plato never mentioned this idea of Democritus, who was practically his contemporary. If we had only Plato's Dialogues we would have never known about the existence of Democritus.

We now have a new development, the idea of being composed of elements, of στοιχεῖα.

Plato takes yet another step. For him over and above the elements and over and above Parmenides' sphere there is something else, what he calls the εἶδος, the "idea," not in the sense of ideas of the human mind, but of the ultimate, radical and essential configurations of reality. The atoms are infinite in number, but *the* idea of an atom, the εἶδος of the atom, is only one. Parmenides' being is a sphere, but this entity of Parmenides corresponds to one idea, the very idea of being. Movement or change corresponds to an idea, the *idea* of movement, which does not move, but is an idea of movement, which is in intimate relation with the idea of being. {50}

We now find ourselves here with a kind of escape from the world of reality in which we have been thinking up to now, from Anaximander to Democritus, to enter a kind of duplicate of reality, viz. the world of ideas. Naturally, Plato resisted this simple dualism and said that the ideas are present in things, they are παρόντα. Thus they are present in reality, although he never explained in what that presence (παρουσία) consists, except by referring to the metaphor of light.

As we can see, here we have some fundamental concepts upon which Aristotle's philosophy rests. They include the idea of beginning or principle, the idea of limitation, the idea of the harmonic assembly (that Aristotle called τάξις);), the idea of the sameness of being, that being is something which underlies (κεῖσθαι); and the idea that what is essential to things is a form or figure (εἶδος). With this we have given a brief explanation of what Aristotle must have had in mind when he said, "And indeed the question was raised of old and is raised now and always...." Which question? For what do we search? Precisely for the reality of what there is, what entity is, what the reality of things is. This includes any beginning or principle, any limitation (πέρας), the one, the same, etc. Plato's ideas are characteristics of the ὄν. This is what has always been the object of searched, τί τὸ ὄν, what is "that which is".

§2

DIFFICULT CHARACTER OF THIS SEARCH

Where is the difficulty, the *aporía*, that Aristotle mentions? This *aporía* was clearly presented by Plato in the *Sophist*, "Ye [he is thinking of Empedocles], who affirm that hot and cold or any other two principles are the universe, what is this term which you apply to both of them, and what do you mean when you say that both and each of them 'are' (εἶναι)? How are we to understand the word 'are'? On your view, are we to suppose that there is a third principle over and above the other two—three in all, and not two?"[9] This is the great *aporía*. Plato himself will go on to tell us, "Up until now, in fact, we believed that we knew in one way or another, with a greater or lesser degree of uncertainty, what things are. But now however we see that when we seek to fix precisely what things are, we are submersed in an *aporía*. It is clear that for a long time (πάλαι—the word we saw earlier in Aristotle) we thought that we understood all these things, but now, it seems, we are submerged in difficulties (ἠπορήκμεν).[10] This *aporía* is just what gives Plato the energy to say, with respect to all previous philosophy, that everything it did seems like an enormous gigantomachy or battle of giants (γιγαντομαχία περὶ τῆς οὐσίας) because of the controversies among philosophers. What is this gigantomachy about? It is about what Plato has just {52} mentioned, viz., what is the ὄν, the εἶναι, that εἶναι present in all affirmations when we say that things are hot, or that things are cold, but which nonetheless seems to be something that escapes us. The imperceptibility of the diaphanous; the diaphaneity of substance, of being, of the εἶναι, of "is," has become a great problem for Plato.

Next we have to ask how Aristotle approaches this great problem.

§3

THE ARISTOTELIAN QUEST

Philosophy in Aristotle, as in all previous Greek thought, is absolutely a philosophy of concretion. Therefore let us ask, for what does Aristotle search? And, secondly, what is the moment of encounter with that for which he searches? That is, what is the moment of truth?

I. *Aristotelian idea of* ὄν, *the* ὄν *and the framework of change*

First, for what is Aristotle searching? To be sure, Plato has just told us, and even Aristotle repeats it: τί τὸ ὄν, what is "that which is"? This is usually translated as "entity," a translation that will have to be corrected immediately. Let us point out that instead of saying *entity*, it might be more convenient to do what, in a neutral and absolutely common way, a Greek might say (just as we do), viz. that things "are." And for Aristotle τὸ ὄν means, in the first place, simply that "which is." Then Aristotle, who begins the search for this "which is," carries out his investigation (ζήτεσις) in four steps.

The first step is to try to say exactly what it is that we are searching for when we say that something "is." Aristotle, with a titanic intellectual effort, has told us that "which is" is said and understood in various different ways (πολλαχῶς λέγεται τὸ ὄν). His immediate disciples—for example Theophrastus, his {54} closest and most intimate disciple—made an affirmation that seems truly astounding to us, that it is "manifest and evident" (φανερόν) that "to be" is said in multiple ways. "Of course," we might say, after Aristotle invested a titanic effort in it.

But then, how many meanings does the expression "which is" have for Aristotle?

In the first place (let us begin the list from the end), we say of something *that it is* in the sense that it is true; later we shall see what Aristotle understands by "truth." The idea of *that it is* as true comes to Aristotle from Plato, from Parmenides, and above all from Sophists like Protagoras; *being* in the sense of "telling the truth" is the way of truth, in other words.

Against this, error (ψευδός) functions as non-being, it is that *which is-not*. Here Aristotle is not thinking primarily about the "is" and the "is-not" as copula of a phrase. Parmenides' *Poem* is full of negations: "being" does not move, being has no differences, etc. Here, we are not dealing with affirmation or negation as formula of a copula, but of the *inherent truth* of that affirmation and that negation. And we say that the "it is" is true in the sense of an affirmation, e.g., that this wall is white, and that it is true that it is not red. So here we have the first sense or meaning of the "that it is", the "is" as truth.[11]

But this meaning of truth refers back to some internal moment of the thing, by virtue of which we can talk about truth. Which moment is that? {55}

Let us look at the second meaning of the expression "that it is" for Aristotle, a meaning that comes to him from the most remote origins of Greek philosophy. We said earlier that things are perfectly delimited (πέρας). Hence, Aristotle thinks that if things begin to be produced and to be made, the fact that a thing is made, and therefore delimited, means that it is finished, that it has its end (τέλος), its completeness, in itself. Because of that, he makes it more precise and transforms the concept of πέρας into a new concept, the concept of "act" (ἐντελέχεια), to have the τέλος in itself (ἐν-τέλοσ-ἐχειν). In this sense and in this measure, things are precisely act (ἐντελέχεια). Against this, of course, we have non-being. We say about something that "it is not" in the sense that it does not yet have that actuality. Of an acorn, for example, we say it is not yet an oak tree; we do not say that the acorn is nothing—that thought never crossed Aristotle's mind—, but that the acorn, whatever it is, is destined to be an oak tree. The acorn is precisely what has in itself its finished act (ἐντελέχεια), the delimited plenitude of its reality. The acorn has it in a certain way since it can be distinguished from other seeds found on Earth; but within it, *qua* seed, is what Aristotle calls the *capacity, power* or *potency* (δύναμις) of producing the oak tree.[12]

So the second fundamental meaning of the expression *that it is* signifies saying of something that it actually is (ἐντελέχεια). But this is not enough for Aristotle, since he is never fully satisfied.

In a third meaning, Aristotle assumes Plato's legacy. We have mentioned the ideas, the εἶδος. When Plato {56} spoke about the εἶδος in general, for example, of the εἶδος of justice or courage, what he understands by εἶδος is something that properly belongs to that of which it is predicated.[13] However, one of the great difficulties Aristotle presented to his master is: what happens to the properties that are accidental in a reality?

If a man who is a slave were given his freedom, Plato would say that while he was a slave he participated in the idea of slavery, while now he participates in the idea of freedom. But, what is that liberation? Plato never resolved this difficulty satisfactorily because he understood that when it is said of something that it is, we understand this to mean that we are dealing with something that properly belongs to the thing "through itself," i.e., insofar as it is. For example, we say that white is nothing but white, and is not gray; whiteness as such is what belongs to the εἶδος.

Aristotle tells us that the third meaning of "that it is" is just what we intend when we tell what is essential to it. For example, we say that Socrates is a musician, but he might not have been; and in this sense, that characteristic does not properly belong to Socrates' being. However, when we say he is rational, this is something that properly belongs to him on his own, precisely because of his essence.

This then is the third meaning of "that it is": being through itself, on account of itself, καθ'αὐτό. Here Aristotle pulls together the enormous mass of the Platonic inheritance. But, as he was wont to say, he was a friend of ideas, but a greater friend of truth.

So now a fourth meaning appears.

Aristotle understands that we say of something "that it is" when {57} it is fully sufficient unto itself, in such fashion that it cannot be an attribute of anything else, nor can it be predicated of anything else; however, other things can be predicated of it. In this case Aristotle will say that the thing, in its fullness, has the totality of the resources that constitute its independence;[14] and this is more or less what a Greek would understand by the term οὐσία.[15] I leave the term without translation; do take the explanation I have just given because every attempt at translation lowers the unitary richness of the concept of οὐσία. Even today in Modern Greek, wealth or fortune inherited from parents is called περιουσία; fortune or assets is what constitute the resources for the independence of a reality.

And so, "that it is," in the sense of being true, presupposes the actuality of reality as ἐντελέχεια. The actuality of reality as ἐντελέχεια is understood to mean that it is something such that it is constituted through itself (καθ'αὐτό). And this reality involves all the resources by virtue of which it is independent; it is χοριστόν, separated and independent from all others. On this fourth sense of being Aristotle is going to center all his reflection, after telling us what entity is (τί τὸ ὄν), viz. that it is the χοριστόν, the οὐσία.

Second step. And now, what does Aristotle understand by this οὐσία, in what does the ὄν consist, the entity?[16] {58}

At the beginning of book Γ of his *Metaphysics* Aristotle gives us the example of health. "Health" is predicated of a man who is healthy. A medicine is called "healthy" because it restores health. Taking a stroll is said to be healthy because it tends to preserve health. Color is said to be healthy because it expresses health, etc. Aristotle says that even those things that constitute the fundamental characteristics of an οὐσία, that which gives it independence, can be understood in many ways. Certainly all the meanings we have just enumerated and others that Aristotle mentions can be reduced to a fundamental one. It is from the health of man that all those things receive the qualification of healthy: the medicine, the stroll, the color, etc. Therefore, Aristotle says, with respect to οὐσία all these things are called *beings* simply by analogy (καθ'ἀναλογίαν). And let us remember that Aristotle never used the expression "analogy of being" (ἀναλογία τοῦ ὄντος); however, he does say that the unity of all modes of being with οὐσία is a unity through analogy.

"Analogy" here does not mean similarity, but has the sense of what we say with respect to the good color of a man referred to something else, such as the health of a healthy man. Consequently, when we speak about something and say "that it is," Aristotle tells us that in the very fact of saying "that it is" in this ultimate and radical sense of οὐσία, all these variations we have just mentioned are manifested. If the color is healthy it is because it manifests health, etc.

However, "to manifest" is rendered in Greek by the term κατεγορεῖν. What Aristotle means is that even in the simplest logos, in a diaphanous way and without being aware of it, we are {59} manifesting the *different ways of being*, the *categories*. If we say that something is white, what we naturally say is that it is white, not that it is red; but in the very fact of saying that it is white, we announce the way in which the real is white, i.e., as a "qualification" of a subject. If we say it is large because it measures twenty meters, we say it has twenty meters, but manifested in an underlying and presupposed manner is the way in which the large is real with respect to that which is large, i.e., quantification; etc. Then, Aristotle establishes his list of ten categories, of which nine, the ways of being with respect to a subject, are condensed and grounded in the very way of being of the subject, in the οὐσία.

With this, Aristotle has made philosophy take a giant step. Basically, what he has done is to conceptualize in a grand manner the issues that were making the rounds in philosophy from Anaximander to the time of the Platonic Academy. First was the meanings of being, and second, being as οὐσία. What do we understand by οὐσία? Here begins what is specific to Aristotle.

Third step. Aristotle remembers that Parmenides had said that entity is something that is here-and-now out there (κεῖται), that "lies there" without change or movement. By two ways that we will immediately indicate—the way of the logos and the way of change (κίνησις)—, Aristotle is going to say that entity does not just lie there (κείμενον), but is "underlying" or "subjacent" (ὑποκείμενον), that it is a *sub-jectum* or a *sub-stance*. The idea of οὐσία as substance is specifically Aristotelian.

That reality is οὐσία is something that Plato had noted in a more or less vague manner. That this οὐσία might be related to a way of being was often mentioned and had been searched for since ancient times (πάλαι). But to say that οὐσία is *subjectum* (ὑποκείμενον), is something specifically Aristotelian. {60}

Aristotle accomplishes this third step in two ways, the two ways in which all of Greek thought takes place, i.e., very concretely. On one hand, Greek thought is directed towards things, which are born, perish and endure from their birth to their death. On the other hand, it is a way of thinking that stems from the logos, whereby man says what things are: the κίνησις and the λόγος. Aristotle reaches the idea that substance is a subject (ὑποκείμενον) in two ways, by way of the logos and by way of change.

If I say of something that it is white, the subject of that predication is a *subjectum*, a subject of the qualities we predicate of it; but the subject itself is not predicated of anything at all. This is the vision of substance as subject from the point of view of the logos. In book Z the *Metaphysics* Aristotle says he is going to proceed λογικός, but he never develops the subject in this manner.

The other is the way of change, *viz.* that things are born, perish and die. At this point, he encounters Parmenides' great difficulty. Aristotle now ponders that what Parmenides says is true, but realizes that underlying motional change there is an underlying *subject* of the change. Substance, which is not just the subject of predication and of the logos, is the subject which underlies the varieties of change.

However, Aristotle just makes both ways (predication and change) identical, and that is one of the most difficult problems in his philosophy. Is this a legitimate move? When we say that everything is changing, does it mean that what is changing underlies the change? Does it mean that what is subjacent, what is underlying, is indeed the subject of predication? This is far from being true, because anything can be turned into a subject of predication, even being itself; and we can say that this is a being or that

that is a being. But simply being a subject of predication does not mean that in reality the thing has a {61} subjectual structure, still less that this subjectual reality is what underlies change. It is one thing to say that motion affects the totality of the thing that is changing, and quite another that the changing thing is a kind of subject to which what we call "change" is occurring. Nevertheless, Aristotle centers his thought on this subject; but here again he finds himself facing a serious difficulty: *what is that subject?*

Aristotle, eternally unsatisfied, again confronts all the difficulties of earlier philosophy. n the first place, "subject" is understood as the matter from which all things are made, because something cannot appear from nothing. That matter, Aristotle says, is *subjectum* (ὑποκείμενον), but strictly speaking is not substance because it lacks any specific determinations. At this point Anaximander's perspective reappears. We could say that those determinations are impressed on matter and are the ones that constitute essence (οὐσία), as something καθ'αὐτό. This may be true, but consider the case of humans: every mortal is born and dies. Is the form, i.e., the essence of each one of those humans the subject, the true substance? Not quite, Aristotle would say, because actually each human is born and dies, but he understands that being born and dying means separating the prime matter from some of its essential determinations. The line of generation is indefinite; therefore, even though it is true that every human dies and every living being dies, yet, prime matter and its essential determination—its substantial form (μορφή), in his terminology—are immortal. What we understand by *subject* is the complicated interweaving (συμπλοκή) of matter and form.

But we can ask Aristotle whether this does not dilute the concept of substance.[17] When I talk about Socrates, {62} am I talking about Socrates being a man or am I speaking of the concrete humanity of this Socrates I have here in front of me, which after all is what really matters? As a typical Greek, Aristotle shows that he cannot handle the problem if it is true that *reality is changing*,[18] being born and perishing in the way he has just described. Therefore he posits the question: what is it that provokes this change?

Prime matter on its own would be indifferent with respect to this or that form; pure form would be the Platonic *eidos*. Who or what is going to impress these forms on matter? For this, Aristotle has a solution that we might call "clever," which consists in saying that the world has not been made by any god (θεός), that God does not move the world, but "provokes" the motion of the world without this God being affected at all. Aristotle's θεός is the only substance, not generated and incorruptible, that does not have as a function to produce the other substances of the world, or even to put them in motion, but only to "provoke" motion in them. How is it provoked? That is the favorite example from Aristotle: as the object of love and desire it moves without moving. It provokes the desire; but to him, the beloved, nothing has to happen. Something would happen to him, if at the same time he were in love with the other; but by himself he moves without being moved. The function of the God of Aristotle is not to make the world, or even to set it in motion, but to provoke its internal motion. That is why Aristotle called this God a "separated substance," because it is the only one that fully realizes {63} the idea of separation (χοριστόν), of the substance that needs only itself.

II. *First philosophy as a science that is searched for*

Based on these elements, we are going to take a fourth step and persist with the question, *what is Aristotle searching for?* He is searching for what is "that which is" (τί τὸ ὄν)! Certainly, but Aristotle himself places us in a difficult situation. He mentions that we have several ways of referring to being, that we use being in four senses, that the fourth way in turn is said in ten ways, which are the categories, and in turn substance is said three ways (matter, form and their composite). One may ask, where is reality? Aristotle never answers this; the idea of what he is searching for is completely diluted.

Nevertheless, Aristotle tells us via the double way of logos and change that he is searching for something that *until now* has not been searched for.

Up to his time, Aristotle had the impression that Greek philosophers had discovered different zones of reality. The zone of the material, the zone of the physical elements of reality, the entity of numbers and figures; Democritus discovered the atoms; Socrates discovered rhetoric, politics and virtue (ἀρετή). Aristotle thinks that all these things "are," but none of them tells us "in what being consists." All these regions of being delimit a section of reality and say about it "that it is". But none takes the term in its *universality* (καθόλου), in its omneity[19] as applied to everything real, and none bothers to tell us {64} what is "that which is," not merely as just, virtuous, hot, cold, divisible or indivisible, but purely and simply as "that which is." And this science or knowledge of things that are, insofar as they simply are (ἐπιστήμε τοῦ ὄντος ᾗ ὄν), is what he calls προτή φιλοσοφία and we call "metaphysics."

Stated that way, this is nothing but a formal definition. But Aristotle, as a typical Greek, is immersed in the framework of change and motion, and understands this "that it is" from that viewpoint.

Change functions two ways in Aristotle's philosophy, as a content, a determination of some of the things that are, and also as the framework within which being, the ὄν, is discovered. This happens not only in Aristotle's philosophy, but in all other philosophies. We shall see that this involvement can be problematic for philosophy. In medieval theology and philosophy, both creation as total production of reality, and the intervention of God in each thing, are always involved; and it is not easy to delimit this double involvement.

Aristotle carves a special region out of change, that of beings in movement. Another special region of being is that of things that are born and die, of things which naturally are (φύσει ὄντα). But when Aristotle understands in what being consists, *qua* being, he sees it from the point of view of movement. He understands that being, in one form or another, consists in always being (ἀεί). What sometimes is and sometimes is not cannot be called something that always is in the fullest sense. Consequently, when Aristotle has to give us the last word about this φύσις, of these movements or changes that happen through time, he has no hesitation in making his own the notion of time as a cyclical, as an eternal return, a notion probably {65} going back to the Orphic tradition. In one of the pages that most impressed me in the *Metaphysics*, Aristotle tells us, "A tradition has been handed down by the ancient thinkers from the most remote antiquity, and bequeathed to posterity in the form of a story, a myth, to the effect that first substances are gods, and that the divine pervades the whole of nature." [20] A few lines later we read, "We believe that every divine art and philosophy have probably been repeatedly developed to the utmost and have perished again...These opinions, however [that the gods are the ultimate separate substances], have floated as relics of the shipwreck of ancient wisdom up to our days." This idea that wisdom has been found and lost multiple times should have had a better and more profound treatment in the conceptualization of Aristotelian metaphysics.

Of course, all this motion is provoked by the θεός, which is the only separated substance. And then Aristotle claims that this separated substance is exempt from any change. To say it is the first unmovable mover (πρότον κινοῦν ἀκίνητον), that moves without being moved, is to see God within the framework of motion or change. Aristotle calls this "theology" (θεολογία), something that has nothing to do with our theology, and metaphysics is also involved with it. These two definitions of metaphysics have given rise to numerous discussions among philosophers and philologists, but they are not important here because we shall see what happens to the two definitions at the hands of medieval philosophy. {66}

The only thing yet remaining is for Aristotle to tell us how we attain the truth about that "which is", considered as such.

Aristotle once again draws upon the inheritance of Parmenides: intelligence (knowing) and being are the same. What does Aristotle understand by that sameness? Is it the case that intelligence and being are formally identical? This never occurred to a Greek mind; for this idea we shall have to wait until Hegel.

Is it simply that intelligence is made for being, as Parmenides said? This is true, of course, and we shall see it immediately; but for Aristotle it was not sufficient. The Aristotelian affirmation of the moment of identity (ταυτόν) as true is not limited to intelligence, but is also applied to the senses. If we hear a certain sound, we say that the act of our perception is auditive since it has a certain sound as an object. But for Aristotle this is not enough and he will tell us that my very act, the one intrinsically determined as such an act, is an act of a sonorous or sound making type. Precisely then is when the sameness appears, between the sound that is heard by audition and the auditive quality of the act. There is among them a formal identity, this is precisely the same ἐντελέχεια as before, carefully understanding that the reality of the sound is not the reality of knowing because there are many sounds that we do not hear, and one can be sensing many things that have nothing to do with hearing. Nevertheless, this happens with all the senses.

Indeed, the same thing in a greater degree occurs with intelligence. Intelligence, when it understands being intellectually as such, and things insofar as they are, has the structure of entity as such, of the entity that always is. That is the reason why, for Aristotle, intelligence, at least considered in {67} general, is immortal and is anchored on the always. This has nothing to do with the idea of eternal life.

Aristotle will tell us next that on this sameness, which is the first radical truth, he grounded the logos that enunciates what things are (λόγος ἀποφαντικός). It refers to complex things, those that can be unfolded as subjects and attributes. The truth of that logos will consist in the fact that the things we say are united are indeed united, and that things we say are separate are indeed separate. The famous "adequateness" between thought and reality never appears in Aristotle.

This means that intelligence (νοῦς) in a certain way is made to be capable of being all (πάντα πῶς ἐστίν), precisely all "that is".

* * *

At the hands of Aristotle, this is the great gigantomachy or battle of giants that Plato mentioned (γιγαντομαχία περὶ τῆς οὐσίας). It is not strange that Plato himself, who did not reach Aristotle's level, at one point said, "I felt overwhelmed scrutinizing reality."[21]

We, the barbarians, have received Greek philosophy for an adventure completely different and alien to it, that of constructing from it a theology, a project begun in the Middle Ages. It is almost as if philosophy were not, *in and by itself*, a grand problem that must be continued as a problem and applied to it what St. Augustine said, "Let us search like those who have not yet found, and let us find {68} like those who still have to search, because it is written: those who have reached their goal have but begun."[22]

Briefly viewed this is the general picture of Greek metaphysics, which culminates in Aristotle. We have surveyed it not in order to say things that are not generally known, but to bring to the fore notions and ideas that will turn out to be quite important in subsequent chapters. We shall end by saying that if we squeeze the idea of the object of metaphysics in Aristotle a little, the following comes out:

1. This idea springs from a very concrete framework, the framework of the change or movement of the real.

2. Fundamental reality, the οὐσία, is always viewed from this perspective of change, as something delimited and separate from the rest of things.

3. In that idea of reality as an οὐσία, separate and determined, Aristotle searches for what is (τί ἐστίν), something that in one way or another corresponds to the idea of the "always" (ἀεί).

4. This idea of entity is taken by Aristotle along the lines of the logos, a term I left without translation precisely because there is no need to distinguish between *concept* and *judgment*—a distinction Aristotle never made nor did any other Greek, at least up to his own time. Aristotle takes οὐσία from the point of view of the logos, and views the problem of the ὄν similarly.

5. From that point of view truth appears as an intellective possession of what always is, said through the logos and seen by the νοῦς.

These five points do not represent a simple summary of what the object of metaphysics is for Aristotle. What they {69} constitute is the inseparable internal core of the idea that Aristotle has of the ὄν. This core is not something extrinsic, as if the ὄν were something that is just there and about which Aristotle tries to investigate, viewing it from the perspective of motion and change, explaining it through the logos, etc. The core belongs internally to the very structure of the ὄν, and precisely because of that, these five points correspond to what is enunciated by the title of this present course, which I tried to explain in the Introduction, "The fundamental problems of western metaphysics." In this case it is not the Western, but the Greek metaphysics; however, these five points constitute the very core, five times problematic, of what for Aristotle the idea of being (ὄν) is, what the idea of reality is.

---

[1] Met Z 1028b 2-4, translation of W.D. Ross.

[2] Diels-Kranz B 1.

[3] *Zubiri's marginal note:* "Later the Pythagoreans gave a clearer conceptualization of this delimitation. For them, numbers and figures constitute delimited itself".

[4] [For the Greeks "motion" and "change" were regarded as more or less the same thing, and the Greek word κίνεσις can be translated as either, depending on the context. The reader should bear this in mind when reading Zubiri's references to movement.—trans.]

[5] *Zubiri's marginal note:* "That is the idea of τάξις".

[6] *Zubiri's marginal note:*

"Insert the idea of *kósmos* here Hep."

"τάξις greater than κόσμος (infinite κόσμοι)".

"The first one who called κόσμος to that which involves the whole was Pythagoras, because of the τάξις in it (Diels I 105, 25)".

[7] [Cf. Diels, H. and W. Kranz, *Die Fragmente der Vorsokratiker*. Zürich/Hildesheim, 1964.—trans.]

[8] Zubiri refers here to the classic work of K. Reinhardt, *Parmenides und die Geschichte der griegischen Philosophie*, Bonn, Friedrich Cohen, 1916, p. 24.

[9] Plato, *Sophist* 243 d-e. Jowett translation, available on the Internet at http://classics.mit.edu/Plato/sophist.html.

[10] *Ibid.*, English rendering of Zubiri's translation, in order to make his point clear.

[11] *Zubiri's marginal note:* "Obscure. We have to say: ψευδός is not the same as negation, ἀληθής is not the same as affirmation, but rather that ψευδός is not true of the affirmation or the negation, and ἀληθής is true of the affirmation and the negation."

[12] *Zubiri's marginal note:* "It is not the case that δύναμις may not be ὄν; Aristotle expressly says the contrary (*Met* Δ 1017 b 1-9). But in its full meaning ὄν is ἐντελέχεια ὄν."

[13] *Zubiri's marginal note:* "καθ'αὑτό: What always and necessarily (or as ἴδιον, or rather I would say, as *constitutive* of something, what belongs

to the τὶ ἐστίν): *Met* L 1073 a 3-4". "*Met* Δ 1022 a 25-36. Synonym of κατὰ φύσιν and καθ'οὐσίαν."

14 *Zubiri's marginal note*: "(Brentano, ch. I). Independent *Met* Z 1028 a 34. Not every ὄν καθ'αὐτόν falls directly on a category (Brentano, § 11). But, careful: Aristotle seems to identify ὄν καθ'αὐτόν and ὄν as species (?) or *category*". [The reading of this manuscript note by Zubiri offers several doubts, and therefore, we give the most probable. It has not been possible to identify the reference to Brentano, if that is really the reference, as it seems].

15 [The term is almost always translated as "substance," as Zubiri discusses further on. His point is that the word was given this meaning by Aristotle.—trans.]

16 *Zubiri's marginal note*: "The ὄν has four senses: 1) To be true. 2) To have actuality. 3) To be itself. 4) To be independent (οὐσία). Each sense is grounded on the following one.

17 *Zubiri's marginal note*: "Here we must clarify the συμπλοκή and the *first* and *second* οὐσία. Two senses of ὑποκείμενον, as τοδε τί (first substance), and τί ἐστί (second substance)."

18 *Zubiri's marginal note*: "Here second substance is viewed from the horizon of change".

19 This term was written by Zubiri with a question mark

20 *Met* Λ 1074 b1 ff.

21 Here Zubiri freely quotes a passage of the *Phaedo* (99 d). It is a passage that Zubiri quotes several times along his works. Cf., for example, *Nature, History, God*, p. 21.

22 St. Augustine, *De Trinitate* IX, c. 1

CHAPTER 2
WESTERN PHILOSOPHY (1)
ST. THOMAS

INTRODUCTION. THE FRAMEWORK OF NOTHINGNESS

Western Metaphysics develops along a line seemingly very much like that of the Greeks. The Greeks, and above all Aristotle, spoke to us about first philosophy (προτή φιλοσοφία) as a θεολογία, that is to say, as a λόγος of the θεός. We already discussed briefly what the θεός is for Aristotle; now we must make this more precise.

Aristotle considers the θεός as an οὐσία, as something that is fully self-sufficient. All realities in some form or another are sufficient, i.e., they are self-contained, and in this sense they are οὐσία. But this special οὐσία, the θεός, has an absolutely full sufficiency and independence. The θεός of Aristotle is purely and simply an οὐσία that is completely self-sufficient and needs no other to occur and attain being. In this sense it is πέρας, something perfectly determined. As such, the θεός is quite removed from what, for us, is infinitude. About this substance Aristotle says that {72} it is ἀκίνετον, immutable, or if you will, unmovable. It is such not only in fact, but also by its internal condition. It is immutable because in itself it is pure actuality, pure act, and that means for Aristotle that God is a pure subsisting "form," with no matter at all. Not only does God not need anything else in order to be, but in addition he is self-sufficient in terms of the fullness of his operations.

Aristotle provides the θεός with an intelligence and a will, but an intelligence and a will that are fully self-sufficient. Precisely because of this, they lack an object different from or outside of themselves. For Aristotle the reality of the world is not knowable to God. Aristotle did not even consider the question of whether God could know the world, because in that case God would depend on the reality he knows. The intelligence and the will that Aristotle assigns to the θεός as the root and supreme explanation of his internal sufficiency do nothing but think and desire themselves: intellection of intellection (νόησις νοήσεας). It is in this self-sufficiency that Aristotle makes the perfect volitional happiness of God consist.

Consequently, there is nothing here that would make us think immediately of what is going to be, in Western philosophy, the idea of an infinite God; that is something absolutely alien to the Greek world. The θεός of Aristotle is something perfectly determined by its internal, formal, and complete sufficiency, in the sense that he has no need of another to be, nor even to perform his operations.

This being, the divine οὐσία, has usually been considered from the perspective of motion or change. So much so, that when Aristotle tells us what that first substance is, he says it is unmoved (ἀκίνετον), that it is the first unmoved mover. This God thinks about himself and loves himself; but Aristotle is far from imagining {73} that this internal knowledge and that volition have any resemblance to what, in Western philosophy, will be self-referentiality. Aristotle makes the divine intellect an "object" of its own intellection and everything ends there. He does not raise the question of the way in which intellection may return upon itself—a notion that Aristotle would find completely alien. God is only concerned with himself, just as we humans are concerned with ourselves, and to a certain extent with others.

This determines one's *relationship with the world*. From God's viewpoint, this relationship is nil; Aristotle's θεός has no relationship with the world. Not only is he unmoved or unchanged (ἀκίνετον) in himself, but he is purely and simply something that sets the world in motion (πρότον κινοῦν). Note that, in the first place, this God has not made the world, since he is something that is just there absolutely. In the second place, not only has he not made the world as efficient cause, he has not set it in motion as efficient cause. Cosmic motions (changes) emerge from the characteristics proper to the substances that compose the world, from their οὐσίαι, and do not depend at all on any divine action. The only thing that this unmoved mover does is to put the world in motion by evoking it. As the perfect substance—here there is probably a vague Platonic resonance inside the Aristotelian metaphysics—there is a certain desire (ὄρεξις) on the part of things, not a desire to go towards God, but a desire to be in motion. For this reason, if God sets the world in motion, it is similar to the way an object of love puts the lover in motion and draws out the desire, without the loved object being altered at all.

But when faced with this God of the Greeks, Western metaphysics {74} inscribed its thought in a completely different framework. It will be easy to repeat the term "theology" and translate θεός by *Deus*. But what lies behind these terms and concepts is something totally different from and alien to Greek thought.

Above all, God, considered in himself *prior to any metaphysics*, is conceived by the whole of Western theology as an existing reality by itself, but in addition endowed with a the character of a person—an idea completely foreign to the Greek world. Not only is God personal, the sufficiency of that person does not reside in self-knowledge. Rather, just the opposite: God knows himself by the intrinsic infinitude in which the divine being consists. Because of this, while for Aristotle God is something susceptible to "replicas," polytheism is completely excluded from Western thought. At first, Aristotle thought that the first unmoved mover was only one, and therefore he repeats the famous Homeric verse, "It is not good to have many sovereigns, let one be the ruler".[1] Somewhat later, probably because of the influence of astronomy, which was then being elaborated in Greece, Aristotle assigned to the forty-seven astronomical circles a similar number of unmoved movers. Just as the sphere of Parmenides was capable of being replicated in the atoms of Democritus, the θεός of Aristotle could be replicated in a series of forty-seven unmoved movers because God lacked the characteristic that excludes any multiplication, that intrinsic infinitude proper to the God of Christianity.

But in addition the relationship between God and the world is totally different in Western metaphysics from the one {75} that the Greek world was able to imagine. Precisely as a matter of faith Western metaphysics has always believed that God created the world out of nothing.

It is true that the two concepts of creation and nothingness may be somewhat fluid at many points. Actually, the verb *bârâ* in Hebrew, which appears in the first line of Genesis ("In the beginning God created heavens and earth") does not etymologically mean "to create", but "to make"; the proof is that the Septuagint sometimes translated this by "made" (ἐποίησεν). However, it is true that throughout the Old Testament this term has the meaning of a creative action, and for that reason it is properly translated as, "In the beginning God *created* heavens and earth."

This idea of creation is still susceptible to several interpretations. One interpretation, quite popular, appears in the second chapter of Genesis and presents God somewhat like a potter who is making man with earthen clay. However, we must keep in mind that the first chapter of Genesis was written many centuries after the second chapter; the first chapter belongs to the exilic or post-exilic era, while the second proceeds from the Yahwist tradition that was set down in writing probably in the ninth century before Christ. Appeal to the potter image is out of the question at this later time. Affirmation that creation is a "creation out of nothing" appears for the first time in the Book of Maccabees (2 Mc 7:28), which says [in the Septuagint], "from things that are not" (οὐκ ἐξ ὄντων) God has created. The important point is not only that this phrase is in Maccabees, but that it is placed in the mouth of a woman of the people, which means more or less that it was a commonly held belief among all Israelites of that time. {76}

To create the world out of nothing means, in the first place, that something is produced that was not there before, *ex nihilo sui;* otherwise, there would have been no production; this is something that happens to anyone here on earth who makes something. Something is made insofar as it had not been made (did not exist) before, and therefore, something appears that is *ex nihilo sui.* But what is proper to creation is to be *ex nihilo sui et subjecti,* because in the end all the productions and creations we witness in the world are productions that operate on something already existing, on a primary subject. Consequently, all these creations, regardless how great they may be, are always "alterations." That is why I have sometimes thought that the formula that best translates the idea of creation would be to say that it is, on God's part, the placing of otherness without alteration. That is, putting (or creating) the *other,* but without alteration, either on God's part or on the part of the subject that receives it; that is the pure and simple placing of the other as other.[2] This shows that the relationship of God to the world is completely different than the one conceived by Greek metaphysics.

God, as creator *ex nihilo,* is the first efficient cause of the whole reality of the world. But he is at the same time the last or final cause. In his double aspect of efficient and final causality, creative action is a fact of faith that as such has nothing to do with what constituted Greek metaphysics. This has a decisive importance for the framework in which the history of metaphysics will be inscribed from that moment until our time. For a Greek, "to be" would mean in the end "to truly be," that is to say, "to be always," to be more or less incorruptible in one way or the other, at least during a certain period of time even though segmented and fragmentary. For the Greeks the world starts by being something whose internal vicissitudes and internal structure man tries to study. Now, on the other hand, {77} the first thing we think about things—and reasonably so—is that they might not have existed, i.e., they might have been nothing. There appears, then, next to the framework of motion of the Greek world, the framework of nothingness.

Given that the first thing that Western metaphysics thinks is that the world, whatever it is, might not have been, or could have been different than what it is, it follows that being does not mean *being-always*, as the Greek thought, but *being not-nothing*, that is, created being. That moment of "not-nothing" is going to constitute, for better or for worse, the framework within which Western metaphysics will develop from the beginnings of Christianity. Therefore man is not, as he was for a Greek, an being that with his *lógos* is going to say what things are, but primarily and radically a traveler between the almost-nothing, which man is, and God, the full reality. This idea of traveler between the world and God is what St. Bonaventure expressed in his famous treatise, brief but full of metaphysical substance, *Itinerarium mentis in Deo*, a journey of the mind towards God. This framework and this vision actually have nothing to do with metaphysics; it is a strictly theological vision. Its theological version in the sense of *lógos* was the object of the earliest Greek and Latin speculations, something that does not concern us now because we are unraveling the structure of a particular metaphysics.

Within this theological framework Greek ideas are going to be received, and the *organon* of concepts they bequeath to us will be used to understand and make intelligible not only God, but also things within the framework of nothingness. Instead of presenting its history we shall concentrate on this metaphysical vision in St. Thomas.

St. Thomas receives the ideas of Aristotle's metaphysics {78} and with them does on a smaller scale what Aristotle did with his predecessors. Above all, he beautifully and neatly purifies and sharpens the concepts received from Aristotle. But it would be a mistake to stop there, as if St. Thomas thought that metaphysics was already fully developed. The metaphysics of St. Thomas *does not stop* there but *begins* there when, with that *organon* of concepts, he interprets what being is within the framework of nothingness.[3] We have, therefore, two points, first the purification of Aristotle by St. Thomas, and second, the Thomist view of being. We shall start with the first.

§1

THE PURIFICATION OF ARISTOTELIAN CONCEPTS

We ask, first of all, what is St. Thomas' purifying reception of Aristotelian concepts?

This purification can be observed in two areas. First is the idea St. Thomas has of what metaphysics is. Second is the idea St. Thomas has of the proper object of metaphysics.

I. *The idea of philosophy as metaphysics*

We have seen that Aristotle's metaphysics (a term he never used) or, if you prefer, Aristotle's first philosophy, was on one hand the science of being as such (ὄν ἦ ὄν) and, on the other hand, "theology." On this duality much has been written. I tend to believe that Aristotle thought that the θεός was the supreme substance, and one can always characterize a body of knowledge *a potiori* by what constitutes its terminus. But, regardless of whether this is the solution to the problem, the fact is that a duality of concepts is present in Aristotle.

Aristotle tells us, in the first place, that as "theology" metaphysics aims towards these separated substances (χωριστή οὐσία), which the gods (θεός) are, or *the* God, if we refer to the single unmoved mover he initially admitted. In the second place, with respect to things he tries {80} to find out what they are insofar as they are. In the third place, about those things, insofar as they are, he tries to find their explanations and ultimate causes.

In the first page of his commentary on Aristotle's *Metaphysics*, St. Thomas says, "According to these three perspectives three names appear." An important remark follows, "It is called 'divine science' or 'theology' insofar as it deals with separated substances,"[4] and this would seem to suggest that St. Thomas merely repeats what Aristotle said about the θεός. But here is where the important inflexion of thought begins, because that separated substance of which St. Thomas speaks is not the θεός of Aristotle, but the God, personal and infinite, who is certainly "separated" from the world. And it is to Him that St. Thomas refers the Aristotelian definition of "theology" as logos of God. Hence "theology" is a science that refers to God as object of religious acts. The theology in which St. Thomas is going to inscribe his idea of God—the separated substances of Aristotle—is a theological and religious vision of the world. No one would think of praying to the first unmoved mover; on the other hand, supplication (εὐχή) is directly addressed to God, the separated substance that for St. Thomas constitutes the God of Christianity. The difference is considerable.

In the second place, in just a few words St. Thomas expresses the second concept, "It is called 'metaphysics' inasmuch as that science considers being [ens] and everything that follows from it".[5] Here {81} it seems that St. Thomas again just repeats the Aristotelian formula; but in this same chapter we shall also see important changes. The "*ens*" about which St. Thomas speaks as primary is *being*, which for Aristotle is not really primary. For Aristotle, as we have seen, ὄν strictly speaking is not properly translated by "being". Though in many cases this may be a good translation, when Aristotle says τὸ ὄν λέγαται πολλαχῶς, "There are several senses in which a thing may be said to 'be',"[6] he is not thinking about being, but about what we express when the logos says of something "that it is", and this is said with many (four) meanings. Still, we might think, at least in the sense of the categories, that ὄν means a "being" or an "being." However, we shall see that even this is not completely accurate.

Continuing with his explanation of this second concept of metaphysics, St. Thomas says, "This trans-physics is found by way of resolution and conceptual analysis, since what is more common is known after what is less common".[7] Here there is another important inflexion with respect to Aristotelian thought. For Aristotle, what we call "metaphysics" was purely and simply "first philosophy," with respect to which the investigation of nature, for example, is second philosophy (δεύτερα φιλοσοφία). The subject is completely different, so different that the editor of Aristotle's works found some writings placed directly after the *Physics*, and not having a title, called them, "What comes after *Physics*" (τὰ μετὰ τὰ φυσικά). St. Thomas does not take this circumstance into consideration and tells us directly that the characteristics of being as such are "transphysical," where {82} "trans" does not mean that they come *after* the *Physics*, but in one form or another are "beyond" the *Physics* and transcend it. We shall have to see in what sense St. Thomas affirms this; but what cannot be done is to simply assimilate that meaning of the term to Aristotle's text, because the translation of μετὰ by *trans* is a great change that will be decisive in the history of Western metaphysics. While metaphysics in the hands of Aristotle was a "first philosophy," here first philosophy is called "metaphysics" because it studies something that certainly belongs to all things, but in one way or another is "trans" to them, beyond them. That is why, although not the most common expression in St. Thomas, first philosophy is identified with metaphysics in the sense that the transcendental is what defines the metaphysical.

St. Thomas has added something further in this commentary. While being, the ὄν ᾗ ὄν, is for Aristotle a characteristic that all things have by the mere fact that they are, because they form that compact unit that we call "world" or "cosmos," here something different appears. Those characteristics, which we may call "entitative" to simplify the exposition, appear as belonging to a very special type, viz. the most common, the most universal characteristics that all things have. Here Aristotle's καθόλου takes on the very concrete meaning of universality, the one that fits everything by the mere fact of being, and thus has become *magis communis*.

St. Thomas provides a third conception of first philosophy by telling us "it is said that it is first philosophy inasmuch as it considers the first causes of everything".[8] {83} Since this first cause is the Creator God for St. Thomas, it means that as theology and as transphysical, first philosophy—what St. Thomas simply calls "metaphysics"—is converted into a metaphysical theology of creation.

For Aristotle metaphysics was, on the one hand, the investigation of being as such (ὄν ᾗ ὄν), and on the other, it was "theology." In St. Thomas both concepts appear unified because he tells us—and certainly this he could not have taken from Aristotle—that being *qua* being has God as a first cause. Consequently, here we are not dealing with a naming process *a potiori* as happened in Aristotle, but with something that forms part of the *internal context* of St. Thomas' metaphysics.

In summary, the interpretation of the μετά as *trans* and the conversion of "meta-physics" into "trans-physics" shapes the conceptual purification that St. Thomas carries out on Aristotle's "first philosophy." But much more important are the purifications St. Thomas elaborates on the object of that metaphysics.

II. *Object of metaphysics and the idea of being*

We can consider the object of metaphysics at two levels, the order of knowledge and the order of reality.

1. The order of knowledge.

St. Thomas does not hesitate to accept directly and without question the *conceptive* concept of human understanding. In this view, to understand is to form concepts, and to understand intellectively is to form concepts of things.[9] This is an idea completely {84} alien to the Greek world, among other reasons because the Greeks never had the term or notion of "concept." It has a Latin

origin and probably goes back to Cicero, who perhaps was inspired by the Stoics; at any rate, up to the time of Aristotle it did
not exist.

For St. Thomas, then, knowledge is viewed as conceptive.
Confronting Plato, St. Thomas tells us (apparently repeating Aristotle) that every conceptive order is the product of an abstraction
(ἀφαίρεσις). Every abstraction seems to be a merely negative operation. Ignoring some aspects of things and considering only
others is not only how we do abstraction, but without it there
would be no abstraction. But the problem is much more serious
because in that apparent *negativity*—i.e., disregarding certain
characteristics of things—what we do is to *positively* constitute
the pure object for viewing by intelligence. In this sense, abstraction is something eminently positive, and that abstraction, according to St. Thomas, may assume several forms.

In the first place, there can be an abstraction where we prescind from the individuality proper to each of the things that constitute the world. If we only pay attention to individualities, St.
Thomas tells us, there would never be knowledge (*scientia*), but
something else—we do not know what. For this reason we have to
prescind from, we have to abstract from the individual characteristics of things; and then, what remains before our eyes is just a
sensible reality with its individual characteristics removed. That
remaining sensible reality can be the object of science, what St.
Thomas and the medieval philosophers in general called "physics." Let us remember that "physics" for a Greek was the theory of
being or entities in motion (undergoing change), something with
which {85} St. Thomas will indeed concur, though after a small
conceptual purification. While for a Greek what essentially constitutes physical knowledge (ἐπιστήμε φυσική) is being or being in
motion (ὄν κινετόν) *qua* in motion, for a medieval philosopher this,
though still true, is put on a secondary level. What is now taken
as the *first* level is sensible substance *qua* sensible substance,
which is something quite removed from what later became known
as physics. This gap cannot be easily closed. In general terms,
what the ancient world, the entire medieval world, and even the
beginning of the modern world concentrated on when considering
movement (or change) in the cosmos is the *situation of that which
is in motion*. In other words, they considered motion as a "state" of
whatever is in motion, and that is why we have "physics" as a science of being or entities in motion. But present day physics completely ignores motion considered as a *state* of something in motion; the only relevant thing is the "functional" relationship of one
reality with respect to another. Motion, considered as a "function," and not as a "state," is what characterizes physics from its

first steps in Galileo to its culmination in our days. Here then, we have a first type of abstraction.

There is a second type of abstraction, seemingly much more profound. It consists in prescinding within the sensible substance from all its qualitative elements (e.g., hot, cold) and retaining purely and simply the fact that it *is* a quantitative substance. What remains would not be a *sensible quantity* (considered by physics), but an *intelligible quantity*, proper to mathematics as then conceived, though something quite far removed from modern mathematics. Despite its clumsy repetition in textbooks, no one can one still maintain that mathematics is the science of quantity. {86} Modern mathematics has moved beyond the science of quantity; it is rather a science of abstract sets, whether of quantity or not. It is also erroneously repeated that geometry is the science of continuous quantity and arithmetic the science of discrete quantity. This is false, because in the first place, there are non-continuative geometries (non-Archimedean geometry), and in second place, because there is a numerical continuum. The introduction of irrational numbers (e.g., $\sqrt{2}$), conferred upon the field of numbers a strict continuity. Therefore, no intrinsic difference between continuous and discrete quantity exists.[10] In addition modern mathematics does not always deal directly with quantity. The elements comprising a set may be quantities, and it is evident that there are sets of numbers; but there are also sets of polynomials, of functions, etc., that by themselves are not defined by their reference to quantity. A set is defined if a univocal criterion is given so that considering a particular thing, it is possible to say if that object has a certain property or not; if it has, it falls in the set, if not, it falls outside the set. That the property may or not may be quantitative is something completely accidental and, in addition, quite limited. Modern mathematics has nothing to do with the notion of quantity considered by medieval philosophers.

There is still a third type of abstraction, much more profound. If we prescind from any quantity, sensible or intelligible, we are simply left with substance *qua* substance. Then we have something much more abstract, something that is just being, the *ens*, what remains before the intelligence following this action. Through the abstraction of individual notes and of any sensible and intelligible quantitative consideration, the idea of being is constituted before our eyes, the idea of {87} that which is insofar as it is. When the object of metaphysics is so defined, we cannot but inquire as to the characteristics of an object constituted in this way.

In the first place, from the cognitive point of view, for St. Thomas being is the highest abstraction, the most abstract thing that can be given. That is why St Thomas is able to say—justifiably from his point of view—that the considerations of *prima philosophia*, the trans-physics, are the *magis communia*, not only "more" but the *maximally* common. The idea of being represents the greatest abstraction, but only by utilizing a hypothesis that should have been questioned: is it true that the first thing intelligence does is to form concepts?

In the second place, and proceeding further along this line of thought, not only is the concept of being for St. Thomas the most abstract that we can imagine, but it also has a radical primacy. St. Thomas says that in the concept of being, all other concepts of understanding are resolved. Indeed, to conceive is only to conceive what this is and what that is; in "what is", in being, all other concepts of understanding are resolved. However, the concept of being will be primary only if the primary function of the intellect is to frame concepts. But what if that were not so? I say this not to criticize St. Thomas, but to point out that the title of the present book, "Problems of Metaphysics," really announces *problems*, and metaphysics is not like a heavy block that is just there, to be taken or be left alone.

In the third place, since every concept represents a unitary moment with respect to conceived things—for example, the concept of man referred to the human species covers all possible men in that species—we must ask, *what type of unity does the concept of being have?* {88}

St. Thomas accepts one of Aristotle's favorite ideas, that being is not a genus. For example, life taken as a genus is divided into different types of living things—vegetal, animal and human—and humans can be determined by means of a division among the properties that distinguish them. But this cannot be done at all in the case of being, simply because in order to make it "differ" there would have to be a difference with respect to being. But then, that difference cannot be in being, because if it were, it would have been something added. To the idea of being nothing can be added. The supreme genera to which Aristotle refers, the categories—substance and the nine accidents—are not in any way "species" of beings, but the primary and radical *diversity* of beings. Within being there is no difference, there is nothing that would correspond to the verb *to differ*, that is, to take being at some point and break it into two parts. Substance and the accidents are not, then, *divisions*, but as a Scholastic would say in a very graphic and very exact way, *primo diversa*, a primary and radical diversity. Therefore, the concept of being does not have a generic unity, but is a separate concept with respect to all other concepts.

This does not mean that the concept of being is not realized in all things that are. On the contrary, each thing that is, is resolved one way or the other in being. This means that what we call "being" is something realized in each and every thing, and furthermore, it does not differentiate specifically or generically some from others; it is in all of them, but in a certain way happens in depth and over all of them. This *being-there-in-and-over* is the exact meaning of "to transcend." The concept of being has a unity that is not generic, but transcendental; it is found realized in all things that are, in all entities, but {89} is not limited to any of them. That is why St. Thomas says that while species and the supreme genera are "divided" into subordinate species, with respect to being no division is given, but a "contraction." The concept of being is not divided into species of entities and supreme genera, but contracts in its own way in each of these supreme genera; it is a conceptual structure of contraction and not a conceptual structure of division. The unity of being, therefore, is not generic; it is a transcendental unity.

The question is, then, *what is proper to transcendental unity?* Here St. Thomas appeals to the idea of analogy in Aristotle. Let us be clear that although the idea of analogy is found in multiple locations in Aristotle, the expression "analogy of being" is never found in him. Let us not make an issue of this now, but concentrate on the points St. Thomas is going to make precise, and outline the associated Aristotelian thought.

We shall not engage in a lengthy discussion of what analogy is, which Thomists and non-Thomists alike might expect at this point. We shall limit ourselves to something simple and fundamental. The important fact is that being, envisioned in the manner explained above, is in all things that are, but in each one of them in its own way; this is precisely the idea of analogy. Perhaps some Thomists might say that this is the analogy of attribution and not of proportion; but let us not deal with that distinction, the important idea is the first. We are dealing with concepts that are realized in each thing, but in a different way in each; and if not in each taken individually, at least in the different supreme genera. We are concerned with the way a quality is *being*, a quantity is *being*, a substance is *being*, and a relation is *being*. These are beings in the sense that they answer the question "what is it?" and correspond to the universal concept {90} of being, but in each case connected to a *mode* of being. Therefore, by virtue of that, the concept of being has a non-generic unity, a transcendental unity, and in addition it is analogical. The idea of being is the supreme abstraction in which all other concepts of understanding are resolved, in a transcendental and analogical way.

As we can see, St. Thomas has been slowly and progressively purifying Aristotle's ideas, and although this accomplishment was not exclusively his, we can concentrate our exposition on him. However, this only affects the order of concepts.

So in our next step, we must ask, in the order of reality, what is it in things that corresponds to that which we understand in the concept of being?

Here matters become more complicated because now it is not the case of the *concept* of being, but of the *entityness* of each thing. I use the term "entityness" to deliberately avoid that difference between *being* and *entity* that has been canonized since Heidegger. This would not be important if we were dealing with Heidegger's philosophy, but once again it is the problem of trying to push notions from a modern philosophy onto an earlier one. When Husserl published *Phenomenology*[11] and "essences" were mentioned there, the Scholastics said they knew about them, and then phenomenology appeared as a purified and psychological version—or transcendental version—of what essences are in Scholasticism. When Scheler published his *Ethic of Values*[12] {91} and said that values are objective, again the Scholastics pointed out that they had defended the idea, with only the difference of referring to the "good." Once again modern notions are pushed onto Scholasticism. Heidegger tells us (*Sein und Seiendes*) that there is a difference between being and entity, and it is alleged that this is what we mean when we affirm that "being" is one thing and "entity" another. But this cannot be admitted; if Heidegger's proposed distinction had existed since Parmenides, as he assumed, the history of philosophy would have been different; nor can we accept the inference that from Parmenides to our times philosophy has misunderstood that distinction.

To avoid these incongruities let us refer to the being of things. We do not talk here about the conceptive order, that is, about the concept of being, but about the real and effective being of each thing. To do this we have to ask three questions.

1. What does St. Thomas understand by "being"?
2. What are the characteristics of being?
3. What relationship is there between these characteristics and the being of which they are characteristics? This question is completely justified, since nothing can be added to being.

1. *What does St. Thomas understand by "being"?*

St. Thomas apparently just repeats some ideas of Aristotle, but with an important modification. In a concise way St. Thomas tells us that "being is everything whose act is to be" (*est ens id cujus actus est esse*).[13] This is a completely alien idea to Aristotle, because while Aristotle referred to being {92} in act, he never said that being was the act of a thing. In addition, what St. Thomas understands by "act" is always subject to interpretation.

Be that as it may, we must ask, what is that *id*, that *something* whose act is *to be* and yet seems outside this *to be*? Is it nothing perhaps? Because then *to be* is not an act. Is it something? Because then *to be* is not what is ultimate and radical. St. Thomas considers things inasmuch as they are "beings" or as individual things, "entities," This is what for many years and in many seminars I have been calling *the entification of reality*, which subsumes and articulates reality within the concept of being.[14] The importance of this will be seen below. Entification of reality consists in believing that what is primary and radical about things is that they are "entities," which supposes that what is primary and radical about things is "to be." But what if this is not so? What happens with languages that lack the verb "to be" or with those languages that, although having it, make little use of it, as it happens in the ancient Semitic languages? There is always a problem here.

Nonetheless, St. Thomas does not question it and just accepts *res* as synonym for *ens*. In this sense, St. Thomas has taken *things* (and here I give the term "thing" a completely innocuous meaning) as "entities," in a radical entification of reality.

2. *What characteristics does being have?*

This entification brings certain characteristics with respect to things that we can quickly enumerate.

In the first place, we may consider being absolutely, that is, taken in itself, any kind of being *qua* being. If we consider it in an affirmative, positive way, {93} every being is an *ens* that has an essence, a quiddity. The term "essence" has a very concrete and precise meaning that has nothing to do with what I, modestly, clumsily and probably ignorantly call "essence" in my book;[15] here "essence" means the essential content that every being has as a quiddity, insofar as it is a being considered intrinsically.

But we can consider it in a negative way and then, together with that *res* that the essence would be, we have what we call the "unity," the *unum*. St. Thomas says that this consideration is negative because, purifying once more the thought of Aristotle, he refuses to consider the problem of unity in the way that Plato did. Plato thought that the *one* opposes the *many*, and devised that fantastic dialectic of the one and the many, which culminates in the *Parmenides* and the *Sophist*. Aristotle never followed this line of reasoning, and understood that what is essential is not that there may be other *ones*, but that *one* (thing) might be another (different) *one*, which is a separate question. He also thought that this "one" of the "other one" can be constituted by its internal indivisibility, since if it were divisible we would not have *one* thing, but two or several. Unity is a transcendental characteristic, albeit negative, of being. St. Thomas, following Aristotle, says that there are many classes of unity, that there are accidental unities, collective unities, etc.; but what is of most interest to him is the unity *per se*, that which constitutes the one. For example, in the case of the human species, the internal unity of animality and rationality is not the same as the unity between Socrates and music, since Socrates might not have been a musician, while the unity of species is intrinsic and formal. {94}

But if we take being not in itself, but relative to others, then we also find two considerations, positive and negative. The negative would consist in saying that every being, as we have just seen, is a *quid*, a *quidditas*; but is *other* than the others, it is *quid aliud*, it is *aliquid*, which is just the origin of the term "something".[16] To be "something" does not mean to be simply *res*, but also to be something *different* than the other. As we shall see below, this poses the problem of determining whether all the characteristics that are flamboyantly called "transcendental" are really such, strictly speaking. Can it be said of God that He is something in this sense with respect to the world? We shall leave this question in abeyance for the time being.

We may also consider the matter positively. In that case the positive relativity of a being with respect to another is a transcendental respectivity, since it must be established along the lines of being *qua* being. St. Thomas says that of this there are only two possible types. One is the being that, because of its own entityness, is called to apprehend every being by the mere fact that it is; this is the *verum*, intelligence. The *verum* mentioned here is not the *verum logicum*—i.e. it is not the case of true knowledge—but of the intrinsic and formal condition through which every being in principle is object of a *verum*, of an intelligence. Something similar can be said with respect to the will. Being can be in agreement with the will, not in the sense of truth, but in the sense that every entity is intrinsically "that which all desire," as St. Thomas says repeating the first phrase of the *Nicomachean Ethics* of Aristotle. In other words, an entity is that which has in itself the very reason for desirability.

The *verum* and the *bonum* are {95} transcendental properties or characteristics of being, referred to intelligence and will, and therefore, to that ψυχή of which Aristotle said that in a certain way it can be everything, a phrase that St. Thomas repeats at this moment, *anima quae est quoddammodo omnia.*[17] Since this all (*omnia*) is such along the line of being *qua* being, it means that this concordance in the order of truth and in the order of goodness is a strictly transcendental concordance.

We now have five transcendental characteristics of being: its *res* or quiddity, its unity, that it is something (*aliquid*), truth and goodness.

Yet, this is rife with significant difficulties, as Scholasticism realized. Thus, for example, to the concept of being as such definitely belongs the idea that there be no multiplicity of "beings" (as opposed to entities); then, in what measure can it be said that these notes are simply transcendental? In the best case they would not be so absolutely, but only hypothetically. In the second place, is it true that every entity is by itself intrinsically intelligible? That depends on what is understood by "entity," because not even Christ's intelligence was able to have a comprehensive intellection of his own divine filiation—something that only the Word was able to have *qua* God, and this was quite well known to St. Thomas. With this, we begin to see that even within this new framework, those things that first appear neatly outlined do not stop presenting problems.

3. *What is the relationship between these characteristics and being?*

We have already mentioned that nothing can be added to being, {96} unless from within the being itself. Assuming that we have a being of a particular genus, we can make all kinds of divisions and subdivisions. But to being as such we cannot *add* anything from the outside because that which could be added would be "nothing."

From St. Thomas' metaphysics one observes that these characteristics of being, regardless of what they may be, are grounded in entityness; were it not for entityness, we would be unable to say anything about transcendental characteristics. These transcendental characteristics, precisely because they are grounded on entityness, accompany every being that exists and is real, *cirumeunt omne ens qua ens.* Because of this, I have taken the liberty of translating with another root that same term and call those characteristics "trans-grounding."[18] Being and its characteristics trans-ground all beings that exist; and this translation is not so arbitrary because, referring to a different theological problem, St. Thomas says that God is "a *profundens* first cause to every being and its differences".[19] Therefore, these characteristics are grounded on being, and because of that they are trans-grounding.

Furthermore, these characteristics are not added to being. How could we possibly add them? Where could they possibly come from? From non-being? In that case they would be nothing. For this reason St. Thomas makes use of an Aristotelian notion and says that, formally considered, being and the one are not identical, but "accompany each other." In this case, Scholasticism has translated the verb ἀκολουθεῖν by *conversio* and that way each of these characteristics is convertible (*convertitur*) with being. However, inasmuch as it is convertible with being new difficulties appear because, if all of them are convertible with being, then all of them {97} could be taken as a starting point. The history of metaphysics from this point on is going to be the development of that possibility.

What exactly does this "conversion" mean for St. Thomas? It is something that he never tells us; these characteristics are not characteristics added to being, but are being itself conceived in a more expressive way, according to the different points of view we have been taking. Then, we must ask, is it the case that these transcendental characteristics are nothing but some type of "expression"? A dedicated Scholastic would say that we are facing distinctions of reason *cum fundamento in re*, grounded in things. But this takes us back to the starting point. And then, what is the ground, in being, for this new and different consideration?

Here the problematic characteristic of this expression arises, which again directs us to the function of conceiving and judging. Is this function going to be primarily the expression of characteristics, which man conceives *cum fundamento in re* by means of concepts with regard to being?

At any rate, as a result we have (1) that the order of being is transcendental; (2) that it is transgrounding; and (3) referred to a first cause, that it is an order supported by something transcendent. The unity of these three terms is not merely semantic or conceptive, but going beyond the purification of Aristotelian concepts it takes us to something much more important and radical. How does St. Thomas actually see being in the framework of nothingness? Everything else is the purified conceptual organon needed to address the question of what being is in the framework of nothingness.

As we noted earlier, St. Thomas has subjected Aristotle to a purifying operation, more or less the same as the purification {98} Aristotle imposed on all previous philosophy. St. Thomas' own metaphysics begins at the moment he asks a key question: what happens to being, conceived in that purified way, rigorously delimited, and viewed from the framework of nothingness? This is the radical and fundamental problem of metaphysics in St. Thomas. Of course, at the very start resides St. Thomas' idea of what metaphysics is, as we pointed out above. Seemingly he adopts

Aristotle's formula: on one hand, he deals with God as separated substance; on the other, he deals with being as such; and thirdly, he refers being to the ultimate and supreme cause, namely God. In the end, this means that St. Thomas' metaphysics consists in seeing how being, conceived as far as St. Thomas can determine quite rigorously by Aristotle, is referred to God.

We are going to cover this metaphysics of St. Thomas in two parts. In the first, we shall examine his positive vision of being. In the second, we shall examine how it is possible to have a true intellection, that is, the type of metaphysical knowledge that deals with this being.

§2

THE VISION OF BEING IN ST. THOMAS

Let us repeat it once more: the being (ὄν) of Aristotle is viewed from the framework of motion; things that change and cease to be pose the problem of what, in one way or another, never ceases to be, but is truly always, and which in one form or another tries to be always. St. Thomas sees being from a completely different framework, since he starts from the perspective that the beings that surround man are created beings. This is not the framework of motion, it is—if I may be permitted the neologism—the framework of "creatureliness." This framework changes the internal structure of metaphysics from top to bottom, because in this framework of creatureliness things appear as creatures, and therefore, not only do we have a vision of things, but also of God himself. When we take God and his creation simultaneously we have what might be called a "creational vision," and it is in this framework of creatureliness that St. Thomas erects his metaphysics. When we indicated above that St. Thomas inscribes Aristotle's notions within a new framework, what we tried to say is that he develops his idea of being within the framework of creatureliness, and his whole purpose consists in interpreting being from the point of view of creatureliness. As we shall see, this is not going to be an easy task.

In this framework of creatureliness St. Thomas observes, on the one hand, things in the framework of nothingness, and on the other, a creator God within that framework. {100}

I. *Entification of the real. Framework of nothingness and the intrinsic finitude of created being*

Things in the framework of nothingness are created. For St. Thomas, what the fact of creation, "creationality," thrusts into the foreground is the finitude of created things.

At first glance appears to be nothing but a repetition of what the Greeks said, viz. that things are limitations (πέρας). But ultimately it is something quite different. When a Greek mentioned πέρας, what he understood by this term are the intrinsic characteristics that internally delimit and thus positively constitute what things are. St. Thomas thinks of something different.

St. Thomas thinks that whatever things may be in the sense we have just mentioned, they have an intrinsic finitude by virtue of which we say that they are imperfect. Only God is the perfect *res*, and finitude consists precisely in the *imperfection* of things that are, insofar as they are created. From this we obtain the idea of Creation in a radical and fundamental first dimension. Although he does not mention it directly, St. Thomas understands that created being consists in being something imperfect. St. Augustine earlier put it in a formula with a Platonic resonance. "To be created is not to be God by nature" (*Creatam esse est natura Deum non esse*),[20] and insofar as God is a perfect being, this not-being-God by nature consists in not being perfect by nature, in being an intrinsic imperfection. For this reason, strictly speaking, while for a Greek the ὄν begins by being something that we have to explain, for St. Thomas it begins by being "not-nothing." Here he is using a term taken from the mystics, not in the sense that it is unimportant, but that in a {101} formal way it constitutes a "not-nothing." Inasmuch as there is a reference to "nothing," there is an imperfection; inasmuch as it is "not-nothing" it points to whatever created things have that is positive. Clearly, this is but to talk purely and simply about Creation

However, at a second level—that from my viewpoint we must consider in addition to the first level just presented—St. Thomas carries out a different operation, viz. the "entitative interpretation" of this imperfection. And here he uses two Aristotelian concepts, purified by him and referred to something that never entered the mind of the Greeks. What is radical about things, St. Thomas tells us, is that they are *beings*; this is what I have called the "entification of reality." For St. Thomas things are synonymous with *beings*, and he did not question whether the entitative characteristics are actually something as primary and radical as he presumes or if, on the contrary, "to be" is some characteristic grounded in a deeper dimension. If we place a subject in the phrase we mentioned earlier—*id cujus actus est esse*—one may ask if there actually is an identity between the *id* and the *act of being*. If there were none, what is radical in things would not be to be entities or beings, but that in which the *id* consists. St. Thomas does not question this, but takes things as beings and completely entifies reality. As a result, since it is the case of a radical finiteness, what St. Thomas wants to say when talking about imperfection and the finiteness of things is that *what is primarily and formally imperfect is their own act of being*. The internal imperfection of the act of being, as act, is what for St. Thomas constitutes the intrinsic finiteness of things. This is clearly an entitative interpretation of something prior and fundamental, viz. the very creatureliness of things. {102}

When all is said and done, at least when this latter is regarded as creation *ex nihilo*, it still does not follow that it is a *truth of reason*. Indeed many theologians have suggested it is only a *truth of faith*. Be that as it may, upon this aforementioned stratum of the creatureliness of things St. Thomas projects his entitative interpretation of reality. He turns the imperfection of things, insofar as they are not God, into the internal imperfection of their own act of being. But this is an interpretation—the most obvious and plausible perhaps, but still an "interpretation." Because of this, St. Thomas, when conceptualizing the transcendental characteristics of being through Aristotle's purified concepts, says that these transcendental characteristics are "what is most common in all things" (*magis communia*). This has a very precise meaning: these transcendental characteristics are what is most common in all created things, *qua* created.

This completely changes the meaning and perspective of the interpretation of being. What is common to every created being, *qua* created, is what the transcendental characteristics express. St. Thomas does not stop with having viewed the entitiness of created things in themselves; he refers entity to its first causes. Then, we must ask, how does St. Thomas view those first (or ultimate) causes of entityness as such?

Since what is most radical in things is to be entity, what God primarily and formally causes is just the entitiness. St. Thomas tells us, "Being itself is the most common and most intimate effect of all the other effects" (*Ipsum enim esse est communissimus effectus primus et intimior omnibus aliis effectibus*).[21] Probably, {103} this *communissimus* reaches St. Thomas from the Neo-Platonists; Proclus [412-485] said that "the first of all created things is being." St. Thomas would never admit this, but he does admit that the entitative aspect of things is the primary end—formal and radical—of Creation as such.

This point of view leads to an entitative interpretation of creative action. In the same paragraph St. Thomas tells us two things that seem to be equivalent, but perhaps are not so after all. First, he tells us that Creation is "the emanation of every being with respect to the universal first cause, which God is".[22] We shall not now stress this "emanation" because St. Thomas is not an emanationist like Plotinus, and here he understands "emanation" as being an effect of divine causality. In this passage St. Thomas takes Creation from the point of view of the entification of reality, and he takes reality as understood entitatively. It is no longer the case, as in St. Augustine, of not being God by nature (*natura*

Deum non esse), but something more concrete. With things considered as entities, Creation formally consists in every entity emanating from the first and universal cause that God is.

Second, at the end of this same paragraph he tells us, "Just as the generation of man is from non-being, which is not man, in the same manner Creation, which is emanation of all of being, is from non-being, which is nothingness".[23] Of course, if the primary effect is the entitiness itself of {104} things and this is created, the entitiness of things proceeds from that which previously is not, i.e., *ex nihilo sui et subjecti.* St. Thomas, therefore, has accepted an entitative interpretation of created reality; he has taken Creation (that as such is not in solidarity with this complex system of metaphysical concepts) and gives us an entitative interpretation of it. What is primary and radical is that created things are created by God. And for St. Thomas the creative action consists in every entity proceeding from God; and precisely because of that this entity is produced *ex nihilo, ex non ente.* It is, therefore, an interpretation of the creatureliness of things from the entitative point of view.

We must emphasize that naked Creation and Creation interpreted entitatively are quite distinct.. Many[24] will think that in the third verse of Genesis, "God said, let there be light and light was made," is where the verb "to be" appears. But the Hebrew verb *hâyâh* means "to be" in the substantive sense, in the sense of existing or there being reality, which renders the literal translation of this passage of Genesis as, "And God said, let there be light and there was light". This indeed is the Creation of things. But the fact that the "there being"—and the "saying"—have entitative characteristics is just the second moment (Creation interpreted entitatively) that St. Thomas couples to the first (naked Creation). Thus we have the entitative interpretation of the creative act. Because of that, when referring to a different problem such as human freedom, St. Thomas can say, "God is a cause that transgrounds every being and all its differences" (*Deus est causa quaedam profundens totum ens ac omnes ejus differentias*).[25] That the "differences" in this case are freedom and {105} necessity does not change the basic point. This trans-grounding idea that St. Thomas has of the creative causality is indeed quite explicitly enunciated. It is an entitative interpretation of the creative causality.

Therefore, we have in the first place that everything created, by the mere fact of being created, has a finite being. This is an entitative definition.

In the second place, Creation consists in the fact that every being is produced and proceeds from non-being.

In the third place, it is in this characteristic of produced from non-being that the very finitude of reality formally resides.

Consequently, in St. Thomas the two definitions of metaphysics that Aristotle gave us acquire a much deeper significance. On one hand there is "theology," and on the other, the science of being as such. St. Thomas has understood reality as entified. In that case metaphysics is at the same time the science of being as such viewed, within the framework of nothingness, as created and referred to the creative cause also interpreted entitatively. In other words, it is at the same time theology *and* the science of being as such. As we shall see, basically the metaphysics of St. Thomas is the entitative theory of Creation, however obvious, but in the end still a "theory." Indeed, St. Thomas gives us more than just a vision of created things in themselves and in their first cause. But the very serious difficulty begins for St. Thomas when he sees God from this framework of creationality.

II. *The entification of God*

With this framework, to conceive God rationally, through pure reason (let us leave aside Revelation, since it does not enter into {106} metaphysics), is simply to understand God as creator; other things such as the Trinity is something that has nothing to do with metaphysics.

God is infinitely perfect and that infinite perfection can be expressed with just one term and concept, the *transcendence* of God. But the problem lies in is the explanation of that transcendence. The transcendence of God has, in my estimation, three elements that we must distinguish. They are important because they are different, and furthermore each one of them depends on the previous one; just to lump them together means to consider as obvious something that is not at all obvious in metaphysics.

In the first place, we have what we just mentioned, the element of God as creator of everything, i.e., of all *things* rather than all *beings*. Here is the radical difference with Aristotle, whose θεός did not produce things out of nothing; he is not even the efficient mechanism by which they are put in motion. He is simply a τέλος, and besides, he is extrinsic to things, something that merely provokes motion. On the other hand, for St. Thomas, God, as perfect infinite *res*, is the cause that produces all things out of nothing. It is what we might call the "stratum of the transcendence of God as *creative transcendence*," the basic and radical stratum upon which the other two elements are grounded, since they are more problematic than the first.

In the second place, if created things as such are beings—this is the entification of reality—then the creative transcendence of

God is something that is also the object of an entitative interpretation on the part of St. Thomas. Indeed, created things are primarily beings, hence the creative causality of God, when producing {107} things, produces being outside of Him. In this sense, transcendence has received a second, different determination—at least in some measure—with respect to the first (mere creative transcendence). Here there is something more, since God appears as the one that entifies reality; this is the *entitative transcendence*. Despite popular impression, St. Thomas never proves the existence of Creation starting from the concept of being, but the other way around: he interprets the entitative transcendence of God starting from the fact that things are created. Let us not indulge in wishful thinking, anything else would be a false perspective based on a conceptist[26] order. Therefore, the transcendent God appears not only as creator, but also as entifier; and in that sense God is beyond all creatures. Cajetan [1469-1534], who obviously does not stand in opposition to St. Thomas, says, "The divine *res* is prior to being and all its differences because, in fact, it is above being, above the one, above truth, etc.".[27] God is not only creator of things, but even of their very transcendental order. As entifier of reality and in his entitative transcendence, God is not only the origin of things, but the origin of that which in them constitutes for St. Thomas their transcendental order, their being with all its characteristics. However, up to now God appears to us only as the cause that produces this order, so the inevitable question is what about God in himself?

This is the third stratum we have to consider. {108} What is this first cause in itself? The matter appears simple, but is quite far from being so, even including the entitative suppositions we have been dealing with up to now. In order to answer this question, it is possible to take two completely different paths, both of which are well represented in the history of metaphysics and Medieval theology.

The first starts at the time of Marius Victorinus [†303] and consists in saying that because God is transcendent in the entitative sense, He is beyond being; in himself He is not being. Marius Victorinus tells us that God is not "being" (ὄv), but "ante-being" (πρo-ὄv),[28] i.e., He is not "being" but pre-being. Even towards the end of the thirteenth century and the beginnings of the fourteenth—therefore, right after St. Thomas—the great master of speculative mysticism, Meister Eckhart, will say "Being is not formally found in God; nothing of what is in God can be reasoned as being".[29] From this it follows that as far as metaphysics is concerned, being as such is intrinsically finite. Also, that God acts as creator of this finite being, but never as something to which one may attribute entitative concepts.

St. Thomas does not take this first way and only makes a slight concession, viz. if we call "entities" the things that are, inasmuch as they do not intrinsically resemble God, God would be non-being. However, this is but a slight concession, {109} one of the many St. Thomas makes to assimilate the thought of those who preceded him; because despite having called David of Dinant[30] "stupid"—*stultissime posuit...*—, St. Thomas does not easily lose his equilibrium.

But there is a completely different second way, which is the one that St. Thomas follows. It consists in saying that God, as cause of the transcendental order, is beyond this transcendental order, but he is so as something that primarily and radically produces the entitiness of things. In an eminent manner—we shall have to explain in what this eminence consists—He is also something that is and the subsisting being itself, *Ipsum esse subsistens*. Here, the transcendence of God is not simply as creator, not even—as in the second stratum—as entifier; it is a transcendence that I might call "hyper-entitative," according to which God is the "hyper-being" *par excellence*, by means of eminence. This is the hyper-entified being of God. The being of God *qua* subsistent makes Him a being through Himself (*a se*), while all other things are beings through another (*ab alio*), that is to say, through God (*a Deo*).

To be sure, St. Thomas tells us that this concept of being, which on the one hand aims towards creatures and, on the other aims towards God, is nothing but analogical. The way in which things are entities, and have their being in Creation, is not the same as the way God is a being, who is the Creator; in other words, this concept is realized in a different way in things and in God. If it were the case of a mere conceptual difference, Duns Scotus, who immediately followed St. Thomas, would say that we can prescind from whether being is finite or infinite, since we understand what the term "to be" means, and apply it univocally to God and creatures. However, here we are not dealing with the problem of the concept {110} of being, but the problem of the real and true entitiness of things; and Scotus does recognize without a doubt that the entitiness of what we call "being" is simply analogous in God and in creatures.

What does "analogy" mean in that case? Does it mean that all things are beings referred to God? Without doubt, but it is a curious inversion of the analogy. Note that analogy of attribution as understood here always supposes there is a first analogue, which is clearly perceived. Let us remember the example Aristotle presented. Above all, "healthy" is the man who has health; medicine is healthy referred to him because it restores health; the stroll is healthy because it preserves health; color is healthy because it expresses health, etc. In other words, they are healthy referred to that first analogue. And in the case of God? No one has seen God! How can we say that things have nothing but analogy of attribution with respect to God? Cajetan says that it is a case of analogy of proportionality, that what being is with respect to creatures is what we call the *Ipsum esse subsistens* with respect to God. This amounts to confessing that we remain completely in the dark.

Things are *ab alio* insofar as they are beings. This is what I would call the "*ab-alio*-ness"[31] of created being as such. In this conception of St. Thomas, being as such is not finite as in the conception of Marius Victorinus or Eckhart and all the Neoplatonists; being is only finite in the case of created being *qua* created. But God is precisely the hyper-being. St. Thomas has accomplished this gigantic enterprise of the entification of divine reality itself—an operation full of problems, regardless of the great enthusiasm it has elicited throughout history. This, as we shall see, is not accomplished without risks.

Nevertheless, we find here three different dimensions {111} of the God's transcendence: the creative transcendence, the entitative transcendence, and the hyper-entitative transcendence. Each presupposes the previous one. The entitative transcendence is possible because there is a creation of things, because God is Creator. A hyper-entitative interpretation is possible because God, as first cause in the conception of St. Thomas would be the hyper-being, and because of that entifies everything He is not. The three dimensions are completely different, but in addition to being different, each one is grounded on the previous one.

The slow pace of this analysis should be forgiven. But I think it is absolutely necessary in order not to accept in a global and routine manner—as it has occurred many times in history—concepts that are in reality very different. Therefore, it is necessary for us to explain them carefully.

To deny the entitative interpretation of things is not to deny Creation. God as creator of things is one thing, and the entitative interpretation of things and Creation quite another. Distinct from both of these is the proper entitative interpretation of God.

This conception of St. Thomas presupposes, above all, that there is an entification of things. Only starting from that entification can creative causality itself be entified. Had he not begun from this primary and radical entification of things, i.e., had he not considered that what is radical in things is that they are entities, St. Thomas would never have arrived at his entitative conception of creative causality. As a matter of fact, this interpretation does not exist at all in the New Testament or in the writings of the first Christian theologians. It only appears when appeal to Platonism influenced the interpretations of some Apologists and Greek Fathers. But regardless of its source, {112} it is still an interpretation, though perhaps one that is obvious and very fruitful. As an interpretation it leaves the door open to other conceptualizations. As we have seen, even in medieval theology it led to the interpretation of God as pre-being, and to the above quoted concept of Meister Eckhart that denied that God had any formal reason for being, which is far from contradicting the idea of Creation. Let us not think that with St. Thomas' metaphysics, and on the basis of his rational theology, the problem of things, Creation, and God has been exhausted forever. In fact the opposite is the case: the door has just been opened.

This is the way being has been seen in the framework of creationality, a framework completely alien to and different from that the Greek world. Of being conceived in such manner St. Thomas will have to tell us what he thinks about its intelligibility. After all, metaphysics for St. Thomas—following Aristotle—is a *scientia*, a real and actual knowledge of that object, of being, which is viewed in that framework of creationality.

{113}

§3

THE NATURE OF METAPHYSICS

What is the *nature of the metaphysics* we have been discussing?. This question must be answered in two stages.
1. What is the unity of the object of metaphysics for St. Thomas?
2. How is a true intellection of this object possible?

Let us begin with the first point.

In order to answer this question we must start from the entification of things. St. Thomas is so faithful to his entification of things that he is never even aware of it. However, a passage we shall cover further on allows us to suspect that at some point St. Thomas may have thought that this is not so obvious after all. Except for this single instance, St. Thomas never questioned it; and for him it is absolutely transparent that things are beings, not only in the sense of one *concept*—as happened with the univocity of Scotus—but also with the single notion of *being*, i.e., things are purely analogous. Considering what we have just said, it is not difficult to understand that for St. Thomas the single object of metaphysics is the unity of being, considered creationally, which at one and the same time involves created things and the Creator Himself. Being as Creator is God, being as created is things. In this sense, the unity in St. Thomas' metaphysics, it seems to me, might be characterized as the *creational unity of being as such.* {114}

Now the full meaning of what has appeared in this chapter many times becomes clear. St. Thomas' metaphysics is the entitative theory of Creation, created things, their Creator and the creative act itself. Therefore, the transcendental order is the creational order.

But there are certain reflections to which that grandiose conception gives rise. In the first place, does the transcendental order of being as such also cover God? If we say that God is the *Ipsum esse subsistens*, does this mean that St. Thomas includes God in this transcendental order? Clearly not, because for St. Thomas God does not "enter" into this transcendental order. But it might be said that at least God is the subsisting transcendental order. Perhaps, it all depends. St. Thomas constantly repeats that God is *ens, verum, bonum, unum* by analogy, but among the transcendentals we still have two others, *res* and *aliquid*. Can it be said that God is a *res*, that He has quiddity? Can it be said that God is "something," that He is an *aliud quid*? In that case, who is the something with respect to which He is *aliud*? That would be the world with respect to God, but not God with respect to the world. Therefore, God is not *aliquid*, because at the very least, creation of the world does not increase the absolute being in which God consists. Can it be said, then, that God is the transcendental order? The treatises of classical metaphysics—including the first of them, that of Suárez—simply eliminate *res*, and *aliquid*. They say that *res* is identical to *ens*; but this is a case of *res* understood as essence, like the quiddity of the Scholastics, and not in the sense I give to the term "essence."[32] About the *aliquid* these treatises say that it is the same as *res*; and in that way we only have three transcendentals left. But this is to amputate the transcendental order, something St. Thomas never intended at all.

In the second place, there is a much more serious problem {115} with respect to the entitative interpretation of the Creator and creatures. Indeed, one might think that the creator God must be something more than the *Ipsum esse subsistens*, in the same way that the creature is something more than *ens ab alio*. We could easily respond to this dialectically by saying that everything that things are as "more" is based on what we said, just as God is "more" precisely on account of being *Ipsum esse subsistens*. But what if it were just the opposite? What if it were the case that God, even as *Ipsum esse subsistens*, is such by reason of what He physically is as οὐσία, by His inner qualifications? It might be said that this is a merely dialectical question; but not too dialectical because in that case being, even assuming it is referred to God, would be an emergence of what God is as οὐσία, as full and infinite *res*, which belongs to itself. Are these subtleties? Let us appeal again to Cajetan, who never admitted that the conceptive essence (or "metaphysical", as they used to say at that time) of God consisted in being *Ipsum esse subsistens*, but rather consists in being the "subsisting intellective knowing itself." In that case the being of God would be an internal position of His own intellective knowing. What could this be except to affirm that it is far from evident that what is radical about God is to be *Ipsum esse subsistens*? To be God is to be, above all, something more radical, and for creatures to be something much more radical than simply *ens ab alio*. The fact is that St. Thomas actually starts from Creation, which is a datum of faith he obviously accepts. Into that Creation he injects the idea of being, and then returns to God by interpreting Creation in entitative terms. Who can fail to see that in this case, with respect to metaphysics, there is an enormous ambivalence? What is metaphysics, the theory of created being or the theory of Creator and Creation? {116}

However, ignoring the foregoing difficulties we see that the transcendental order constituted as such has a set of characteristics in St. Thomas:

(1) The transcendental order is the entitative interpretation of creationality. This is the order of *ens qua ens creationale*, as Creator or creature.

(2) That transcendental order is intrinsically necessary since ultimately God is the *Ipsum esse subsistens*. Anything transcendental that a creature has proceeds in some manner from God necessarily.

(3) This necessity is also ascendent. In other words, if God, as the Neoplatonists thought, were to create the characteristics of things in a cascade, the first He would have created would have been the being of being and then the things that have that being.

In the end, the transcendental order appears as a metaphysical and theological canon, to which the very creative action of God has had to adjust in order to create things existing outside of Himself. If we join the last two characteristics—that the transcendent order is necessary and ascendent—St. Thomas would summarize them by saying that the being of the creature consists in "participating" in the being of God, though it is a participation to which the moment of causality is intrinsic.

That the matter is not so simple St. Thomas himself lets us know it when he poses the question, "whether creating is something proper and exclusive to God." Referring to the creations humans can produce, St. Thomas says they always presuppose a matter upon which creation operates, and that is why in reality it is an alteration. But in the case of Creation, "every created being participates, *so to speak*, in the {117} nature of being because only God is His own being".[33] It probably crossed the mind of St. Thomas how enormously problematic this entification of things is, and above all, the entification of divine reality itself. Indeed, a text of Aristotle can be quoted according to which the "so to speak" would not refer to the gerund *essendi*, but to *naturam*. In fact there is a passage in Aristotle where he says that being (ὄν) and the one (ἥν) are some sort of natures; and it is possible that St. Thomas in his polemic with the Neoplatonists might refer to "nature." However, in that case nature would only be *natura essendi*, and the entified participation would seem to be for St. Thomas something that is such "so to speak."

To the three characteristics of the transcendental order already mentioned we would then have to add two additional ones.

This transcendental order has a transcendent principle. It is God, the highest being, the *Ens a se*. In created things, since they consist of pure *ab-alio*-ness, in being different than God, it means that if the transcendental characteristics concern the pure and formal fact of *ab-alio*-ness, then the transcendental order is concluded and fixed.

However, is this evident? These statements, more than propositions *about* the transcendental order, constitute the very fabric of the transcendental order in the thought of St. Thomas, just as the homologous propositions we enunciated with respect to Aristotle constituted the internal fabric of his conceptualization of the ὄν ἡ ὄν, the *ens qua ens*. Because of this, they are essentially and formally internal problems of metaphysics, problems that are much more than just the consequences and the difficulties that appear within {118} these conceptions. They are, above all, the problems that constitute the inner core and the fabric of the transcendental order as such.

We must ask St. Thomas how it is that the transcendental order intellectually can be understood as truth? St. Thomas will tell us, on the one hand, that this truth is a coincidence of the intellect and things, and, on the other, that it is transcendental.

What does St. Thomas understand by that *coincidence between intellect and things*?

Obviously, it is a case of a *con-venire* or "coming together" between the intellect and things. But that intellect is twofold and here the difficulty resides. On the one hand, it is the divine intellect; on the other, the human intellect, not precisely as human, but as finite; and the same is the case with any other intellect, even the angelic.

With respect to the divine intellect there is a truth that for St. Thomas is inscribed in the framework of Creation and nothingness, interpreted entitatively. God not only knows what He creates, but St. Thomas also tells us that if God were not an intelligent being, Creation would have justification or explanation as being (*ratio entitatis*), but would never have justification or explanation as truth (*ratio veritatis*).[34] God knows what He creates, but there is a much more important subsequent affirmation, viz. that what God creates is precisely what He knows. In other words, each thing is the realization of a preexisting idea in the divine mind. This preexistence may be understood in various ways. It might be an emergence of an act of the will in the Divine mind (as Scotus thought), or it might be the intrinsic imitativeness of the divine essence. Whether it is one or the other does not matter in this case; what does matter is that it is always an idea realized *ad extra*, and its realization is things. God is, in this sense, {119} an *intellectus originarius* because (together with an act of the will) He is the one that produces things in accordance to His internal intellection. This is the basis for the existence of a coming together between the divine intellect and things, a coming together that is not extrinsic but intrinsic, since every created thing, by being such, is already a pre-intellected thing. In such fashion, the radical truth of things will consist in their conformity with the divine idea. This is what afterwards has been called in a formalistic way *ontological truth*. It is not conformity between understanding and things, but conformity between things and understanding, in this case the divine understanding.

But along with the divine intellect we have the poor finite intellect, the human intellect. What happens with respect to it? Repeating Aristotle, St. Thomas says that man fabricates many things with all his ποίεσις and all his τέκνη. These are the artificial things, whose being consists in according with what man had in his head. But that is not the general condition of things. Man does not produce *res naturales* (φύσει ὄντα), and the only thing the human understanding can do is to be in accordance with them. Following Aristotle, St. Thomas says that all things, insofar as they are termini of an intellection, are called in principle to conform to the intellective mind. In this sense, their being possesses a *verum* that is not a *verum logicum*, but the necessary condition for the existence of a *verum logicum*. The necessary condition for a judgment to be in accordance with reality is that things, in accordance with their own structures, conform to the intellect that pronounces something about them. Because of that, things *qua* "knowables" involve a reference to that entity called "soul," and St. Thomas repeats here Aristotle's phrase that the soul, in a certain way, is all things. {120}

But St. Thomas does not settle the question with just that; he tells us, "A natural thing is constituted between two intellects, the divine and the human. And by its adequation to both, it is said to be true."[35] Natural things have an adequation to the divine intellect insofar as they realize what is in the divine mind, and in that sense, we say that they are true. On the other hand, by their adequation to the human intellect we say that the thing is true inasmuch as by its own structure it is destined (*nata est*) to conform to a proper estimation by the mind. Towards the end of the paragraph St. Thomas tells us, "The first explanation of truth, that is, its conformity with the divine intellect, is prior to the second, which is comparison with the human intellect."[36] That is why, even if human intellect did not exist, it would always be said that things are true with regard to the divine intellect.

Indeed, to be constituted between two intellects elicits the second point, which we shall cover briefly. *In what sense and in what measure is this dual coming together transcendental?*

The question is clear. Since primarily and radically things are beings, the divine intelligence is an intelligence, which expands to ideas of diverse entities. It expands to participations of the very subsisting entitiness in which God consists. Human intellect consists purely and simply in the capacity of being formed and conformed by being *qua* being. That is to say, both truths—the truth of adequation with the divine intellect and the truth of adequation with the human intellect—are *transcendental*. They concern being as such and {121} are seen within the framework of nothingness. It is within that framework, because things are something created by God, and therefore, pre-intellected; and it is within that framework, because man has to receive them, but *qua* entities. Therefore, this transcendental truth for St. Thomas has three aspects: (1) it is grounded on being; (2) it consists in the intrinsic intelligibility of the being; and (3) it has two dimensions, one with respect to God, and the other with respect to human intellect. And on account of this latter dimension, human intelligence is enabled and even at times forced to elaborate the most abstract concept of them all, the concept of being. This is the dawn of metaphysics.

That is why I continue to repeat *ad nauseam* that the metaphysics of St. Thomas is an entitative theory of Creation. This might seem to be obvious, and in that case the problem of metaphysics might seem to consist in taking it or leaving it, as if metaphysics were not internally and intrinsically a formal problematic, which is necessary to develop.

Confronting this problem, and also others, we can repeat Plato's phrase, "I fell faint scrutinizing reality".[37] Yes, "fell faint", but not discouraged. With new energy, modern philosophy at the hands of Descartes is going to confront problems very similar to those encountered by St. Thomas, and is going to make us see that metaphysics constitutes the way of its own internal problematicism.

---

[1] *Met* L 1076 a 4, Οὐκ ἀγαθόν πολυκοιρανίη εἷς κοίρανός.

[2] [Zubiri's meaning in this passage is somewhat obscure.—trans.].

[3] [In Spanish there are two words that can mean "being" in English. The verb *ser*, from the Latin *esse*, can be so translated, as can *ente*, from the Latin *ens*. A problem arises however because *ente* can also mean *being*, though there is a separate Spanish word also with that mean-

ing, *entidad*. However, *entidad* can also mean *entityness*. Zubiri generally prefers *ente* for *being*, though he sometimes uses *ser*. The English translation will depend on the context.—trans.].

[4] "Secundum igitur tria praedicta [...] sortitur tria nomina. Dicitur enim *scientia divina* sive *theologia* inquantum praedictas substantias [sc. separatas] considerat", *In Met.*, proem.

[5] "[Dicitur] *Metaphysica*, in quantum considerat ens et ea quae consequuntur ipsum", *Ibid.*

[6] *Met Z* 1028 a 10, translation of W.D. Ross.

[7] "Haec enim transphysica inveniuntur in via resolutionis, sicut magis communia post minus communia", *Ibid.*

[8] "Dicitur autem *prima philosophia*, inquantum primas rerum causas considerat", *Ibid.*

[9] [Elsewhere, in his most important work, *Sentient Intelligence*, Zubiri refers to this theory as *sensible intelligence*. He contrasts it with his own view, *sentient intelligence*, which calls for a much more integrated approach to human understanding.—trans.]

[10] [What Zubiri means is not that there is no difference between discreet and continuous quantities, but that one need not assume totally different branches of mathematics are required to deal with them.—trans.]

[11] This was the abbreviated form in which Zubiri always referred to the work of Husserl *Ideen zu einer reinen Phänomenologie und phänomenologishen Philosophie*, the first volume of which —the only one published by the philosopher while he was alive— came out in 1913.

[12] Again, it is an abbreviated quotation of the work of M. Scheler *Der Formalismus in der Ethik und die materiale Wertethik*, published in 1913-1916.

[13] St. Thomas Aquinas, Opusc. 42 *De natura generis*, ch. 1. *Cf.*, *Quodlib.* 2, a. 3.

[14] [Zubiri discusses entification of reality in his major work, *Sentient Intelligence*.—trans.]

[15] He refers, obviously, to his book *Sobre la esencia*, published in 1962.

[16] [In Spanish, "something" is *algo*, from the Latin *aliquid*.—trans.]

[17] *Quaestiones disputatae de veritate*, q. 4, a. 8.

[18] [Zubiri neologism—trans.].

[19] "Voluntas divina est intelligenda ut extra ordinem entium existens, velut causa quaedam profundens totum ens et eius differentias", *In Aristotelis libros Peri Hermeneias*, L, I, *lectio* XIV, no. 22.

[20] [St. Augustine's *De trinitate*, Book 4, Ch. 2, No. 4—trans.].

[21] *Questiones disputatae de potentia* 3.7.

22 "Emanatio totius entis a causa universali quae est Deus", *S. Th.* I, q. 45, a. 1.

23 "Sicut igitur generatio hominis est ex non ente quod est non homo, ita creatio, quae est emanatio totius entis, est ex non ente quod est nihil", *Ibid.*

24 [Zubiri writes "all" (*todos*) since he is referring to the Spanish equivalent of the Douai-Rheims translation from the Vulgate. Modern translations already take what Zubiri says in this paragraph into consideration—trans.].

25 *In Aristotelis libros Peri Hermeneias*, L. I., lectio XIV, no. 22. Zubiri repeats here the text quoted on the note to page 96, a text also quoted in *Sobre el sentimiento y la volición* (On Sentiment and Volition) (Madrid, Alianza, 1992, p. 158).

26 [Zubiri neologism—trans.]

27 "Res divina prior est ente et omnibus differentiis ejus: est enim *super ens et super unum,* etc." This text from the Commentary of Cajetan to the *Summa* of St. Thomas (q. 39, a. I, VII) also appears quoted in *"En torno al problema de Dios"* (In Regard to the Problem of God), appearing in *Naturaleza, Historia, Dios* (Nature, History, God), p. 442 (1987 Spanish ed.).

28 The text of Marius Victorinus (*P. L.* VIII, col. 11, 29 D) appears quoted in the same context of the previous footnote (*Naturaleza, Historia, Dios*, p. 441). There we find along this same line, a reference to the "unsure" John Scotus Eriugena (*P. L.*, CXXII, col. 680 D), and another reference to the Thomist comentary on Dionysius the Areopagite (*Comm. de Div. nom.* I, L. 3).

29 "Esse non est formaliter in Deo; nihil quod est in Deo habet rationem entis". Zubiri also quotes this same text of Meister Eckhart in the mentioned passage of *Naturalez, Historia, Dios* (Nature, History, God), p. 441.

30 [Pantheistic philosopher, c. 1160-1217. According to his theories, all things—material, intellectual, and spiritual—have the same essence, namely God.—trans.]

31 [Zubiri neologism, from Lt. *ab alio*, Sp. *por otro*, by another—trans.].

32 [For Zubiri's understanding of essence, refer to his book *Sobre la esencia* (English translation, *On Essence*, published by Catholic University Press of America). Zubiri's notion of essence is quite different from that of the Scholastics.—trans.]

33 "Quodcumque ens creatum participat, ut ita dixerim, naturam essendi: quia solus Deus est suum esse", *S. Th.* q. 45, a. 5 ad 1.

34 [Here we encounter the difficulty of translating the Latin *ratio*, and the Spanish *razón* into English, since they can mean "reason," "explanation," or "justification."—trans.].

[35] "Res ergo naturalis inter duos intellectus constituta... Et secundum adaequationem ad utrumque, vera dicitur", *Quaestiones disputatae de veritate* q. 1, a. 2.

[36] *Ibid.*

[37] Again, here appears the free quotation of *Phaedo* (99 d), which Zubiri had used towards the end of the previous chapter.

CHAPTER 3
WESTERN PHILOSOPHY (2)
DESCARTES

Let us recall once more that it is not my intention to synopsize all of the philosophies we encounter as we proceed, simply because this is of little interest and would contribute nothing new. Our purpose is only to appeal to some philosophers who are truly representatives of the history of Western thought, and fall in step with them and their historical parade, as something that manifests to us the fabric and internal problematicism of what we have called the *transcendental order*.

The previous chapter was dedicated to St. Thomas, not just because of the intrinsic value of his ideas, but above all in order to exhibit those few concepts that are fundamental for everything we are going to cover. At the end of that chapter I made five important points about St. Thomas' philosophy: (1) He gave an entitative interpretation of creationality in the transcendental order. The order of *ens qua ens* is the order of *ens* creationally considered, taking this *ens* as creator God or created reality. (2) We discussed the intrinsic necessity of this order. (3) We dealt with the antecedent necessity of that order. And I quoted the paragraph where St. Thomas told us that creation consists precisely in participating —*ut ita dixerim*, "so to speak"—{124} in the nature of "that which is," *naturam essendi*. Precisely because of this, it is evident that this order is intrinsically necessary, with the same necessity as the *esse divinum*; and in addition it is necessarily antecedent. In other words, in a certain way, putting it anthropomorphically, if God proceeds to create, the first thing He has to do is to think that what He has to create is an entity, and therefore, something that fits into the transcendental structure. (4) This transcendental order has a transcendent principle, which is God, considered as *ens*, the *Summum Ens, Ens a se*. (5) In created things this order is concluded and fixed, because it concerns just the nature of what is *ab-alio*, i.e., the *ab-alio*-ness of created entity as such.

In addition, I said that in all of this there is an internal inflexion of Aristotelian thought at the hands of St. Thomas, an inflexion that is decisive for the history of metaphysics, as we shall see. Out of this inflexion, which proceeds from the metaphysics of Aristotle, modern philosophy is born within medieval philosophy of the end of the fifteenth and beginning of the sixteenth centuries, and congeneric with it, modern science is also born. This science concerns the world and man. And, naturally, the problem arises—and this is what concerns Descartes—of how to provide a solid base for this knowledge, an indubitable and certain foundation.

To accomplish this goal, Descartes places himself within the framework of earlier philosophy, God and Creation. Therefore, he is within the framework of nothingness.

Nevertheless, within this framework Descartes is going to elevate something to the highest rank quite different from what St. Thomas did. The framework of nothingness causes St. Thomas to elevate the intrinsic finitude of being to the highest rank; however, for Descartes it is something {125} at first sight completely different, viz. the radical uncertainty of human knowing. Within the framework of nothingness human knowing shows itself intrinsically and constitutively uncertain.

This is an inflection that is enormously important, but always within the framework of nothingness. We shall witness the unfolding of Descartes' thought in two parts.

In the first place, what is the problem Descartes poses? In the second place, concerning the question in which we are interested, what are some of the steps in the development of this problem?

§1

THE FRAMEWORK OF NOTHINGNESS: UNCERTAINTY

Putting it simply, what is Descartes' basic problem?

Descartes tells us in the *Regulae ad directionem ingenii* that all human sciences constitute only one thing, wisdom, σοφία.[1] In Descartes this σοφία becomes the primary and radical subject of his reflection. Bearing in mind that Aristotle said that he created *Prima Philosophia*, Descartes determines that his reflection is a *meditation* or a series of *Meditationes de Prima Philosophia*. Since this σοφία covers everything we wish to know, and partially know, about the world and things—everything we call "science"—Descartes' meditation has to concentrate first and foremost on the character of this science.

Descartes tells us that it is not a matter of taking this science, and therefore the creation of things by God, as a datum of faith, as an object of revelation. His problem is to investigate the intrinsic condition of science and its objects, starting not with other explanations, but from explanations (reasoning) based on our own {127} mind (*rationibus non aliunde petitis, quam ab ipsa et nostra mente*).[2]

Now, what Descartes needs to do is to tell us what he understands by "science." But he never does so; he merely presupposes that we understand what he means. And he presupposes it because he receives from Medieval philosophy a fairly precise idea of what science is, understood not as a scientific "body of truths," but as a "way of knowing," a way of knowing these truths.

Likewise Ockham, for example, told us, "Science is a true knowledge, but dubitable, which by virtue of its own nature must be made evident though reasoning" (*Scientia est cognitio vera sed dubitabilis, nata fieri evidens per discursum*). In the first place, we must have a *cognitio vera*. Here, "true" (*vera*) refers to the fact that things are as the intellect affirms they are. In the second place, Ockham says that it is something *dubitabilis*. Indeed, the great majority of the truths we call "scientific," and form the body of science, are truths that, at least in principle, are dubitable until an explanation or justification for them is given. There is, therefore, an aspect of internal dubitability, which is the fringe that accompanies all knowledge, the body of which constitutes science. And, in third place, Ockham tells us, this truth is true, but dubitable, that is to say, it is not enough that it be true in order to have science, but it has to be certain in some way. And by virtue of its nature this is to be made evident though discourse, whereby its doubt is changed into certainty.

Here we have the three essential elements that comprise the problem for Descartes: truth, doubt, and certainty {128} through evidence. Whereas for previous philosophy the point of departure for all speculation was a meditation about *being*, for Descartes the beginning of philosophy—really more than "beginning," as we shall soon see—is a meditation upon *knowing*. It is a meditation upon knowing that, from the viewpoint of earlier philosophy would be something difficult to apprehend; but Descartes now tells us that it is the easiest to know. And by "easy" he actually means "immediate." The immediacy of knowing to the knower is just what confers preeminent rank on the process of knowing in the structure of philosophy.

Consequently, the finality that philosophy searches for is now the *finality of a certainty that is unchangeable.* How to find this order of grounding of true certainties that are unchangeable is Descartes' problem.

§2

DESCARTES' DEVELOPMENT
OF THE PROBLEM

In this second part we are going to distinguish three steps:
(1) Doubt and certainty.
(2) Certainty and evidence.
(3) Evidence and truth.

I. *Doubt and certainty*

Under Ockham's conception, as in any other akin to Greek thought, uncertainty, insecurity is an almost universal fringe to knowledge in the sense that there are few truths that are evident by themselves. That is the fringe of insecurity that accompanies knowledge.

But for Descartes the ability to doubt, that uncertainty, is something deeper and more profound. It is deeper and more profound because for him it becomes something different, namely a method. "Method" does not mean here a logical operation, but more or less what it meant for Parmenides when he referred to the ὁδός τῆς ἀλεθείας, the way that leads to truth. For Descartes, that way is strictly *doubt*, not only because everything is dubitable, but for another reason as well. Descartes appeals to doubt, not to remain in it, {130} but to see if there is something able to resist it. And it is based on that intention that the method of doubt rests.

"Methodical doubt" does not mean that we should put everything completely in doubt at one time, but rather that we should systematically entertain doubt about all things to see if there is actually something capable of resisting doubt. By employing this method, Descartes, with his intelligence and his thought, ends up closed within himself and his thoughts. Descartes himself said, "I separate myself and remain in solitude" (*solus secedo*);[3] a solitude intrinsically defined by the action we have just described, because to say that man remains alone with his thoughts is something as old as mankind itself. I remember, for example, that Aeschylus in verse 757 of *Agamemnon* placed this phrase in the mouth of the chorus, "Away from all, alone, I find myself thinking on my own."[4] He was referring to the oracles, to the various contradicting oracles concerning the subject being debated. Centuries later St. Augustine would say, "Do not desire to step outside, truth resides in the interior man" (*Noli foras ire, in interiori homine habitat veritas*). But in another paragraph he adds, "I would more easily doubt that I am alive, than doubt that truth exists" (*faciliusque dubitare me vivere quam non esse veritatem*).

However Descartes is going to do something more serious. He goes beyond that solitude that man in his interior self wishes to have for whatever reasons (those of St. Augustine are different than those of Descartes), in order to find the truth that resides in himself. This is the strict and rigorous way to find something formally irresistible and resistant {131} to doubting, something that is not doubtful, but immovably certain.

It is well known that for Descartes the unquestionable fact, the fact where that unquestionable certainty is found, is the very fact of doubt, "I think, therefore, I exist." I am actually doubting everything, but I cannot doubt the fact that I exist; consequently, *cogito, ergo sum.*[5] The philosophy of Descartes, from this moment on, is going to be an *egology.*[6]

However, Descartes is not satisfied with what he has just said, which is quite significant. He has to take another step.

II. *Certainty and evidence*

Why is this incontrovertible fact undoubtedly true? Descartes tells us the answer: because I perceive with clarity and distinctness that, if I think, it is because I exist.

Nonetheless, throughout all of his *Meditations* he never tires of repeating that there could be an evil genie who, despite Descartes' most clear evidences, might be able to deceive him. But Descartes makes a radical exception to this possible deception about the *ego cogito*. He does so because that *ego cogito* is not a reasoning process such as, "everything that thinks exists; the fact is that I think, therefore I exist." No, that is not Descartes' meaning. The meaning that Descartes gives to the *cogito, ergo sum* is that this *ergo* forms part of the *cogitatio* as such. {132} I have the *intuitus*[7] that actually I think, and therefore—Descartes says more precisely—when I say *cogito, ergo sum* what I am saying is *cogito me cogitare*, I think that I am thinking. Here is precisely where the Descartes' viewpoint is anchored. The presumed truth of the premise "everything that thinks, exists" is grounded on this *intuitus* (and not the other way around), which is immovably resistant to any attempt to doubt it.

In the phrase, *cogito me cogitare*—I think that I think—the "I" intervenes twice and this is a serious problem. Descartes has not meditated at length on this serious problem, because for him the *cogito me cogitare* is self-evident—I think that I think.

If we call what is said in the subordinate proposition ("that I think") a *thought that is thought*, then the "I think" with which the phrase begins is what we might call a *thought that is thinking*. This is the "thought-that-is-thinking" that thinks precisely its own thought *qua* being thought. And of this, of this "thought-that-is-thinking," Descartes says he has an immovable certainty.

The "I think" might be completely false from the point of view of the thought-that-is-thought; however, from the point of view of the thought-that-is-thinking it would be an incontrovertible truth, because that very falsehood and error is what is seen and thought. For Descartes, not even divine omnipotence could make that *intuitus* fail. The incontrovertible reality Descartes talks about with respect to thought is not the incontrovertible reality of the thought-that-is-thought, but of the thought-that-is-thinking. That is the issue. {133}

Of this thinking Descartes tells us that it is an *intuitus*, that in which I "see" with all clarity (we shall soon see what this "clarity" means for Descartes) that this thought is a thought that involves existence in itself. Because of this, Descartes tells us that the *ego cogito* is not only a fact but an incontrovertible fact; moreover, its very incontrovertibility reveals to us that it is at least, at the exordium of philosophy, the very essence of man. Not only *cogito, ergo sum*, but *ego sum res cogitans*, "I am precisely something that thinks, a thinking essence".[8]

Several reflections immediately appear with respect to the Cartesian viewpoint. Descartes says *ad nauseam* that he is only moving in the order of truths that are certain, of true certainties. That is what he says; but is this what is happening? Let us call certainty, *a potiori*, the point of departure of the doubt, and then, Descartes would tell us that he is moving in the order of certain truth, that is to say, of an egology whose formal characteristic is the incontrovertible certainty of its own *ego*. But I am not asking if what Descartes says is true in a particular philosophy (we are not interested in that here), but I am asking whether Descartes is really doing that.

Indeed, let us take the thought-that-is-thought, I think that I think. In this "that I think," what is the thought Descartes deals with? It is not the whole of thinking in general or the intellect in general, as in medieval philosophy. Descartes understands that his attempt to doubt aims at the "I think," that I am *actually* thinking. In that actuality is where the characteristic of "that I think" resides. Hence, that actuality is what {134} we mean when we say "I am here-and-now thinking."[9] To say "I think that I think" is, in Descartes' hands of Descartes—regardless of what he says—"I think that I am here-and-now thinking." Then it is clear that all the strength of the *ergo* resides not in the fact that I am *thinking*, but in the *I am here-and-now*, i.e., in the actuality itself of the act. The thinking characteristic drops to a second tier and what remains at the first tier is that "I am here-and-now," I think that *I am here-and-now* thinking. Precisely in the "I am here-and-now" is where the actuality of thinking resides, and therefore its very characteristic of reality. The reality of thinking, and not just its dimension of truth, is what comprises the initial and radical strength of the *cogito*.

So despite what Descartes claims, the thought that he deals with is not precisely thought *qua* certain or doubtful, but thought *qua* actual, that is to say, *qua* reality.

If we now take the thought-that-is-thinking ("I-think-I-am-here-and-now-thinking"), whence does the *intuitus* acquire its incontrovertible characteristic, that radical "I think," this *cogito me cogitare*, the first *cogito*? To be sure, Descartes insists that it is an intuition, *intueri*: an "I see that actually it is so." But that vision is not the vision appropriate to, for example, the evidence of a mathematical theorem. In order to simplify I shall render it this way: the fact is I am here-and-now seeing that I am here-and-now thinking. The strength of the *cogito* resides in the *I am here-and-now*, i.e., in the characteristic that in a certain way corresponds to that intention with respect to the cogito's object; it does not reside in its presumed characteristic of certainty. Indeed, just the opposite: its presumed characteristic of certainty is not grounded on anything but that radical characteristic of reality the intuitive act has, not in whatever intuitive nature it may have, i.e., it resides in what the act has as *real*. The *cogito me cogitare* is not, therefore, "I think that I thought," but rather that I am here-and-now seeing that I am here-and-now thinking. {135}

We now ask, what is the relationship between these two components of the phrase, "I am seeing that I am here-and-now thinking"? One might think that Descartes highlights the logical identity of the subject "I." But that is not true because, as logical subject of the phrase, the *ego*'s are different; one is the *ego* that forms part of the thought-that-is-thought, the other is the *ego* that-is-thinking, and we could continue this way *ad infinitum*. It is not a logical identity; it is the identity of the to-be-there-here-and-now. Really and truly it is the case of *being here-and-now* as "I am here-and-now" thinking, and how "I am here-and-now" seeing that "I am here-and-now" thinking. Man's access to himself is not a question of intuition. It is the condition of a reality—whatever it may be, we are not going to delve into that problem—

of a being here-and-now, that cannot be here-and-now thinking except by intuiting and seeing that actually he is here-and-now thinking. This is just the subject of *reflection*; but reflection is not simply a matter of judgment; it is the real condition of human intelligence itself *qua* reality. How does intuition reach its object? Certainly not through chance, but *through itself*, through its own intrinsic condition; otherwise it would be infinitely doubtable. The identity, that is to say, my being here-and-now in reality reaches its object because it is the case of one selfsame and unique reality, which we express with the expression *to be here-and-now*.

Descartes, with his idea of being, has brought the matter into a merely logical dimension. And if in the metaphysics of St. Thomas we have seen the entification of reality, here we witness something different, but equally important, viz. the "truthification (or verification) of entitiness".

Being enters into truth, at least for us men. The first thing that Descartes discovered about human {136} understanding is just that it is *verum* [true]; but he overlooked the moment of reality in understanding, and in the very act of thinking.

Nevertheless, in this "verification" or "truthification" of reality ("verification" not in the sense of testing, but insofar as he subsumes entitiness and reality under *verum*) there are two cases. There is one that involves the *ego*, the only reality whose reality incontrovertibly involves truth. For Descartes, this is the first principle of philosophy.

But there is a second case in which truth incontrovertibly involves the reality of its *object*, which is God. Descartes tells us that the idea of an infinite entity cannot come from myself; I know I am finite and limited precisely because I have the idea of infinite being.[10] This idea has to come to me from some other reality—the Cartesian version of the famous ontological argument.

So we find ourselves between a truth that emerges incontrovertibly from the reality of the *I*, and a reality that emerges incontrovertibly from the truth of the idea of God. Based on this inherent tension, Descartes explains what he has to tell us about truth.

Given "verification" of reality and entitiness, it is indispensable that we be told what Descartes understands by "truth."

III. *Evidence and truth*

Descartes manipulates four different concepts of truth, however each is {137} grounded in the previous one. We must carefully try to understand these four different strata of the problem of truth in Cartesian philosophy.

1. Truth as firmness

In the first place, as we have just said, Descartes searches for some truth that has unchangeable certainty. Here "truth" means "firmness," an intellective firmness in the face of every doubt or uncertainty. This is something that philosophy has sought from its origins. When Parmenides tells us at the beginning of his *Poem* (1:29) what truth is, he tells us precisely of the "immovable heart of the well-rounded truth" (ἀληθείης εὐκυκλέος ἀρτεμές ἦτορ). That moment of the ἀρτεμές, of the unchangeable, pertains to truth, in one form or another, since the beginnings of philosophy. When Aristotle, more logically, wished to discover the first principle of the logos—the principle of contradiction—he tells us that he is going to search for a principle that may be βεβαιοτάτη, the most secure, the most inflexible. This idea, therefore, that truth is unchangeable belongs in some to a primary and primordial concept of truth. For Descartes it not the case of truth founded on evidence, but of truth that is unchangeable in itself, by virtue of its inner structure *qua* truth. Truth in this sense is *firmness*; truth is firmness by itself.

2. Truth as manifestation

Secondly, we have to point out a different concept of truth in Descartes. Truth, he tells us, {138} is an attribute of a *perceptio clara ac distincta*,[11] of a clear and distinct perception. Here it is no longer a question of unchangeable certainties; it is the case of a *manifestation*. Here truth is manifestation, not simply firmness. In other words, truth is only that which is firmly known, "firmly manifest," and this *perceptio clara ac distincta* by itself is the evidence of it for Descartes. It is also clear for Descartes that this belongs to the realm of truth; after all, evidence is the incorporation of the true into the certain. So we have a second concept of truth.

3. Truth as transcendental

There is a third stratum, which is much more radical and definitely much more problematic than the first two, but to which Descartes expressly appeals.

Descartes tells us that everything I see with a clear and distinct perception is *procul dubio* (without doubt) *aliquid*, "something." When I think objectively a series of evident truths, that which I think, objectively, *procul dubio*—without doubt, Descartes says—is something, is *aliquid*.[12] And here is where the tradition of the previous metaphysics intervenes. This *aliquid* is convertible with the *ens*; this is the conversion of transcendentals. Hence for Descartes, truth thus understood as the terminus of a *perceptio clara ac distincta* is *ens*, but *ens* precisely {139} *because it is true*.[13] This is the transcendental "verification" of being. Everything that is clearly and distinctly perceived is *aliquid* and by being *aliquid* is a *res* that is converted with *ens*. Hence because of that conversion, which is transcendental and evident, this third concept of truth is *transcendental* truth, strictly speaking. It is "transcendental" because it is converted with *ens*, but starting from the understanding. And here we find the important and decisive inflection to which Descartes has subjected all previous philosophy.

When that earlier philosophy spoke of the conversion of *ens* with *verum*, it always appealed to and started from being; it is being *qua* being that fits with the divine understanding and what is supposed to fit, in one form or another, with human understanding. But St. Thomas does something more: he fuses these two dimensions of the truth—I shall come back immediately to this idea—he fuses them into the intrinsic being of the real. The real, *ens*, is intelligible by itself. This means that for earlier philosophy the problem of the *verum transcendentale* was oriented towards *ens*. But Descartes does not orient it towards *ens*; he orients it towards understanding. That is the important, decisive inflection with which modern philosophy will be born.

Truth is the first transcendental. The first transcendental is not *ens*; for me, a thinking thing with intelligence, what we call *ens* is fulfills the transcendental conditions of what the *verum* is, of what truth is. The first transcendental is to be an *aliquid verum*; but it is *aliquid* insofar as it is *verum*, i.e., insofar as it is clearly and distinctly perceived. It is, in the transcendental order, the perfect communication for the verification of entity. {140}

While for earlier philosophy being consisted in the entification of the real that afterwards is trans-grounded to understanding, which knows the real, here we have exactly the opposite situation. It is the *verum transcendentale*, as *verum*, that which involves the being of an *aliquid* that is converted with *res*. That is why the philosophy of Descartes is not merely an egology; it is something deeper and more radical, a transcendental egology. It is "transcendental" because truth is now found to be inscribed in certainty, and in turn being is found to be inscribed in truth. The result is that the certainty of the *ego cogitans* is the ultimate and radical ground of the transcendental order for me. The transcendental order is not based on being; it is based on the *ego* insofar as it has certainties and clear and distinct perceptions of something. Of course, this is for me, for my *ego*, because I am a thinker; but we still have to consider things. Truth not only consists in the fact that I may think with truthfulness objective contents of a concept, but it consists in something more, it consists in the fact that *things are really what I say about them.*

4. Truth as transcendent

We still have to analyze a fourth concept of truth. Descartes does not use the expression I am going to use, but no matter. Let us call that concept "transcendent truth," because it means not only the truth of some objective contents, clearly and distinctly perceived in the mind, but also that those objective contents, clearly and distinctly perceived by my mind (i.e., the whole transcendental order), express the reality of things *beyond* this order. When all is said and done, reason, {141} i.e., thinking and intelligence with all its concepts, moves *primo et per se* in the objective order. But the real, as such, remains in principle *beyond* reason. If reason is going to reach the real, it will have to be in a different manner than that discussed in the foregoing paragraphs. .

Hence this transcendent truth is the one that interests Descartes most. Descartes wishes to ground knowledge as science, not only of God, but also of man and things; this is transcendent truth. This is what is most important to him, but also the most complex.

Indeed, let us think carefully about what Descartes tells us. Descartes moves *a limine* in the framework of nothingness. Within this framework arise both the uncertainty of my own reason and, above all, the radical uncertainty about what the things are that are offered to this reason. Of course, Descartes has already proven the existence of God through his version of the ontological argument (we are not going to investigate now the rest of God's attributes) and considers—reasonably, up to a certain point—that creation is a most free act of God. However, this freedom, as Descartes understands it, radically affects my reason and things.

In the first place, it affects my reason. We are not dealing with the question of whether God was free to create beings possessed of intelligence; this, of course, is a triviality about which there is no dispute. Descartes tells us something much more important, that the *entire objective order* of reason—not my faculty of thinking—but the objective order of thinking and reason, could have been different than it objectively is. The entire objective order of my reason, the whole transcendental order, depends on a most free act of the will of God, who has willed that there should be a reason that has *this* particular objective order. Probably here, Descartes (with perhaps a very logical exaggeration) has {142} continued the tradition of earlier philosophy; after all, for Ockham everything except the principle of contradiction could have been radically different than it is. Descartes reckons that even the principle of contradiction —he never questions it— is an act of the God's entirely free will.

But then, granting that God created the objective order of my reason, Descartes says that this is *procul dubio aliquid*, that it is something, and precisely by being something it has been created by God, and so has God for its author. He tells us, *est aliquid, et a nihilo esse non potest et necessarium Deum auctorem habet.*[14] The transcendental order, the objective order of my reason, is a creation by God. Precisely by being a positive act, it has God as its ultimate creative cause. God is, from this point of view, the transcendent principle of the transcendental order.

In the second place, there is the real world. Let us put reason aside now. This real world has also been created by God as freely as He has created my reasoning reason and my objective reason. If we wish to follow a particular order, first we would have to say that Descartes considers that God created the world in conformity with certain ideas that He had in His mind—and this is why the objective order of reason is definitively (for him) something freely willed by God. But, in addition, Descartes probably considers that these ideas are, in God, an act of His most free will. Here Descartes distances himself from the philosophy of St. Thomas and accepts the decisive influence of Duns Scotus.

For St. Thomas, the essence of God, considered as subsisting being, involves in itself, formally, an intrinsic {143} imitability *ad extra*; this imitability is but each of those possible imitations, i.e., an idea. In that way and with the same necessity by which God is the Supreme Being, He is also the Being that through His ideas makes possible that which is not Him, that which is imitable *ad extra*. The ideas preexist in a certain way in the divine essence, and only because of that does God knows them as He knows himself.

Scotus' point of view is completely different. Scotus says that within the divine essence there is an act of *fontanal* will, so to speak, internal to the divine mind; and this act of internal will consists in creating, within God's mind, the ideas themselves. The ideas are thus an act of the entirely free creation of God within His own mind; and because of this the ideas do not preexist in the intelligence, but rather intelligence sees them as terminus of an internal creative will of God. This is a radically different point of view. Scotus, particularly at the hands of Descartes, has consigned freedom and the contingency of reality to the very bosom of the divine essence. In His act of free internal will is how God has created the ideas, and has produced the ideas within himself in conformity with which He is going to create the real world.

A second point to consider is that this world, which God is going to create, is in conformity with His ideas, and Descartes will not abandon this point of view. In this sense, insofar as reality is pre-intellected—even though consequent to an act of will—it has a *verum transcendentale*. Actually, it is adequate to the idea God had of reality when He created or willed to create, and effectively did create the reality in question. Therefore, this reality possesses a *verum transcendentale*.

In the third place, we must keep in mind the absolute {144} independence of these two *vera transcendentalia*, the transcendentality in the objective order of my concepts, and the transcendentality according to which reality is in accordance with the divine ideas. That is a crucial question. They are, indeed, two absolutely independent transcendental truths.

God could have created a world that had nothing to do with the most evident and most transcendental truths of my own reason. In that case, there would not be transcendent truth; the world would not be, nor would have anything to do with, what my objective concepts say. What my mind conceives is a *verum transcendentale* that has no reason to coincide with the *verum transcendentale* of reality.

But Descartes does not stop here. He says that God freely *makes them coincide*. Why?

One might think of the entitative attributes of God. But that is not the explanation. Descartes keeps working with his favorite idea of the verification or truthification of reality, and in this case, of divine reality. However, the truth of divine being, of divine reality, here acquires a special characteristic that classical theology calls the non-absolute *potentia Dei ordinata*, which Descartes calls "veracity." In fact God is truthful and precisely by being truthful He cannot deceive me; therefore, although He has made a real order that *might* have nothing to do with the transcendental order, He has *actually* made them coincide. He has made the order of reality coincide precisely with the objective order of concepts, and hence that the *verum transcendentale* of reality coincide with the *verum transcendentale* of understanding.

In St. Thomas—here is the difference—there is a necessary coincidence between both orders. Being for St. Thomas is intrinsically intelligible because it has been pre-intellected by God and because, as such, is offered to my mind. {145} For Descartes, being, like my reason, is referred to a free act of divine will; that is why its coincidence is not grounded on the intrinsic intelligibility of the real. That the real is intelligible for my mind is *not* an intrinsic characteristic of reality or being; it is simply a *contingent* fact, the truthful veracity of God. There does not exist *a parte rei* an intrinsic and *a priori* intelligibility of the real. With this, the unity of the transcendental order has been broken. It is true that for Descartes this unity is based (reestablished) on the divine veracity, but we shall see what happens to that divine veracity in the course of history.

At any rate, if it is true that in Descartes we are present at the dawn of rationalism, it is a rationalism that has often been called *voluntaristic rationalism*. The whole Cartesian rationalism is based on a radical voluntarism; this is the *will to reason*. Here "will" is on the part of God who is free to create an objective order in a finite and created reason like the one we all have. It is the will to a free "reason" when creating a world whose internal structures can effectively coincide with the evident and transcendental structures of my reason.

But then it is clear that the two dimensions of the *verum transcendentale*, which the philosophy of St. Thomas had offered to us, have been internally dissociated. For St. Thomas, on one hand the same reality, in its intrinsic condition as being, is the subject so to speak of a *verum transcendentale* referred to God; that entity, actually, is the reality pre-intelected by the divine intellect. On the other hand, that same entity is the transcendental order referred to finite intelligence, because it is the capacity the entity has to inform every intelligence that approaches reality. Descartes does not consider things from this point {146} of view. For him, there is a strict dissociation between these two dimensions because the first transcendental for Descartes is not *ens*, but *verum*. And as truth, this truth emerging out of a free act of God is completely different (or in principle, could be) for real things and for the human mind. If indeed things are intelligible, they are so in fact through an act of freest will, but not by the intrinsic condition of their entitiness. Thus the two dimensions of the *verum transcendentale* have been definitely dissociated. What is going to happen in later philosophy is a complete breakdown of the unity of the transcendental order, and a more radical dissociation of the two dimensions of this *verum transcendentale*.

The verification of reality is an operation as significant as the entification of reality. Descartes stumbled over the real character of thought as a reality that is here-and-now, and was inexorably led to dissociate the two aspects of the *verum tanscendentale*, referred to an act of freest divine will. That divine will, on the one hand, creates various things, and on the other hand, my reason. If God places them in accord, it is precisely though the principle of intrinsic veracity; in the end, He does so by an attribute we might call "transcendental," but of a purely moral order, viz. that God cannot deceive me.

Consequently, we find in summary: 1) For Descartes the first transcendental is not being either in the case of man, who moves in the order of objective evidences, or in the case of God, as terminus of *veracitas*, His veracity. Rather, it is *verum*. 2) Transcendent truth is not grounded on the intrinsic intelligibility of being, but is a characteristic freely willed by God; if things are intelligible, it is {147} because God has freely willed them to be so, not through an internal and intrinsic characteristic of their entitiness.

3) Transcendent truth is a *veritas facti*, it is a factual truth, the fact of the freest creation on the part of God.

4) Speaking metaphysically, this means that contrary to what St. Thomas had in mind when referring to the necessary order, i.e., the necessary characteristic of the transcendental order, the transcendental order is perforated by a radical contingency. This is the *radical contingency of the transcendental order*. The transcendental order lacks any necessary unity when taken integrally; it is purely and simply a contingent fact. I consider it important to emphasize this in Descartes' vision.

Contrary to what is commonly said, the philosophy of Descartes does not simply move in a game of certainties and insecurities; it reaches much deeper, it reaches all the way to the transcendental character of the *ego* and the transcendental character of the divine free will. From this we get four fundamental concepts of truth: firmness, manifestation, transcendentality and transcendence. Manifestation is grounded on firmness; transcendentality is grounded on objective manifestation, and transcendence is a characteristic most freely willed by God. That is why Descartes moves *a limine* within the framework of nothingness.

What I have just said is not something that I have invented. Descartes, towards the end of his Fourth Meditation (*De vero et de falso*), tells us there will not be error—we shall explain why— so long as the will "when issuing its judgments limits itself to what is clearly and distinctly manifested to the intellect." Such judgments will be unchangeably true—this is the first concept of truth—insofar as the will limits itself to clear and {148} distinct perceptions because (here the third concept of truth appears) every clear and distinct perception is, without doubt, something, and therefore, cannot issue from nothing, but necessarily has God for its author" (*in judiciis ferendis ita contineo, ut ad tantum se extendat quae illi clare et distincte ab intellectu exhibentur [fieri plane non potest ut errem], quia omnis clara et distincta perceptio procul dubio est aliquid ac proinde a nihilo esse non potest sed necessarium Deum autorem habet*).[15]

It is just here that the transcendental dimension of truth appears. Truth is no longer convertible with being because it is the intrinsic expression of intelligibility of being. Rather, quite the other way around: truth is convertible with being because being *freely verifies what the objective truth of reason is*, which God has willed to grant me, "God, that supremely perfect being who finds it repugnant to be fallacious" (*Deum inquam illum sumum perfectum quam fallacem esse repugnat*). Here we have the fourth concept of truth, *ideoque procul dubio est vera*: it is, therefore, true without any doubt at all.[16]

So these four concepts of truth appear mingled in Descartes. But it was necessary to see them sequentially, in their internal structure, and to perceive the metaphysical texture of Descartes' thought. Contrary to what might seem to be the case at first glance, Descartes' thought is not a trivial exercise in certainty and doubt, evidence and non-evidence, but touches {149} upon the most serious problems and dimensions of the very fabric of the transcendental order.

Thus these four concepts move *a limine* within the framework of nothingness. Descartes clearly tells us, "I am something between God and nothing, i.e., between the Highest Being and non-being, inasmuch as I have been created by the Highest Being, the Supreme Being" (*me tanquam medium quid inter Deum et nihil, sive inter Sumum Ens et non ens [ita esse constitutum, ut,] quatenus a Summo Ente sum creatus*).[17]

Based on this, Descartes tells us that the assent the will grants to ideas (and which for him constitutes judgment) has two possibilities. One is to rely on what clear and distinct evidence tells us, and with it to rely not only on my transcendental truth, but also on the transcendent truth of things, i.e., on what God has freely willed them to be. The second possibility is the opposite. If the will precedes the order of evidence, I not only err or can err, but I have a more serious problem. In that case, I am falsifying the essence of the will, or at least the act of the will with respect to reason. Because of this, for Descartes, the opposite of truth is not simply error, but a *falsum*, i.e., a sin against reason. Not only has he verified (truthified) truth, but also with respect to judgment—so to speak—he has moralized, in a transcendental sense, its very structure.

The framework of nothingness is thus not only the result, but the very principle of Cartesian philosophy. I am uncertain and insecure, because I am that singular unity {150} of nothing and God, because I am a free creature of God. Uncertainty is not only a fringe of insecurity that accompanies the great majority of our knowledge, as in Ockham, but something more serious. It is something that constitutes the very condition of the *ego*; it is the intrinsic condition of the *ego* as thinker. As we see, nothingness places at the highest rank not the finitude of entity as in St.

Thomas, but uncertainty, and with it the essentially contingent character of the transcendental order as such.

Within this framework of nothingness, first philosophy is a progression from nothingness to God that is full of uncertainty and yearning for evidence.

Philosophy, then, is no longer theology, nor even an entitative theory of Creation, but anthropology open to theology. However, the inflection has been consummated. From this moment on, philosophy will dizzily be transcendental anthropology and not theology.

---

1 No doubt, Zubiri refers here to an important passage of the First Rule, "Indeed, all sciences are nothing but human wisdom, which remains one and identical with itself regardless of the different objects it deals with without receiving from them any other diversity than the one the light of the sun receives from the variety of the things it illumines", *Regulae ad directionem ingenii,* in R. Descartes, *Oeuvres* (Ed. Adam-Tannery), X, p. 360.

2 "Rationibus non aliunde petitis quam ab ipsa et nostra mente posse ostendi" (A-T, VII, 2).

3 A-T, VII, 18.

4 [It is unclear which lines of *Agamenon* Zubiri had in mind here. The reference given, line 757, is not correct since that line is spoken by the Herald and has nothing to do with the idea that Zubiri is trying to get across to us. No other lines of this play seem to fit. It is possible that he was thinking of another play by Aeschylus.—trans.]

5 A-T, VIII-1, 8.

6 [Zubiri neologism.—trans.].

7 "Simplici mentis intuitu" (A-T, VII, 140).

8 A-T, VII, 34.

9 [Zubiri is here drawing a distinction between two meanings of the verb "to be." One is the permanent sense, such as "Socrates is a man," and the other the immediate sense of something happening, something actual here-and-now, such as "I am writing a letter." In English, both of these senses are expressed by the same verb, "to be," but in Spanish they are expressed by two verbs, *ser* and *estar.* Zubiri capitalizes on this to make Descartes' meaning clear. To capture Zubiri's explanation, *estar* is always translated using "to be here-and-now,", while *ser* is translated with "to be."—trans.]

10 "Nec putare debeo me non percipere infinitum"... (A-T, VII, 45-46).

11 "Clara quaedam et distincta perceptio" (A-T, VII, 35 and 62).

12 "Omnis clara et distincta perceptio procul dubio est aliquid", (A-T, VII, 62).

13 "Ideoque procul dubio est vera" (A-T, VII, 62).

[14] "Est aliquid, ac proinde a nihilo esse non potest, sed necessario Deum authorem habet" (A-T, VII, 62).

[15] A-T, VII, 62.

[16] "Nam quoties voluntatem in judiciis ferendis ita contineo, ut ad ea tantum se extendat quae illi clare et distincte ab intellectu exhibentur, fieri plane non potest ut errem, quia omnis clara et distincta perceptio procul dubio est aliquid, ac proinde a nihilo esse non potest, sed necessario Deum authorem habet, Deum, inquam, illum summe perfectum, quem fallacem esse repugnat; ideoque procul dubio est vera", (A-T, VII, p. 62).

[17] A-T, VII, 54.

CHAPTER 4
WESTERN PHILOSOPHY (3)
LEIBNIZ

§1

LEIBNIZ' PROBLEM. THE FRAMEWORK OF NOTHINGNESS: POSSIBILITY

Leibniz also places himself within the framework of nothingness. St. Thomas had seen within that framework, on a basic level, the intrinsic finitude of being. Descartes saw, on a primary level, the uncertainty of man who searches for clear and distinct ideas, who looks for evidence about truth and being. Leibniz places himself in the same framework, but the progression of his thought is much different.

Leibniz tells us quite graphically that "what is good about Cartesianism is actually at the antechamber of truth." Thus for Leibniz Cartesianism is not the whole truth, but only the beginning. Therefore, Cartesianism must be lacking something that for Leibniz is decisive.

Indeed, for Descartes all philosophy is based, in one form or another, on the concept of clear and distinct ideas. However, in Leibniz' view, Descartes ignores {152} something critically important in those clear and distinct ideas. The clear and distinct ideas are *mine*, but regardless how much they are mine they are ideas of *something*, and that "something," obviously, is not mine. To be sure, this "something" cannot simply be the real thing itself, because there are many ideas of unreal things; but if there is no real thing in the objective terminus of an idea, there is nevertheless that which makes it *possible* for the thing to be real.

Therefore, in the first place, the content of an idea represents that which is objective about the thing. In the second place, that which is *objective* about a thing is what is *possible* about it. The idea of a glass of water is not really a glass of water, but the idea of a glass of water contains the *objective possibility* of that which in reality we call a glass of water. Therefore, in the idea there is a moment by virtue of which its terminus is a possible object. According to Leibniz, Descartes forgot that to support all philosophy on ideas means to support the real upon the possible as its ground.

As long as this is only applied to those things that surround man, it does not appear to be a far-reaching truth. Since the beginning of the world we have known that those things that eventually became things did so because they were possible. But Leibniz, influenced by earlier metaphysics, realizes an operation with a much greater scope: not only a few things or many of them, but the entire real universe, according to him, had to be possible before being real. This is what now appears within the framework of nothingness.

For St. Thomas, the framework of nothingness highlights, primarily, the intrinsic finitude of being. For Descartes, nothingness highlights, primarily, the uncertainty of man amid his search for truths. For Leibniz, {153} it is something different; within the framework of nothingness he highlights, primarily, the *possible* as antecedent ground of the *real*. This is what we must now proceed to consider very carefully.

§2

LEIBNIZ' DEVELOPMENT OF THE PROBLEM

To accomplish this, we are going to divide the analysis of Leibniz' thought into three steps.

First. What is the objective content of an idea as possibility of the real?

Second. What are the consequences that this conception of the objective content of an idea as possibility has for the vision of things?

Third. How does the philosophy of Leibniz regard the transcendental order?

I. *Idea and possibility*

The idea as possibility has two aspects.

In the first place, there is the specifically Cartesian aspect. Ideas have to be clear and distinct. Anything else would not be moving among ideas, but among confusions. However, Leibniz understands that this clarity and distinctness must have a very precise character. Ideas are not limited to containing just a few clear and distinct notes; rather, these notes have to be precisely those which are requisite (*requaesita*) to the thing of which the idea is a concept. Therefore these requisite notes must be rigorously defined. An idea is clear and distinct only when it is so defined. What Descartes was missing was the notion of definition, which is not just a *logical* pronouncement, but the *objective character* of a thing; and this objective character {155} is limited with respect to its intrinsic condition of being a note, and it only deserves to be called a definition insofar as it is clear and distinct. As has been often remarked, Descartes' criterion of evidence is itself not evident; and this is due to the fact that it is not well-defined. Leibniz understands that it is always necessary for the clarity and distinctness to be those of an idea rigorously defined.

But though necessary, this is not sufficient for Leibniz; there is an essential second element. Not all notes are an idea of some objective terminus, even if rigorously defined and combined. For that it is necessary that these notes be rigorously compatible among themselves. Compatibility is something that, according to

Leibniz, completely escaped Descartes' perspicacity. Thus it is not just a question of definitions.

What does Leibniz understand here by "compatibility"? Compatibility means the intrinsic possibility of an object. Compatible notes make that of which they are compatible notes an intrinsically possible object. But what does Leibniz understand by "possibility"?

Classical philosophy, since the time of Aristotle, spoke about potential being (δυνάμει ὄν), but that δύναμις had only two meanings. First, it was the *capacity of producing something*, for example, in a seed there is the tree that is going to be born from it in the form of a "force" (δύναμις). Second, it can have a different meaning, that the *same tree has a kind of pre-contained existence* in the seed, and this existence is called δυνάμει ὄν. In this case, the tree is nothing but *potential* or *virtual*. {156}

However that is not the case here. Leibniz, under the decisive influence of Francisco Suárez [1548-1617], considers that compatibility is something more, and that it is intrinsic. This means that the object, in itself, must be intrinsically possible as such. Not only must there be a δύναμις capable of producing it and therefore, that the terminus of that δύναμις be virtually preexistent; it is also necessary that in itself the object must have intrinsic possibility.

What is that intrinsic possibility for Leibniz? Faithfully following Suárez, Leibniz tells us clearly that the intrinsically possible is anything that is not intrinsically contradictory. That is, what makes something intrinsically possible is that its notes are not contradictory among themselves. Let us understand what a judgment is. It does not mean that when we predicate something of a thing our thinking does not contradict itself, because this is something derivative, not intrinsic. For Leibniz—and the same for Suárez—the notes among themselves in fact exclude the moment of non-being by which they would be incompatible among themselves. In non-contradiction, the *non-* that affects the intrinsic possibility is the non-impossible; and the *impossible* on the other hand is the contradictory. Because of this non-contradiction is what constitutes the possible as such.

Now, according to Leibniz an idea that contains compatible notes, in the sense we have just indicated, is what rigorously constitutes a concept. Here Leibniz makes a distinction taken—at least in its vocabulary—from Suárez. If we have an idea that meets all the conditions just outlined, then we have an apt concept (*conceptus aptus*) ... apt for what? Precisely to have reality. This is what turns the objective *terminus* into something *possible*. A concept that does not meet these conditions, but {157} because of a deficient intellectual analysis we were led to believe is apt, yet in the end is not so because it is contradictory, would be a defective concept. Here we can clearly see how the terminus of possibility is antecedent of the real thing in Leibniz' philosophy, just as it was in the philosophy of Suárez.

It is the case that being, the entity with which metaphysics deals, is not actual being in its reality, but that which by aptness *can* have reality, *can* exist. The primary base upon which metaphysics rests is the possible *qua* possible, i.e., apprehended in an apt concept, or if you will the objective terminus of an apt concept. It is true that between the apt concepts and the defective ones Leibniz is going to introduce a third category, which includes, for example, things we perceive or imagine; but we shall not delve into that problem here. Leibniz, in a way quite characteristic of his way of thinking, classifies sensibility as purely and simply a confused intellection. This is such far-reaching affirmation that it will have to be discussed at the proper time. We shall put it aside for now, however.

The concept defined with rigor, the apt concept, is what constitutes the *ens possibile*. This means that existing things, by virtue of this *possibile*, realize what is contained in the possible as such. The possible contains the answer to what a thing is, namely, it is an *essentia*. To incorporate all reality into an idea is not only to incorporate what exists in the possible, but also to make the possible the very essence of what exists. This places essence prior to all existing things and makes it the ground of their existence. The equation between possible object and essence is what confers on Leibniz' thought its greatest precision.

Leibniz, however, still must explain how we form an objective concept from compatible notes {158} under these conditions. He replies that the answer is simply by demonstration. Since we are dealing with rigorously defined notes, the demonstration must be through definitions. Therefore, the priority of the *possible* over the *existent* is the priority of *ideas* over the *real*, and therefore, the priority of *essence* over *existence*. This is absolutely decisive for the way in which Leibniz understands the real with respect to the possible.

Before elaborating, let us stop and reflect on just what this exposition of Leibniz' metaphysics Leibniz suggests.

1. *With respect to the idea of contradiction.* The principle of contradiction is a principle that for very good reasons has been making the rounds of metaphysics since the time of Aristotle, who enunciated it explicitly. Aristotle referred to it as a principle of "speaking," i.e., the logos could not contradict itself. However Leibniz is saying something more. He is saying that contradic-

tion—or non-contradiction—is a structure of reality itself, which could not be affirmed without also saying that entity—real or possible—has the same structure as the logos. But is this correct? If not, contradiction and non-contradiction would not be useful to qualify a real thing. A real thing, strictly speaking, is not contradictory or non-contradictory; it is what it is and nothing more. Contradiction is on the part of the logos, which enunciates or affirms something about the thing that exists; but the moment of *non* has no positive reality in things. Be that as it may, the framework of nothingness has so penetrated and drenched all things that we find it the most natural thing in the world to say that things have an aspect of being and an aspect of non-being. But things are actually what they are and that is where their function ends. {159} In Leibniz as in Suárez it is difficult to maintain that contradiction (or non-contradiction) is something pertaining to being.

2. *Non-contradiction as an internal possibility of a thing.* But what do we understand here by "internal possibility"? We have already seen the answer: that which is not impossible. What does this "impossible" mean? That it cannot be realized by potency? But, in that case, the possibility open to the dimension of contradiction and non-contradiction is the possibility of an intellective potency, capable of knowing and producing the thing; it does not belong to the thing's internal structure. Indeed, the possibility of something, the essence of a thing, is not comprised only of notes that are not incompatible, but possesses an intrinsic and internal unity by virtue of which this thing has its own possibility and when it is realized, has its own entity. This is an idea we shall encounter later on in Leibniz' philosophy, but which is for now eliminated completely from his consideration of essences. The internal and primary unity is something positive, not merely negative. Is it the case that this primary and positive unity is certified intrinsically by non-contradiction or, to put it simply, by pronouncement, by a λέγειν, of any kind at all?

Furthermore, just like all philosophy since the sixteenth century, Leibniz has confused two notions that are different. It is clear that we can talk about the objective possibility of something. But does "objective possibility" mean a possible *object*? That is a different question. The possibility that there can be such an object does not mean that there is a possible object with respect to which the real object is nothing but the addition of existence, i.e., existence is something added to that which is the possible object. The "possibility" of an object is one thing, and a possible "object" is definitely something else. While it may be {160} certain that prior to reality—or at least, simultaneously with it—there has to be an objective possibility, it remains problematic to talk about a possible "object" that, as such, is prior to reality. Perhaps the metaphysics of Henry of Ghent (+1293) hovers over the Leibniz' philosophy. To create is not to add existence to an essence, but to fully place in reality an existing essence. Anything else is a fiction that, in the end, is somewhat anthropomorphic. And here is the proof: when Leibniz affirms that the compatibility of notes has to be demonstrated, we may ask whether such a demonstration is possible.

The famous Gödel theorem demonstrated that in mathematics, with a finite body of axioms, we cannot demonstrate that our conclusions will not be contradictory. It might be said that this demonstration is rigorous, and therefore, based on the principle of contradiction; but it is a principle of contradiction that refers to the λέγειν, i.e., to the mind of the one who demonstrates it. From the objective point of view, there is no possibility for demonstrating the non-contradiction of a finite body of axioms. Consequently, compatibility is not based on non-contradiction, but just the opposite: non-contradiction is based on compatibility.

II. *Possibility and reality*

Now, with this idea in hand Leibniz now must tell us how he views real things. This is the second step.[1] {161}

In the first place, how does Leibniz regard existence? Leibniz recalls Descartes' ontological argument. In the idea of infinite being existence is included. Leibniz attacks this argument, but in view of the foregoing discussion, it will not surprise us that what he attacks is the starting point. Is it true that we have an apt concept of God? To say that an entity is infinite is not sufficient to have such an apt concept. Leibniz must embark on the task of demonstrating that an apt concept of God is intrinsically possible. Here we perceive the decisive influence of Scotus' theology.

Scotus first proves that God is possible, and then continues with a new form of the ontological argument. If God is possible, He is *eo ipso* real, existent. However, even in this case, we can see how Leibniz has conceived the *res divina*. It is not the case that God has passed from possibility to existence, but that in the bosom of the divine entity His own possibility is the ground of His existence. Leibniz is faithful to the priority, at least metaphysical, of the order of the possible over the order of the real.

The same occurs with creation. Creation involves a moment of will, a *fiat*, and it formally consists in that. But Leibniz asserts that this *fiat* is spoken about something that the intellect presents to the divine will. That something so presented is just the order of the possible, what classical theology called the "science of simple intelligence." Because of this, creation is also viewed with respect to possibility. To create is to confer existence upon something that preexists as possible, to confer existence upon an essence; it is definitely to realize something possible.

The case of man is similar. Man—Leibniz tells us—is "rational animal," repeating the classical formulaand emphasizing that reason is {162} what distinguishes humans from the animals. What does Leibniz understand here by "reason"? He understands that reason consists in the capacity to determine what things are essentially, i.e., to determine the primary requisites that make them possible. This determination is what he calls "analysis." Consequently reason in Leibniz is constitutively an *analytical reason*. It consists in analyzing that which constitutes the complexity of what there is, and of everything that is, into its elements, until reaching its ultimate components. Hence, by virtue of that reason, man possesses what are called "eternal truths." Actually, through his analysis man has discovered mathematical truths and other types of truths, all of them eternal truths; that is why, we say that man is a spirit.

The spirit is characterized by reflection or self-awareness. It not only performs certain acts, for example, knowing, but also knows itself when doing so. It has that moment that Leibniz calls *apperception*; and since every human perception is apperceptive, while perceiving everything else, it perceives itself.

Since in intellection we find eternal truths, this means that in one way or another the human spirit has something like an internal and constitutive movement towards such eternal truths, which are innate. They are innate not exactly in the sense that man is born thinking about them, but in the sense that to think about them is something that proceeds from the internal development of his reason. Consequently, by virtue of apperception, when thinking about myself and my own reason, about the *I* which is reason, I am thinking of everything objectively possible. That is, I am thinking about being and every necessary truth. The rational *I* is, in such fashion, the very possibility of the knowledge of being. With this, we again find possibility ahead of real things. {163}

But here we encounter two "reasons," human reason and divine reason. The divine reason has created, and human reason, by means of analytical resolution, reaches eternal truths. How? By thinking about itself. What happens then, in the relationship of this human reason with divine reason? That is the problem of the transcendental order.

III. *Structure of the transcendental order*

Leibniz severely criticizes Descartes, affirming that the transcendental order is not contingent, but intrinsically necessary. It is such "intrinsically" because it is not grounded on divine veracity. Leibniz asserts that what we think about being and what the Divine intellect thinks cannot be separated but are essentially conjoined, not through any act of divine veracity, but through an intrinsic condition. The transcendental order is intrinsically one since it is intrinsically necessary in itself. Why? It is one simply because human reason is an image of divine reason.

Descartes missed this idea. As a faithful heir to the philosophy of the fourteenth and fifteenth centuries, Descartes believed that human reason is a contingent *effect* of the divine will. For Leibniz, this is inadmissible; human reason is intrinsically an *image* of the divine reason. With this, the two orders—the order of transcendental truth concerning my intellect and the order of transcendental truth concerning the divine intellect—are one and the same intrinsically necessary order, as necessary as the very being of God. Therefore, this order is none other than the order of reason *simpliciter.* {164}

We have seen, first, what the order of the possible is as such; and second, that the possible is just the order of the concept. Hence, to affirm that the order of my reason is identical with the order of divine intelligence means to affirm purely and simply that the single and unitary order—which the order of being is—is intrinsically an order of rationality. Here entity remains inscribed in rationality. Because of this, while in Descartes we confront a rationalism that is voluntaristic—the "will to reason"—in Leibniz we have a more profound type of rationalism: his philosophy is an attempt to fashion a *rationalist rationalism.* It is reason that rests intrinsically and necessarily upon itself *qua* reason.

However, this is nothing but a general affirmation. It is necessary to analyze more carefully how Leibniz understands this transcendental order of rationality. This is done in three steps.

1. Transcendentality as such

The transcendental order is the order that concerns the truth of things and the truth about being. Clearly Leibniz here follows Descartes' path and incorporates the plane of entitiness into that of truth. Things are just what their intrinsic truth is.

But in another respect a profound and radical difference arises. Towards what does Descartes orient truth? We saw the answer: he simply orients it towards evidence, towards manifestation. Leibniz—here we have the great difference with Descartes—turns towards something completely different. Indeed, what is understood by truth? For Leibniz a judgment is true {165} when all the requisites of the subject are contained in the predicate. In that case—Leibniz tells us—every truth is an identity, not in the sense of an empty identity like $A = A$, but in the sense of an intrinsic and necessary implication. By virtue of this implication what is expressed in the predicate is pre-contained in the requisites that constitute the character of the subject. Therefore this is not a formal identity, but something much more radical and profound. It is the intrinsic unity of the object about which judgment is made.

This is just what Leibniz' thought decides. As we saw in the previous chapter, Descartes oriented truth towards evidence and found that the evidence in an *aliquid*, and by being an *aliquid*, is convertible with *ens*. Now we find a different solution. Leibniz directs truth towards unity and recalls that the *unum* is convertible with *ens*. This is what constitutes the great novelty of Leibniz' metaphysics. Entity has been incorporated into rationality in a very concrete form because the rational order is the order of unity. *Ens* is incorporated into the *verum*, but the *verum* is incorporated into the *unum*; here is where truth acquires its transcendental character.

By virtue of this, Leibniz finds himself compelled to explain more precisely just what he understands by reason. What is that particular rationality that constitutes the transcendental order? If it were only the case of simple things, as Aristotle said, what has been said would be sufficient; but things are enormously complex and Leibniz does not recoil when confronting that complexity. Faithful to his idea that the possible is always prior to the existent, he tells us that nothing that is real would be real were it not for the fact that the possible, *qua* possible, is determined to be in existence such as it is and in no other {166} way. This is precisely what Leibniz calls *sufficient reason*. Here "sufficient reason" does not mean that there is sufficient reason for a given thing to exist. For Leibniz, it is something much more profound, namely, that the possible *qua* possible—essence *qua* essence—is by means of itself determined to have a certain form of existence.

This principle of sufficient reason is indeed a *principle*, but in a very special way. For Aristotle, a principle is that "from where" a thing is presented to us as intelligible. Here "principle" is something different; it is a series of first truths of reason, unbreakable true judgments because they refer to the simplest ultimate elements into which the whole complex of the things that exist are analytically resolved. This is taken up by Leibniz to such a degree that he has consummated the absorption of the principle of causality into the principle of reason; primary is the principial[2] characteristic of rationality, and causality is a mode of reason.

However, this is very problematic. Is it possible to think that causality can be subsumed under an order of rational principles? The question is left unaddressed.

By virtue of the three characteristics we have pointed out—the transcendental order is an order of truth, this truth is constituted by a *unum,* and this *unum* is the order of sufficient reason—the complete transcendental order is, for Leibniz, an order of strict rationality, of strict rational grounding.

If we turn our attention to things and to God, we gain a better appreciation of what Leibniz understands by the transcendental with respect to God and the transcendental with respect to things. We mentioned this subject earlier from the viewpoint of possibility; now we have to approach it in its {167} deepest stratum, in the constitutive unity of the transcendental order.

How much of this can be applied to God? We already saw that God is His own possibility, but now we know that possibility is sufficient reason, or at least forms part of it. To say that God is His own possibility means, for Leibniz, that God is His own reason for being. The same way that in God His reality is based on His intrinsic possibility, the reality of God is based on His intrinsic reason. His own being is His own reason, but it is still "reason." That man may not perceive the structure of that reason is no obstacle for God to be His own reason, according to Leibniz, for God to be His own reason for being.

2. The transcendental unity of the world. Optimism.

This God has created the world, but He has not created the world without reason. What kind of reason? As we emphasized earlier, it is necessary to stress that the principle of sufficient reason does not consist in giving an explanation of what existence is. Rather, it consists in knowing why, or in virtue of what, the possible is determined to be real in one form rather than another. It is a characteristic that must be based on the intrinsic condition of the possible. Leibniz tells us that the possible for the divine mind is not only a system of notes that are compatible among themselves because of non-contradiction, but also a kind of permanent candidate for existence. Every possible, in its positive unity, is an "attempt" at existence, a *conatus existendi;* precisely because of this Leibniz is able to say that God does not create without reason. What kind of "reason" are we connecting with this concept of the possible?

{168} If Creation had consisted in just one thing, the question would have been answered. But we have many things, an entire universe. So Leibniz, by virtue of the principles he has established, places the possible ahead of the existent. He wants us to see that each one of the things that comprise the universe is a realized possible, that is to say, a case of existence granted to a candidate, to something intrinsically possible. Hence Leibniz can say something that, although it has become part of the history of metaphysics, to our ears sounds bizarre, *Dum Deus calculat fit mundus* ("God makes the world by calculating"). Calculating... what? Calculating just these possibilities, viz. the compatibility of the candidacies with existence. Every *possible* represents an attempt, by virtue of which it is an essence capable of being realized; but that essence has to be compatible not only in its internal notes, but with other essences. Indeed, Leibniz carried out a theological-metaphysical operation that could only be done by the founder of analytical mechanics. The fact is that despite the infinite number of possibles present to the divine mind, there is only a finite (though large) number of essences compatible among themselves. That is the existing world, the world that has the greatest possibility; and while God surely could have made many other poorer worlds, He could not have made any richer with respect to entity. Thus for Leibniz, ours is the world that has the greatest possible entity or being.

Nevertheless, since *ens* and *bonum* in traditional metaphysics are convertible, whatever has the greatest entitiness is what has the greatest goodness. This is the principle of metaphysical optimism in Leibniz, an optimism—properly understood—that is purely metaphysical.[3] {169} Leibniz gave certain moral and psychological resonances to his optimism that even from his own viewpoint would be difficult to maintain. A century later the Lisbon earthquake [1755] shocked the whole edifice of Leibniz' thought and forced Kant to write a pamphlet on optimism (*Über den Optimismus*). Nonetheless Leibniz' optimism remains this transcendental optimism. Our world is the one that has the greatest possible entitiness: it is a world in which the greatest set of essences compatible among themselves is realized. If we consider that each essence is like a kind of force that tends to exist, this real world is the resulting maximum of the infinite forces involved. That is the reason why God has willed it. This is the "principle of the best"; God cannot want anything but being; among several beings He cannot but want the one with the greatest entitiness; and when willing this greatest entitiness He has willed the best. Consequently, for Leibniz this world is the best of all possible worlds.

The transcendental order of the world, as viewed by God, is a *unum* constructed in such manner. This is the *unum* of rationality, that *unum* by which, according to reason, the greatest number of essences are compatible. Optimism is the structure of the transcendental unity of the world.

3. The transcendental unity of being. The monad.

We still must discuss created things. Here also Leibniz is inflexible with his thought, *Omne ens est unum* [Every being is one], a phrase that {170} has made the rounds of the history of metaphysics from the days of Parmenides, "being is one" (ἕν τὸ ὄν). The theme of unity appears among the transcendentals of classical metaphysics.

Leibniz, a great mathematician, had a very precise concept of the *unum*. The *unum* is so radical that not only is it indivisible in the sense of classical philosophy, it consists of a primary unity that penetrates to its internal detail. As Leibniz would say, it is a *metaphysical point*, it is *monás*, monad. The transcendental unity of being is monad, and conversely, monadism is the theory of the transcendental unity of being as such. The metaphysical "point" that the monad is realizes,through its reality, just what was thought in the divine mind. The attempt at existence that was in the divine mind is, in the real and actual monad, a *nisus*, an appetite towards its own internal unfolding.

This appetite is essential in Leibniz' transcendental philosophy, since it is a "transcendental appetite." It is "transcendental" because it is not something *consequent* to the structure of being, as in the philosophy of Aristotle, in the Middle Ages, and in Cartesian philosophy itself; it is instead something that *constitutes* being as such. But it is an appetite and a tendency.

However, upon reflection we may ask, is an *activity* the same as an *appetite?* Leibniz glossed the question, but it is worth considering.

Be that as it may, this impulse and internal appetite is the appetite for the unfolding of something that radically and previously has been a monad; in other words, what that *nisus* produces is the internal development of details. From this it follows that each monad, regardless how much activity and appetite it may have, never acts upon the rest of the others. Each one of the monads, for Leibniz, is closed upon itself, which means that it this is a transcendental closure. {171} Such self-containment does not mean that a monad has no relationship with others. But it is a very curious relationship. Each monad in its internal detail is a little like the other monads in the universe; God has placed them in accordance with a preestablished harmony in such fashion that each monad, without stepping outside itself and only producing its internal detail, is in a certain way a "mirror" of the other monads. As Leibniz says, it is a representation of the universe from its own point of view. The expression was a felicitous one, but not all such things are particularly accurate.

Leibniz had a decisive influence in history; but curiously not on account of his transcendental philosophy. Rather, he has been influential for something different, viz. the application of this transcendental philosophy to scientific matters. Leibniz is the great creator of genius, not just of one science, but of several, precisely because of this idea of the metaphysical point, and his precision in constructing the internals of a monad starting from its intrinsic unity. This is how he discovered infinitesimal calculus. (Newton also discovered at about the same time but it in a different way, by means of fluxions).

Furthermore, for Descartes the science of the physical world was mechanical, but that mechanics was purely *kinematic*, the geometry of motion. On the other hand, for Leibniz it becomes something different, it becomes *dynamics*. He introduces the notion of mechanical force, thus creating analytical dynamics that passed through Lagrange and reaches Hamilton, becoming one of the great achievements of physics during the nineteenth and early twentieth centuries.

Leibniz also created other things. In his polemic concerning {172} space—which we shall not cover here—Leibniz understands that space is the relation between monads. This resembles in some ways the idea that later will surface in mathematics as set theory. While it is certain that Leibniz never thought about set theory, he did think it fitting to make a non-metric analysis of space with what he called "topology." He probably did not go further than giving it a name, but that was decisive. Kant, who did not understand what this term could mean, thought that topology was something like the problem posed by a glove of the right hand and a glove of the left hand, which although being symmetrical cannot be superimposed. This was a limitation of Kant's thought, because at almost the same time the great Swiss mathematician Leonhard Euler [1707-1783] solved the first strictly rigorous problem of topology, not of the topology of sets, but of combinatorial topology. The famous problem of the *Seven Bridges of Königsberg* consists in determining if one can go from one side of the city to the other by going over all the bridges, traversing each only once, and then returning to the point of departure. A lot of prizes were offered, but no one could solve the problem until Euler demonstrated it was impossible in the general case. He also showed under what conditions the problem is solvable, and under what conditions it is unsolvable. This was one of the first great conquests of combinatorial topology.

Leibniz created still other sciences, for example, the idea of mathematical logic. He discovered the fourth figure of the syllogism, which until then had not had a place in logic, and created the idea of the *ars combinatoria*; though perhaps the erudite will say that the idea had been making the rounds since Raymond Lully [Raimundus Lullus, 1235-1315], but only acquired relevance with Leibniz.

However, his transcendental idea of the monads had no philosophical consequence whatever except in the case of {173} two Jesuits. One of them, Palmieri,[4] about a century ago gave a different metaphysical interpretation of Transubstantiation using the idea of monads, a perfectly orthodox idea, as Franzelin defended,[5] certainly someone with impeccable Scholastic credentials. The other repercussion is represented in our times by Teilhard de Chardin.[6] His idea is that the elementary particles of the universe have a kind of germinal psychism, which by means of *enroulement* (whorl, scroll) of particles continues to emerge through evolution. This is simply monadism. Of course, it is difficult to conceive that in the bosom of an electron there can be a germinal psychism.

Leibniz, to be sure, has had much greater scientific than philosophical influence. However, with respect to man, his transcendental conception that man is an image of God has been enormously important. Leibniz, based on his view of the priority of the possible to the real, said that when thinking of myself, I think about being and about all necessary truths. The human monad is just as closed as the other monads, but since this necessary order of eternal truths is the very content of the divine mind, through it man is an image of God. God is the same for all; consequently, when thinking about myself and discovering my own transcendental apperception of the order of being, I am discovering an order of truths, which is thought in identically the same way by all other thinking reasons, i.e., all other humans. Precisely because of this, the human monad is not only a mirror, but an "image" of God. As Leibniz would say, the intellectual monads are *de petits dieux*, small gods. With this Leibniz eventually tells us that we see all things in God, an affirmation also made by Malebranche in a different sense. This kind of vision of all things in God is enormously problematic; perhaps in the other world it may be true, but is it in this one? {174}

Nevertheless, in Leibniz the unity of the transcendental order is the unitiness and identity of the transcendental order, included in the order of reason.

We now understand that:

1) The transcendental order is not contingent, but necessary,

2) The transcendental order is the order of entitiness considered as objectively possible.

3) This order of entitiness as objectively possible is an order of rationality.

4) This order of rationality is formally constituted by the unity in which rational truth consists.

IV. *Philosophy as science of the principles of reason*

Because of the foregoing, Leibniz' disciples—disciples are always a terrible thing in philosophy—were able to say, together with Christian Wolff [1679-1754], that philosophy is *sciencia prima cognitionis humanae principio continens*. In other words, that general metaphysics—"ontology" as Wolff called it—is the science that incorporates the first principles of human reason. We should understand that this includes the principle of identity, the principle of sufficient reason, and everything that can be derived analytically from both of them. On this point, Wolff, through Leibniz, was most likely influenced in a decisive way by Suárez.

Suárez has the merit of being a great debater. When the Suarezians are told something with which they do not agree, they not only say they do not agree, they articulate a syllogism. This comes from Suárez, and Leibniz acquired much from Suárez. I say this with no irony intended since I greatly admire Suárez; but each one of us has his own style.

Returning to the discussion of Leibniz and his disciples, we note that their philosophy has, in addition, a few special subdivisions. It has {175} a science about the cosmos, a "cosmology," which consequently is called "natural." There is also a psychology that is natural and deals with man. And there is also a science about God, which is a natural theology. Of course, here the term "natural" means that it does not proceed from supernatural reasons or from faith, but only from the order of reason. Because of that, natural cosmology, natural psychology, and natural theology will also be called "rational cosmology," "rational psychology," and "rational theology." The "rationalist" rationality of Leibniz, followed by Wolff and Baumgartner, was decisive throughout eighteenth century philosophy.

At first glance, this philosophy appears to have nothing to do with what we said about Descartes. Descartes' philosophy was anthropology open to theology, but it rapidly became a transcendental anthropology. Is this the case with Leibniz?

Apparently, it seems that the opposite is true. Leibniz tells us that man is an image of God, that human reason is an image of the divine reason. But let us ponder what he says about divine reason for a moment, just to be sure that fundamentally he has not simply conceptualized divine reason as human reason raised to the infinite. Leibniz presents divine reason as calculating with possibles, as someone who knows the complete infinite analysis of the mechanical forces that compose the universe would calculate. However, is this a calculation that can be attributed to divine reason? This can be done only by hypostatizing with the adjective "infinite" that which constitutes the peculiar condition of the human reason. According to Leibniz, God calculates with the possibles as a poor mathematician on this Earth might calculate with available data in order to solve a problem. {176}

Secondly, Leibniz says that the divine will is ordered by the divine intellect, which is true to a certain extent, at least in almost all theologies and metaphysics, except those of Descartes and a few others. However, does this mean that the will is *constrained* by that which the intellect offers? This only happens in the case of human will. To conceive that our science of how God knows is a kind of order that constrains the divine will with respect to His creative *fiat* amounts to thinking that our science of how God sees is a kind of vision of a will determined by our simple science of knowing. But this is pure anthropomorphism.

This becomes quite clear when—in the third place—Leibniz emphatically says that God does not create the world without a reason. What does he mean by "reason" here? This is a pronounced anthropomorphism, because for Leibniz it is a reason determined by possible entity or being, *qua* possible, by virtue of its attempt to exist. Basically, what God did in Creation is to give willful acquiescence to the maximum possible entitiness. God would inexorably submit himself to the principle of the best, something that does not even happen in the case of the human will. Contrary to what is generally said, the human will does not decide what is best ("best" not in the moral sense, but in the sense of the here-and-now); rather the *fiat* of the human will consists in the fact that it declares what is here-and-now desiring to be the best. Leibniz' ideas are rationalism that cannot be applied to man or God.

Leibniz has made divine intelligence a kind of calculus of possibles. He has made divine intelligence something quite intrinsically dependent upon this simple intelligence of God. Above all, he considers that it is determined by possible entity or being *qua* possible. Because of all this, {177} we discover in the bosom of Leibniz' whole metaphysics a germinal anthropomorphism. This makes Leibniz' metaphysics a hyper-transcendental anthropology, so "hyper-transcendental" that in the end it has conceived God in the image of man, instead of conceiving man as an image of God.

We can now contrast the different philosophies we have covered. For St. Thomas, what appears in the framework of nothingness is the *intrinsic finitude of being*. For Descartes, what appears is the *uncertainty of truth, uncertain man*. In Leibniz, in the framework of nothingness, the *possible appears ahead of the existent.* So at these pinnacles of thought we are presented with the curious spectacle of great philosophers in disagreement, and it would be chimerical to try to make them agree. But this is never what is most essential, because these men who are not in accord are nonetheless understood, and this is what is truly decisive.

* * *

In the previous chapters we have tried to clarify the fabric of the metaphysical problem of Western metaphysics. We have seen that Western metaphysics moves *a limine* in the framework of nothingness, no doubt motivated by the idea of Creation, although not limited to it exclusively. Things begin by being "notnothing," things that have come into being, and not only with respect to each other. Indeed, the totality of the universe has come into being.

St. Thomas, whom we take as an example of medieval philosophy, places in this framework of nothingness the ideas of Aristotle. This emplacement, details of which are outside the scope of this book, fundamentally consists of introducing Aristotle's idea of being {178} into the new framework, and then utilizing this framework and Aristotelian concepts to interpret, in an entitative fashion, the whole of creation and its creator-being. We saw that for St. Thomas this being has its own entitiness; otherwise, the act that produces it would not be a creative act. That entitiness is *ex nihilo sui et subjecti* or as St. Thomas says, *ex non ente quod est nihil;* therefore, the very idea of being as intrinsically finite and separate is the Aristotelian expression of the creationality of being as such, of created being *qua* created. This created being has some transcendental characteristics: unity, quiddity, somethingness (*aliquid*), *verum* and *bonum.* These characteristics are *grounded* on the intrinsic entitiness of being as such; they *express* the entitiness of being as such, and therefore, are *convertible* with that being. This being with all its characteristics is placed between two intelligences. On the one hand, we have the creative intelligence, which has put into existence what was already in the divine intelligence. Not only does God know what He creates, but He creates what He knows. In other words, reality considered as being is the realization *ad extra* with respect to God of what the divine intelligence of that being is. On the other hand, there is the human intelligence with its intrinsic finitude, which also addresses that being, not to produce it, but to understand and comprehend what it is. Therefore, the created thing—*res naturalis,* St. Thomas says—is situated between two intellects, the

divine and the human, and in both respects is intrinsically intelligible. It is so with respect to the divine intellect, because created
being is the realization *ad extra* of what is a previous intellection
by God. It is so with respect to the finite intellect, because that
intellect is made in such a way that on its own it may understand
everything along the lines of being. Consequently, the truth that
refers to being as such is and should be called {179} *verum transcendentale*, grounded, of course, on the intrinsic entity of things.

From Descartes on, matters change. Descartes moves within
that same framework of nothingness; there is no doubt about that
and he expresses it clearly, "I am in the middle between God and
nothingness." What happens is that Descartes sees at the outset
that this finite intellect—which St. Thomas quickly handled by
saying it was made to understand being as such intrinsically—is
disoriented and uncertain. For Descartes, the uncertainty of finite
intellection is what the condition of being created places at the
forefront. He slowly moves out of that uncertainty by steps we are
not going to repeat now, steps that in the end are reduced to
thinking that in the clear and distinct perception of ideas—that
intuitus, of which Descartes speaks—we actually have an *aliquid*,
which according to the medieval doctrine of the transcendentals,
is convertible with being. This being must be called "transcendental" in some sense from that moment. But to the order of reason
the order of things is basically alien, and God could have made
things that have nothing to do with that order of my reason,
which is a free creature of God, just as things are also creatures
of God. From this it follows that the adequacy of the transcendental order with respect to things is perforated with an intrinsic contingency. Descartes surmounts the difficulty by saying that God
is infinitely truthful. Therefore, it is through a truth, a *potentia
Dei ordinata*, the medieval theologians called it, that God has created a reality having the same structures my reason has, in its
rational and transcendental evidences. Perhaps this is not something transcendental in the sense we just explained, but it is at
least a kind of moral transcendentalism. {180}

{180} In such fashion, philosophy, which began for Descartes
by being implanted in an "egology," at least has been opened towards God, and in that opening has found the way to real things.
But the inflection has been consummated. From this moment on,
philosophy is going to be grounded more and more on this type of
ego.

In fact, Leibniz finds that all the steps of Cartesian philosophy
are problematic because, in the end, Descartes is only moving in
the antechamber of truth. He says "Antechamber" not because it
is untrue that ideas must be clear and distinct, but because the

clarity and distinctness as they appear in Cartesian philosophy
do not offer a sufficient starting point for a philosophical structure. They do not offer it because, according to Leibniz, Descartes
went astray on the proper condition for clear and distinct idea,
which is to contain the objective possibility of a thing. While for
Descartes at the outset the framework of nothingness presents
the uncertainty of the *I*, for Leibniz what appears at the forefront
is that things, prior to being *real*, are actually *possible*, not only
with respect to a particular thing, but with respect to the entire
world. The desire to understand the whole world, which Leibniz
accepts as the inheritance of Descartes, requires us to understand what actually exists against the background of the possible.

From my perspective there are three fundamental ideas in
Leibniz: possibility, existence, and transcendentality. First, possibility is constituted by the compatibility of a thing's notes among
themselves, which happens when they are not contradictory. Following Suárez, Leibniz affirms that the intrinsic possibility of being is its internal non-contradiction. Second, we have existence.
Real things now appear as something that has an existence supported by their own possibility, and this happens first of all in the
case of God. {181} Leibniz' exposition of the ontological argument
has a different form than in Descartes since it must be demonstrated that the *idea* of God is an *objectively possible* idea. If God
is possible, *eo ipso* He exists, and He appears as the reason for (or
explanation of) his own being based on his own internal possibility. Therefore divine existence itself is supported by its own intrinsic possibility.

The same occurs in one form or another with respect to the
spirit of man. Were he nothing more than the elements that comprise his intrinsic spirit, he would be just another thing among
the many we have in the universe. But the entity man is has reason, and with it he proceeds to think, not only about the things
he encounters, but also about being and all the necessary truths.
In that fashion, the *I* appears as the ground for the possibility of
my intellection of being as such.

Third, with these notions, Leibniz tells us what he understands by the transcendental characteristic of things, which for
him is concentrated in two areas. First, the unity of being, its
transcendental unity, is the *monad*, and therefore, monadism is
the theory of the transcendental unity of being. Moreover, the entire universe as such has an intrinsic unity, which is the maximum compatibility of the possibles, the greatest entitiness, and
with it, the maximum goodness. The metaphysical optimism of
Leibniz is the theory of the transcendental unity of the world. In
this way, we find that man, by being an image of God, does have

in himself internal movement towards comprehension of being. Thinking about himself, he thinks about being because in himself he is discovering the image—finite, but authentic—of what the divinity itself is, of what divine reason itself is.

---

1 Zubiri's marginal note: "At some point, refer to contingency, that whose contradiction is possible".

2 [Zubiri neologism from "principle"—trans.].

3 Zubiri's marginal note: "VX,D nihil sunt quam possibilium optima", etc. Cf. other important passages in H., Leibniz, p. 242.

4 [Domenico Palmieri, S.J. (1829-1909), born in Piacenza, Italy, philosopher and theologian.—trans.].

5 [Johann Baptist Franzelin, S.J. (1816-1886), born in Aldein, Austria, Cardinal and theologian. Apparently, Zubiri does not count him as a Jesuit since he was raised to be a bishop and Cardinal.—trans.].

6 [Teilhard de Chardin, S.J. (1881-1955), born in Orcines, France, controversial scientist and philosopher.—trans.].

CHAPTER 5
WESTERN PHILOSOPHY (4)
KANT

§1

INTRODUCTION. THE FRAMEWORK OF NOTHINGNESS: OBJECTUALITY

Kant is not satisfied with Leibniz' conceptualization of metaphysics. However, Kant begins by accepting the same philosophical framework as Leibniz and Wolff. That framework is creation *ex nihilo*, i.e., the framework of nothingness. For Kant, God appears as creator—an idea Kant never abandoned throughout his entire philosophy—a creator-God that surely has an intellect; *intuitus originarius*, he calls it. Here "original" is not original just with respect to human intellect, which is something derivative (we shall soon see in what sense it is so). "Original" means that it is *originator*. Divine intellection, required for a creative *fiat*—Kant never disputes this—is an *intuitus originans*. Things, insofar as they are produced by an act of divine will, but along the lines of that {184} originating intellection, are *Dinge an sich*: things-in-themselves, things as they are in themselves.

Kant expressly tells us this in the *Critique of Pure Reason*.[1] Things-in-themselves are the terminus of the *intuitus originarius*. There is another very meaningful paragraph of Kant written a few years before his death where he tells us, "God is creator of the world as a thing-in-itself; but as it appears to us, it is a creation of our own sensibility."[2] Putting aside the second part of the affirmation, let us pay attention to the first. Things-in-themselves are just things *qua* terminus, originated by an *intuitus originans*, *originarius*. Up to this point that is exactly what Leibniz would say. But within this framework humans, as possessing finite reason, carry out a certain kind of knowing. They acquire a particular knowledge about being, about entity. This knowledge is what constitutes metaphysics. Indeed, Kant has no doubt in saying that this is what metaphysics is: "Philosophical knowledge by pure reason (*aus reiner Vernunft*) in its systematic connection, is called 'metaphysics'."³ This is exactly what Wolff and Leibniz said when affirming that metaphysics is the science of first principles of human reason. Although he puts it in a different way, Kant faithfully reproduces Leibniz' idea.

That Metaphysics, according to Kant, has four parts.⁴

    I. Ontology
    II. Rational Psychology
    III. Rational Cosmology {185}
    IV. Rational Theology

This is just the division proper to the philosophical encyclopedia of Leibniz and Wolff. But here is where the difficulty begins for Kant.

Kant must tell us how these two ideas are related: (1) the *intuitus originarius* produced things having some characteristics, i.e., what things are in themselves; and (2) what human reason can know about things through concepts. That is the problem: the relationship of things-in-themselves and knowledge about them that can be acquired through a system of concepts. In other words, what is the relationship between metaphysics and things themselves?

Kant exposes that great difficulty first in a manner that we might call "extrinsic," which is the most telling from the historical point of view, by showing what has happened to metaphysics, to that presumed strict science of reason, over the long course of its history.

Thus, in the first paragraph of the "Introduction" to the first edition of the *Critique of Pure Reason* Kant tells us:

> Human reason has this peculiar fate that in one species of its knowledge it is burdened by questions (*dass sie durch Fragen belästig wird*) which, as prescribed by the very nature of reason itself, it is not able to ignore, but which, as transcending (*übersteigen*) all its powers, it is also not able to answer. The perplexity into which it thus falls is not due to any fault of its own. It begins with principles which it has no option save to employ in the course of experience, and which this experience at the same time abundantly justifies it in using.⁵

Here we find again the term "perplexity" (*Verlegenheit*) with which Aristotle described metaphysics. It is the Kantian version of the Aristotelian *aporia*, which will reappear once more in Hegel, as we shall see. Reason finds itself in this *aporia* through no fault of its own (*ohne ihre Schuld*).

Next Kant makes an exposition as to why {186} reason has fallen into that predicament, and has had to reach for principles that transcend experience and therefore are not firm. This has been the origin of all kinds of discussions and arguments. Kant says, "The battlefield of these endless controversies is called 'metaphysics' (*der Kampfplatz dieserendlosen Streitigkeiten heisst nun Metaphysik*)."[6] As Kant tells us in the Introduction to the second edition of the *Critique of Pure Reason*, he means that Metaphysics, with all its presumed knowledge of things by pure reason, does nothing more than spin its wheels without getting anywhere;it is a *blosses Herumtappen*[7] that, as Kant says, has not yet entered, has not undertaken the secure way of science (*den sicheren Gang einer Wissenschaft*). As an historical affirmation this is undeniable. What is important now is to see what Kant thinks has produced this situation, i.e., what he believes to be the root of the problem. That is where the difficulty resides.

If we think about what Descartes and Leibniz said the matter seems obvious enough. In one form or another, for Leibniz as for Descartes, human reason actually knows things. But which ones? It knows those that exist by themselves, no doubt about that. To be sure, this is not free from difficulties; but Descartes resolves them by saying that divine veracity exists, which has arranged things to be in accord with human intellection. It is not the case that God has placed *human intellection* in accordance with things, but the other way around: He has placed *things* in accordance with human intellection. Thus the world has a rational structure. This does not mean that reason has a {187} cosmic structure, only that the world has a rational structure. Of course, God's creational paradigm—if you will—is just the order of reason, the transcendental order. In the case of Leibniz, the matter is clearer still. We know things-in-themselves simply by the very type of our reason, which in contrast to what Descartes claimed, is a reason similar to the divine reason, and so is an image of that reason. Therefore, by its very structure it is made for a limited knowledge of that which, in an unlimited and infinite way, the divine reason knows, namely things as they are in themselves.

But here is where the difficulty begins for Kant, because for Kant human reason is essentially different from divine reason; nonetheless, it is intrinsically necessary. In the first place, divine reason makes things. Human reason does not make them; it has them right in front of itself, and has to know them, indeed, it wishes to know them. Human reason has an intrinsic *finitude*, something with which Leibniz and Descartes would agree, and a point to which we shall return forthwith.

In the second place, reason has to *receive* the things that are given to it in order to know them. Here an aspect appears, not only of finitude, but if you will, of fact, of donation.

In the third place, reason must do more: it must make of the given an *object* of knowledge, which means an object of thought.

These three moments, finitude, receptivity, and objectuality (with thinkability[8]) are what together constitute the essential differentiator of human reason from divine reason. Of course, each one of these moments is directed to the other. Thus, finitude—we shall see this immediately—is expressed in terms of receptivity, and receptivity in {188} terms of being a candidate for objectuality. Therefore we might say that human reason is a reason constituted by objectuality.

Thus, the framework of nothingness, which for St. Thomas had thrust the intrinsic finitude of being to the forefront, for Descartes the uncertainty of intelligence, and for Leibniz possibility before reality, plays a different role for Kant. For him, it places objectuality ahead of the thing itself. Kant will anchor his entire reflection about metaphysics and the transcendental order.

To analyze Kant's thought we shall divide it into two parts. First we will examine the nature of the problem as Kant sees it. Second we will consider his development of the problem

With this, let me note something to which I shall return soon, namely that all efforts to present Kantian philosophy as a philosophy of science are completely mistaken. Of course, science has its place in Kantian philosophy, but Kantian philosophy is not a theory of science; it is rather a transcendental philosophy, as he clearly indicates.

§2

KANT'S PROBLEM

What is Kant's problem? This must be studied concretely, not only with respect to the characteristics of things, but also with respect to the characteristics of human reason that knows them.

We begin, first, with the characteristics of things. These are the three moments we have just covered. By reason of its turning to objects, human reason is intrinsically finite; it moves among respectivities, and makes of what is received an object of its own. It is necessary to make these three terms sufficiently precise, something that is not as simple as it might seem at first glance.

What does Kant understand by finitude (*Endlichkeit*)? He tells us that human reason does not produce things, but knows them. This is true, but Kant's intention of Kant goes much deeper. He is trying to tell us in what the very finitude of human reason consists, a finitude accepted by Descartes, Leibniz, and St. Thomas. Does this finitude simply consist in not having the same reach as the divine? In other words, is it because it knows things less and knows them poorly? This is clear, and is what the earlier philosophers said; but Kant's position is completely different. It is not only the case that human reason knows less and that its knowledge poorer than divine reason, but that what it knows is known in a different way. And for Kant knowing it in a different way means that human reason knows it *finitely*. It is, then, an internal and intrinsic way of finitude. The *way* of knowing, not {190} the *what* is known, constitutes the radical finitude of human reason for Kant.

In what does this radical finitude consist as a way of knowing? Here the second note appears. Human reason knows in a finite manner because it needs for the objects to be given, that is it needs receptivity. On this point there would not be any real disagreement among Kant, Descartes, and Leibniz. Clearly, in one form or another, for Descartes and Leibniz things are given, because human reason does not pull them out of its head.

But the difference is greater in Kant. Because for Kant, even though the objects are given in their perfect individual concretion within what he rightly calls (together with almost all earlier philosophy) *intuitus*, intuition, that intuition is not originating, is not original, as we have already seen. But we must issue a warning that previously "original" was not opposed to "derivative." Here, on the other hand, original *is* opposed to the derivative. It is not the case that human intuition is derived from the divine intuition, but that it is *derived from things*, while divine intuition *produces things*. In contrast to the *hervorbringen*, the producing, there is the *empfangen*, the giving, which involves receptivity; the given exactly and formally means that which is received. Of course, not everything that is given must necessarily be received. Putting it this way in the abstract, to have confused the *given* with the *received* is one of the great arguments with which the Thomists have criticized Molina,[9] thinking that the *scientia media* substitutes knowledge of things for knowledge of God. If by "substituting" we understand that there have to be things for God to know them, there is no doubt about this; but that does not mean that the divine intellect is receptive; it means that it is *a posteriori*, which is something different. Be that as it may, here the moment of receptivity is absolutely necessary. Intuition *qua* receptive is just {191} what constitutes sensible affection. So man has an intuition (a sign of his intrinsic finitude) in which objects are not only given to him, but are given through an affective intuition, i.e., in an impression, internal or external; it does not matter because it is a sensible intuition. With this Kant completely roots out something that was dear to the philosophy of Leibniz, namely, intellectual intuition. Leibniz considered that there was an intelligible intuition, the intuition of being, and by the spirit intuiting itself, it was more or less intuiting being. For Kant, on the other hand, there is no other intuition but sensible intuition.

What happens is that this sensible intuition is not knowledge in any order. To intuit an object is not to know it, in this world or in the other. To see the Holy Trinity face to face in heaven is not to understand it, a thing that no one can do, not even the finite, human intelligence of Christ; that can only be done by God, who is the Word. It is not enough to have intuition in order to have knowledge. They are two different things.

For this reason, man has to fall back upon what is given under the form of sensible affection; man not only has to receive it passively, but also has to make it an object of thought.

What is intuited as object is precisely the third characteristic of the difference between the human reason and the divine, and the second characteristic of the finitude of human intelligence. Reason is finite because it knows in a *different* way, because after something is received in a sensible intuition, what has been received must be made into an object of thought. Though it might appear that Kant sees no great problem with Descartes' and Leibniz' thought, the difference is in fact radical and essential. {192}

To return to our starting point, Kant distinguishes in a radical way *things such as they have been produced by the originative intellect*, and *things man proposes to know because they are given by sensibility through sensible intuition.* This means that for Kant, to be a *thing* and to be an *object* are two completely different dimensions. There are many things that are not an object of human intellection (not only in fact, but they can never be). But, in second place, and more importantly, for those that are objects, the conditions that make them possible as *things* are not the same as the conditions that make them possible as *objects.* The conditions that made them possible as things were carried out, since the thing is there; however, *I* have to make an object of that thing, and to be an object is not given. Here is where we must pay extra attention in order to try to unravel the Kantian problem.

Since the time of Aristotle reality, i.e., the primary being of reality, has been termed a ὑποκείμενον, a *sub-jectum*, a substance, something that underlies properties, which as such cannot have a separated existence. If they had a separated existence they would not be properties, but independent substances. Naturally, here the *sub-jectum* is a *sub* with respect to the properties it has. And this understanding of reality remained more or less the same throughout medieval philosophy. So for a medieval philosopher to say that something is *sub-jectivum* means that it has the maximum degree of reality. Not "subjective" in our modern sense, it is a real and effective *subject*, a ὑποκείμενον, in the Aristotelian sense of the term. But this reality, which is a *sub-ject*, suffered an enormous shift during the history of philosophy from Descartes to Kant.

Indeed, the first thing we ask is how {193} human reason can know it. With this, the difference between the *sub-jectum* and its properties completely recedes to a secondary plane. What remains on the first plane is that this, towards which the human mind is directed, is certainly a *jectum*, but a *jectum* that is not a "sub," but an "ob," right in front of me, an *objectum*. In this situation, the *objectum* is not contrasted to some properties which it underlies; that makes no sense. The only thing that would merit the name of "subject" and would underlie not some properties, but the very character of the *objectum*, is the human *subjectum*. With this the term *subjectum*, for all entities in the universe, has ceased to mean the physical reality of the subject in order to mean purely and simply that the only authentic and real subject in this philosophy is the human *subjectum*. It is just to this human *subjectum* that an *objectum* is present. The primary characteristic of things, for Kant, is to be *objecta*, not *subjecta*. In German the matter is clear, *objectum* is *Gegenstand*, what is in front of me. Not having distinguished those two dimensions of the problem, the *objectuality* of things and the *subjectivity* in the Aristotelian and classical sense of the term, is what for Kant is the dogmatism of earlier metaphysics. It is not dogmatism in the sense of unconditional criticisms or poorly made criticisms; it means, purely and simply, to have just taken the "object" of thought as a *subjectum reale*. This is what dogmatism is for Kant: failure to distinguish between the *objectum* and the thing itself.

We can now understand why objectuality has taken first place within the framework of nothingness. It is because in fact humans, abandoned to their intrinsic finitude in that framework, encounter just *objecta*. The first thing they must investigate is what these objects are {194} with which the human mind has to deal. Here we have, then, the Kantian problem with respect to things.

Let us now consider the Kantian problem with respect to the character of reason itself. Reason has to make "objects" out of things in order to investigate what they are, since intuition in itself is not knowledge. So, what is that making and what is that thinking? Kant's answer is final and clear: to think in this case is to judge (*Urteilen*). Human reason, inasmuch as it carries out this function of judging, is what Kant calls "understanding."[10] What is judging? At Leibniz' hands "to judge" was to refer one concept to another by means of an exhaustive analysis of the concepts of subject and predicate, in order to see how the requirements of one are included in the requirements of the other. A judgment in this form would be a process, an essentially analytical function of reason. The judgment would consist in decomposing things down to their ultimate elements and from them, to see how, through sufficient reason, the complexity of things emerges.

But this is not what Kant understands by judging. Kant understands that judging—let us not forget that he cannot put aside sensible intuition—is a function of concepts. This means to refer a concept to something already given, to something that exists *prior* to the concept, and in this sense something present beyond the concept. Consequently, the function of judging does not consist in analyzing concepts, but in going from a concept to something that is not in the concept itself, to something that has a face that opens onto what things are. In Kantian terms, the formal {195} and radical structure of reason is not analytical, but synthetic; synthesis consists in precisely going from concept to thing.

In contrast to Leibniz, reason for Kant is essentially synthetic.[11] It is so because of what we have just said: in its intrinsic finitude it has to make itself an "object," but from something given to it. Consequently, reason necessarily has to return to the given—to intuition—in order to know what the object is.

Reason is synthetic. But, what is the nature of this synthesis? It is not just a synthesis that we might call "psychological," i.e., that I associate my representations, this with that; nor is it the case of a subjective synthesis of representations, which would not be of any interest. Nor is it a mere logical synthesis; i.e., it is not the case that, when objectively considered, the content of a concept (a predicate) is in the concept of the subject. Rather, the entire order of concepts is referred to something given to it. In other words, this is an objective synthesis, and what the concepts enunciate is in fact in the given. It is not the case of a psychological synthesis, or a logical synthesis, but of a synthesis that contains (or at least tries to contain) truth, which is to say that concepts are in the things that are given.

This truth is the *conformity of thought with things*, and Kant never doubted it. What happens is that Kant's philosophy is often presented from perspectives completely chimerical and fanciful.

Besides, this truth is a synthetic truth. Therefore, {196} it unifies concepts and reality. What kind of unity is it? That is the question. Leibniz thought it was a unity of the predicate as concept and the subject as concept. For Kant this is not so; it is the unity between an order of concepts and something that has been given–a completely different kind of synthesis. Here the question of truth leads to unity, just as in Leibniz; but the way to unity in Kant is completely different from that in Leibniz. Indeed, if the unity in question is the one we have just indicated, viz. unity of the concept with what is given, then we have to return to things to find truth. If it were only this, all our truths, and therefore, all synthesis and all the unities would be empirical, would be factual truths. Human beings would compile a catalog of truths and in the measure that they are true they would be properly realized in things; they would be unities and truths of fact. But humans, the human mind—Kant tells us—naturally incorporates some truths that are necessary and universal. In other words, not only are there in fact truths in the things effectively given to us, but that for whatever reason—we would have to investigate this—these truths are valid truths for all kinds of possible objects and possible circumstances. This universal and necessarily absolute validity is what Kant calls *a priori*. Therefore, it means that together with empirical truths that are unitary syntheses, here we encounter a synthesis, strictly speaking, that is *a priori*. This is because of the intrinsic necessity with which certain truths present to us, from the point of view of concepts, something that cannot but be fulfilled in any possible object. The unity of concepts and of things is then an *a priori* synthetic unity. {197}

Of course, here Kant appeals to what we said above, to the *factum* of science. Clearly, Kant is not concerned now with Newtonian mechanics as such, although he may find inspiration there. He is interested in science not so much for what it contains in our sense of the term, but for what it has of truth. Kant is interested in a theory of truth, of course as exemplified by science. His is not a theory of scientific knowledge in the style of the positive sciences, but something different; it is a theory of truth as such. Kant tells us, thematically and expressly, that to deny that human understanding is capable of incorporating this type of truths would amount to radical skepticism. That is the critique he directed at all of Hume's philosophy.

Nevertheless, that these truths may enunciate something that refers to every possible object as such is what Kant would say is a *transcending (Übersteigen)*. These are therefore *transcendental judgments*. By "synthetic *a priori* judgments" he only means, purely and simply, the order of transcendental truth as such. That is what interests Kant: that the truth of every possible object is transcendental. Because of this, to ask how synthetic *a priori* judgments are possible (in the rough Kantian terminology, very much of his era) is simply to ask how the transcendental order is possible.

As a result, when Kant talks about science (*Wissenschaft*), he is not referring to the science elaborated beginning in the seventeenth century; rather, he understands by *science* a "knowledge" (*Wissen*) that is in a certain way absolute and radical. In a similar way, years later, when Fichte writes his *Wissenschaftslehre*, this does not mean "theory of science," something like a methodology of science. On the contrary, the meaning of "science" points to a science of transcendental truth, an absolute science, {198} a transcendental knowledge. This is what the issue is all about. That is the pure and simple formulation of the Kantian problem.

So that problem, following the thread of these historical considerations and the logical and critical engagement with Leibniz and Wolff, comes down to this simple formula: how is the transcendental order possible? This refers to a transcendental order directed towards some objects that as such are not identified with things-in-themselves, but an order that is still necessary, i.e., transcendental. We now must answer the question of how is this possible. That forms the second part of our considerations.

§3

KANT'S DEVELOPMENT OF THE PROBLEM

How does Kant answer this question about the possibility of the transcendental order? Without forgetting what we said above concerning objects, let us examine Kant's three step reply:

1. The principle of the transcendental itself.
2. The internal constitution of the transcendental.
3. The characteristic of this knowledge of the transcendental called "Metaphysics."

I. *The principle of the transcendental*

As we have seen, the very principle of the transcendental has been centered on the unity in which truth consists. This truth is a unity that humans do not encounter as something finished, something complete. Indeed humans must make things an object of their own thought in order to possess the truth. Hence the problem of objective unity is strictly and formally the problem of a "doing" or "making."

Kant tells us that unity, the synthesis, is a doing (*Tun*), an action (*Handlung*). For him, the synthesis is not something that can be seen and received, because in such case it would not have a transcendental character. Rather, it is something that is *made*. Hence, it is something that is to be done, and as anything that is to be done it is determined {200} by the action that does it. The unity, the unitary synthesis, as Kant says, is a blind faculty (*ein blindes Vermögen*). What is important for us here is not whether it is blind, but what it is that interests Kant, i.e., that such a synthesis is not something *seen*, but something *done*. Kant must tell us *what* is done and *how* it is done.

So what is it that the understanding does when it makes an object out of something? To begin with, the understanding does not make what we might call the content of the object. This is a complete fantasy, not only in the order of pure reason, but also in the order of sensibility, a fantasy that never entered Kant's mind. It is one of the many naiveties that have been dumped onto his philosophy. For Kant, synthesis does not "make" the content of the object; what it does is to make of that content something mine, that is to say, *it makes the objectuality; it does not make the content of the object.* Kant must now provide us with greater details as to how the making of this objectuality is accomplished. Let us remember that the thinking Kant is going to work with is the thinking of the understanding, the thinking that judges. To make an object out of something is to propose it as terminus of a judgment, a judgment that is going to try to tell us truly what it is that constitutes its proper object. Consequently, for something to be the terminus of a judgment—Kant is the least possible subjectivist we can think of—means that it is something intelligible. Were it not intelligible it would not be a thought, but an imagination, a fantasy. Because we are dealing with the terminus of a judgment, which says that *A* is *B*, it is obviously understood that the synthesis opens the ambit of intelligibility that belongs to *A*. And precisely because to think is to become aware of something, {201} we are dealing with a function of knowing under the concrete form of a judgment.

Nevertheless, what does it mean to make something intelligible, to know it? It can mean two things. It can mean that it is intelligible for me, and this can be accomplished in myriad different ways. But for Kant it is not enough that it be intelligible for me; he needs for the object to be intelligible *qua* object. Of course, Kant never doubts that the conditions that make intelligibility possible are the same that make intelligibility possible *for me.*

Why and in what does this sameness consist? It consists simply in the fact that I am the one who makes the thing an object for my intelligence, because I am the one who in a certain way defines the ambit and the area of intelligibility with my function of judging. That is why the object is intelligible. So could there be objects that are not intelligible? No, they would not be objects, perhaps they might be "things," but the least that one could say of them is that they would never be objects. An unintelligible object is a kind of transcendental impossibility for Kant. What the "I think" makes in the synthesis is the intelligibility of the object. So not only can I not understand the object except in a certain way (by synthesis), in any other way it would not be intelligible at all. The object is an object *because it is intelligible,* and herein consists the proper job of reason: it makes what is given to be intelligible. Precisely on account of this that intelligible thing is an object of thought.

But then, making something intrinsically intelligible is, from St. Thomas' old formula, convertible with the thing that is intelligible. St. Thomas was dealing with being. Kant would say he is not dealing with things-in-themselves, but purely and simply with the case of the object. Inasmuch as *intelligibility* is convertible with *objectuality* it is the first and radical transcendental characteristic. The object is object because it is intelligible, {202} and intelligibility consists in its own transcendentalness, so to speak. The proper task of the human mind therefore consists in making the transcendental. Granted that this intelligibility is what since St. Thomas has been called "truth," Kant does not hesitate to say that this is a *verum transcendentale*; it is a truth that affects things. Kant tells us, "The relationship of our knowledge to the empirically given objects is a transcendental truth (*transcendentale Wahrheit*). And that relationship makes transcendental truth possible, which precedes any metaphysics."[12] There can only be as much logical truth and scientific truth as there is transcendental truth, that is to say, insofar as the object is intelligible to human intelligence. The intelligibility of an object is what human intelligence makes, simply by approaching it in the form of a judgment.

Kant tells us that we are the ones that make the unity of our judgments, a unity not of the *content* of the object—this is held by the thing itself—but that unity in which the *objectuality* consists. We make it, because what we really make is the intelligibility of the given. This intelligibility is the intrinsically *verum* and *transcendentale* character of what is given; and because of this the given acquires the characteristic of object. Thus, to say that human intelligence makes the objectuality is to say that it makes the intelligibility. Object is everything intelligible; anything that is unintelligible would not be an object. The transcendental order, for Kant, is the order of objectual intelligibility. Therefore, this transcendental order does not rest upon itself, as for example, in the case of Aristotle; but neither does it rest upon God, as Descartes and Leibniz suggested, though in different ways. Descartes {203} thought that divine veracity is what confers upon reality a rational structure in conformity with the transcendentalness of my own understanding, as a free creature of God. Leibniz thought that it was accomplished by making human intelligence an image of the divine. For Kant, the human and the divine are two essentially different types of reason. The transcendental order does not rest upon itself and does not rest upon God, it rests upon me. It is my own subjectivity, as principle of the transcendental order, that should be called the "transcendental subjectivity." Transcendental subjectivity is purely and simply subjectivity in the sense of a *subjectum* as opposed to an *objectum*, to a *Gegenstand*; it is subjectivity as a principle of the transcendental order. Here "principle" does not mean what Suárez and Leibniz understood, i.e., that it is non-contradictory; this, Kant would say, is mere thinking (*blosses Denken*); we can think of many things that are non-contradictory, but that does not mean they are objects. For Kant, "principle" means principle of the possibility of the object *qua* object (*Grund der Möglichkeit des Gegenstandes*), *qua* given object; and properly understood, insofar as the given has sufficient intelligibility to be thought by the understanding, which judges about the given. It is a principle of the given as intelligible object. The synthetic action of the understanding is the principle of the intelligibility of the given.

We can now understand the sense of the paragraph mentioned at the beginning, which anticipated what we have just indicated, "God is creator of the world as thing-in-itself; but as it appears to us, it is a creation of our own sensibility".[13]

This gigantic progression of Kantian thought is not {204} quite something accomplished, but rather a program. Now Kant must tell us concretely what is involved in making (or creating) the intelligibility of the objectual order. In other words, what is the internal constitution of the transcendental order? Secondly, what is our possible knowledge of this transcendental order? Indeed, what is metaphysics? This is what we must now analyze.

We divided the progression mentioned above into three steps. In the first place, what is the *principle* or *ground* of the transcendental order, i.e., of those universal and necessary truths that constitute the *verum transcendentale* of objects? In the second place, what is the *internal constitution* of that transcendental order? In the third place, what is the presumed *unity* of this transcendental order, i.e., the unity of metaphysics?

Before proceeding, let us briefly summarize the road we have thus far traversed. We inquired as to how this transcendental order is made. Kant says that this is an action of the *I*. The action of the *I* is just what is called "to think"; *Ich denke*, I have to think. Kant tells us that to think is to unite some representations with others. Let us put ignore the fact that definition may not be correct *in re*; Kant tells us *ad nauseam* that to think is to unite representations. Where are these representations united? Kant is not referring to the fact that they can be united in my conscious mind, since that would be a mere psychological unity. Nor is he referring to the fact that they can be united from the logical point of view, for example as Leibniz suggests—a kind of inclusion of the notes that constitute the requisites of the predicate with the notes that constitute the requisites of the subject. Instead Kant says that it is an objective union by virtue of which the multiple, the multiplicity of things, cannot be thought of unless a subject with an objective intention unifies it. Therefore Kant says that the {205} "I think" is something that must be able to accompany all my representations. Hence, the "I think" as possibility in principle accompanies all my representations.

Here, in a transcendental dimension, the notion appears that was introduced in Leibniz' metaphysics, namely, *apperception*. The understanding, when judging, not only perceives or apprehends that *A* is *B*, but also co-apprehends itself in the form of thinking subject, of a thinking *I*. This apperception is transcendental by virtue of what we have just discussed:; because it is not a subjective unity, but a rigorously objective one. When uniting some perceptions with others, what I want is just to assert that the *A* is truly *B*; not simply that I think it is so or that it appears to be so, but that it is so really and truly. The apperception is, in this sense, transcendental.

Hence, when we say that to think is to judge, Kant tells us that what underlies the function of judging is the radical function of thinking. By virtue of this thinking the given is placed within a perspective of the structures proper to thinking, i.e., thinking in the way referred to by "I think." Then it is clear that to submit everthing to the unity of apperception means that everything is subjected *a priori* to the objective structure of judging. Nothing is intelligible as object unless it is made intelligible by me; nothing is made intelligible by me if it is not in conformity with the structure of my own function of judging. This tells us that the supreme principle of the understanding is the "I think," which is thus the principle of any possible intelligibility of the object. Therefore the "I think" is the basic principle of the transcendental order. The transcendental order, formally, consists in objective intelligibility; but principially[14] it consists in the "I think" that makes it possible. {206}

The object has to present itself this way to the understanding in order to be intelligible, and therefore, to be object. Since we are here moving in the order of pure understanding, Kant might find himself facing the situation of an object that is not intelligible. However, according to what he says, such a situation cannot occur—it would be a transcendental impossibility. With respect to things-in-themselves, the great majority will not be intelligible for me; but we are not dealing with that issue. If something is an object, it is such precisely under the above conditions, because to be object means to have these conditions of intelligibility. Hence, if it were not intelligible it could never appear as an object.

This is just what characterizes Kant's philosophy on this point. The transcendental impossibility of an unintelligible object depends essentially on the fact that intelligibility is made by my own function of judging. This intelligibility is what constitutes the objectual characteristic of the object, of the given.

All of this is quite abstract and in need of clarifications, which is logical since Kant had to write his great work *The Critique of*

Pure Reason in order to clarify it. We shall appeal to that book in order to proceed to the second step, one that at the same time serves as clarification of what we have covered in the step just concluded.

II. *Constitution of the transcendental order*

The transcendental order is first and foremost the order of the *verum transcendentale*, of the transcendental truth, properly understanding that transcendental truth is in its very transcendentalness something made by the "I think" itself in its judging dimension. {207}

With this Kant gives the impression of having created a new science, one that up to now was unsuspected. Kant himself says this to Christian Garve (1742-1798). According to Kant, he has made a science that "is not metaphysics at all, but is a completely new science, and one that up to now has never been attempted (*eine ganz neue und bisher unrersnchte Wissenschaft*), that is, the critique of a reason that judges *a priori.*"[15] Though he says that this new science is not metaphysics, somewhat earlier he had written that this science of his "contains the metaphysics of metaphysics" (*enthalt die Metaphysik von der Metaphysik*).[16] It is a metaphysics—if you will—raised to the second power, a meta-metaphysics.

This metaphysics is a philosophy of the transcendental order. In another letter also written to Markus Herz (1747-1803), Kant says, "I shall be very happy when I finish my transcendental philosophy, which strictly speaking is a Critique of Pure Reason."[17] He adds that later he will take up metaphysics as such.

Summarizing, Kant tells us his work is indeed a transcendental philosophy. This is what the *Critique of Pure Reason* is. He also tells us that this transcendental philosophy, in the sense in which Kant takes it, is a completely new science because he grounds it *a priori* on the very structure of human understanding. Therefore, it is necessary to inquire about the internal structure of this transcendental truth. This structure comprises two moments. The first is the moment of objectuality. {208}

1. Moment of objectuality, the categorial.

As we have said, things, objects, are that *about* which human understanding is going to judge. But then, judgment as a determinant of the intrinsic intelligibility of the transcendental order has its own proper structure. This structure is the one that allows us to answer the question that probably has been stirring in the reader's head just as it has been doing in mine for many years, viz., what is it to make a thing intelligible? Kant is now going to attempt an answer to that question through a relatively simple consideration.

Let us imagine that I take an object, prescinding from the question of whether it is real or not, and I say that it has a particular color, for example, white. When I say that it is white, I have made a true statement, but at the deepest level I am presuming something else. We should remember that this same thing takes place in Aristotle's philosophy. Thus, when I say about A that it is white, not only do I say that it is white—a superficial statement, perhaps—but I also understand at the deepest level the real and factual way in which the thing is white, i.e., its being-quality. In every affirmation, besides what is said, there is also this "accusation," this imputation or charge. We make an accusation in the affirmation about the charactistics of the mode of being of the predicate, that is, the quality enunciated in the predicate accuses the mode of being in the subject. Since "accusing" is κατεγορείν in Greek, Aristotle introduced the idea of the *categories*.

Kant performs the same operation, but in a different dimension. It is true that when I say that this is white I accuse..., but what? The way of being? Not at all: what is accused is the *way of being true*, the *way of being intelligible*. Indeed, the categories are just that: the ways in which the intelligibility of the object for the human mind is accused. For example, the idea of causality is not a property that belongs to *things*; it is a property of *intelligibility*, {209} to which it belongs *primo et per se*. If it were not through the causal way, nothing would be intelligible to me; but *causality does not enunciate something real and objective about things, it simply enunciates their intelligibility*.

Although we are not going to run down the list of categories, we are only going to recall that Kant enumerates twelve (Aristotle listed ten) and takes them from the structure of judgment. Judgment, Kant tells us, has quality, quantity, relation and modality. Each one of these four is subdivided into three, etc. In this way Kant obtains the list of categories, which are the twelve aspects that have to be given in judgment for an object to be intelligible. To make a thing intelligible consists in representing it from the point of view of the twelve dimensions that judgment has. This is really what Kant intended. And then, of this transcendental philosophy that Kant has told us is the metaphysics of metaphysics, he will tell us that its axioms "are simple principles of the exposition of phenomena (*sind blosse Prinzipien der Exposition der Erscheinungen*)." And what is important to us, he tell us that, "the pompous name of an ontology, which proposes to offer synthetic *a priori* knowledge with respect to things themselves, has to recede before something more modest, before a pure, mere analytic of human understanding (*muss dem bescheidennen, einer blossen Analytic des reinen Vertandes, Platz machen*)".[18]

Ontology is, in fact, the science of these categories, and these categories are nothing but the dimensions of the very intelligibility of the object. The concepts that constitute the principle of the intelligibility of things do not *proceed from things*, as claimed not just in empiricism but also in all earlier philosophies, for example, in Descartes and especially in {210} medieval philosophy. They do not proceed from things; they proceed from my "I think." Also, they do not *produce* things, they only *make them intelligible*. We can now see that to make things intelligible means to make them transcendentally true; that is, to make them representable as substances, as qualities, etc. Hence, since intelligibility is convertible with object, to make something intelligible is just to make it an object. Thanks to these twelve categories, that which the synthetic action of judging makes is the object as such.

But Kant notes that there is a serious problem lurking that he must address. One might put it this way: I can now reason about a particular object by virtue of the twelve categories, and my reasoning will take me to a series of conclusions or consequences that comprise whatever else can be known about that object. But Kant says that this is completely illusory because while it is quite true that the categories and the capacity that the human mind (the "I think") has of making things intelligible determine the characteristics of intelligibility of these things, that is not the whole story. If we use terminology that Kant himself did not use to express his thought more precisely, what the categories determine is the character (Kant says the "form") of every object, i.e., its *objectuality*. But, an object's objectuality is not one more object. Regardless of how many ways we turn the categories around or how many times we turn around the pure concepts of understanding, the only thing we will obtain are precisions. These precisions may be very rich, but in the end they will only mean that if there is an object, it must have such and such conditions. So the objectuality of an object is not one more object, it is the character that {211} every object must have *if* it is actually an object; but the objectuality is itself not a real and positive object.

For this reason Kant says that the categories have a transcendental meaning; that is, the categories do not consist in my subjective representations, but consist in assembling and structuring something that belongs to the world of the object, viz. its objectuality. They do not have any *transcendental use* at all, in other words, they do not permit any determination, by pure reason, of the character of a particular object. The only thing they can determine is the character that an object must have in order to be an object, but never the content or the reality of that object.

The categories have a transcendental *sense*, but they completely lack transcendental *use*. In order to have transcendental use something else is needed. It is necessary for the understanding, which has that structure and by virtue of that structure makes an object intelligible, to be given something that indeed constitutes that object.

This is precisely what corresponds to the second moment of the transcendental order, *the given*.

2. Moment of given

The given and what we have just indicated about the categories together constitute something, and that something is just a real and factual object. The synthesis of the categorial and the given is precisely what Kant called the *transcendental deduction*. With this, beforehand, we understand that the Kantian transcendental deduction is not an expression of the *being* of things, or even an expression of the *intelligibility* of the object, but a positive *constitution* {212} of the intelligibility of the object. It is the order made by man and by human intelligence. Therefore, the transcendental order does not *express* the object, but *constitutes* it. And constitutes it because intelligence constitutes intelligibility and intelligibility converts precisely with objectuality:

1) In the end, the transcendental order is, for Kant, starting from intelligence, the order of the objectual intelligibility of something given.

2) It is an order imposed by the understanding upon the given.

3) It is a necessary *a priori* order. In this Kant will be inflexible.

4) It is an order grounded on a principle, the "I think".

But in order to have the transcendental order nailed down, we must be given an explanation about the given, and also about the synthesis of the categorial and the given. Otherwise, we would not have a full description of the transcendental order for Kant.

To begin, the synthesis depends squarely on the character of the given. And the given may be of two types. Here is where the great task and the great Kantian speculation begin. I proceed here in a different order, the given after the categorial. Though I seem to be reversing Kant's table of contents, in fact I am not. First, the *Critique of Pure Reason* has shown that the categories, the pure concepts of the understanding, do not have an empirical origin, but have their font and their *a priori* source in the pure understanding. Second, it has shown that these categories can be applied to objects independently of any intuition of these objects.

And third, they can only {213} lead to a theoretical knowledge when these objects are empirically given. And it is at this moment when practical reason offers to us a given object, one that is in the moral order, which leads to a knowledge, to an intellection, and to a thought of the supersensible as such.[19] Thus Kant explains the progression of his thinking: first, the constitution of the transcendental order, which the categories are; and second, the two types of the given, according to the two types of given that will also be the result of the transcendental order. With this, a third question will arise: in what does its transcendental unity consist?

a) The empirical fact. Synthesis of the categorial and the phenomenal.

In the first place, Kant will have to tell us what the transcendental order is, dealing precisely with the given in an empirical intuition. We are not going to summarize the *Critique of Pure Reason* here, but only indicate the central idea.

What is given in sensible intuition is a serious {214} problem for Kant. Things have to be given, but for humans, in the order we are here considering, what is given is given by way of a sensible intuition, of an empirical intuition. This means that for Kant we humans cannot have knowledge of things unless things become visible to us. But to become visible to us in Greek is φαίνεσθαι, that is, things have to be "phenomena."

"Phenomena" for Kant means neither a mere subjective appearance nor an extraordinary thing, as when it is said that someone is a phenomenal person; here it is the case of φαίνεσθαι, of "becoming visible". The object is what becomes visible. But since I am the one to which it has to become visible, it will only become visible if it meets the conditions I have in order for something to become manifest to me. These conditions, Kant says, are *space* and *time*.

For Kant, space and time are not *entia,* they are not beings, they are purely and simply the conditions for the possibility that objects become sensibly visible to us. That is why he calls this part of his *Critique of Pure Reason* "Transcendental Aesthetics," where "Aesthetics" means it is the domain of αἴσθεσις, of sensing; this is the *Transcendental Theory of Sensibility.* The Transcendental Theory of Sensibility is nothing but the transcendental theory of the manifestation of an object through the way of the senses.

We can then put the question this way: how is it possible to have a synthesis with the categorial order? Because when all is said and done, things are not actually concerned with what I have in my head or with my capacity of judging with the structures of my purely subjective categories.

But it is not that simple, because in fact the conditions for things to manifest themselves to us, viz. {215} time and space, are there *a priori*, that is, are present beforehand, as a transcendental condition of every sensible manifestation. Space and time are properties of the subject, they are *a priori*. But then, the order of the categories is also an *a priori* order. The result is that we have a common moment, the "a priority" of the two orders that constitute the insertion point or the synthesis of the categorial order and the order of sensible manifestations. Indeed, let us consider something, for example, the sun. The sun that astronomy deals with is not a system of luminous sensations or luminous perceptions that I have; the astronomer is not concerned with my sensations and perceptions, he or she is concerned with the laws of the sun. Of course, nothing can be known of the sun if it cannot be seen in some way through perception (in photographic plates, by direct inspection or whatever). What is the difference? The difference is that what I perceive I see as a series of properties of an object, of something that is there. And that is just the sun, which I perceive it as such, as an object, precisely because it is in time and space. But then, this second operation, seeing it as an *object*, depends on me; that is why in the most modest of perceptions, the transcendental synthesis of the categorial and the phenomenal is given.

For Kant, it is in this unitary synthesis of the categorial and the phenomenal that the transcendental idea of experience is constituted. Experience for him does not simply mean sensible experience, or as it is often said, sensations or sensible perceptions. Experience means the *system of sensed objects*.

The transcendental order, with respect to these objects whose unity constitutes nature, is transcendental experience, that is, the synthesis of the categorial and the phenomenal. {216} According to Kant, it is only then, when we have an object constituted as an object, that we can have science. Astronomy and the celestial mechanics of Newton are constituted as sciences precisely because of this. They are not just a system of perceptions, but a system of objects provided with some laws; however I make the object in its objectuality. Certainly, I do not make the sun, but I make the set of sensations and perceptions that the sun gives me intelligible as manifestations of an object that is there, at such and such a place in space and time, and called the "sun."

This knowledge of objects is called "science." It means that science is made with concepts, and this is what we have been commenting upon for some time. It is a synthesis of the conceived with the given.

But humans may attempt something else: not only can they try to know *things* with concepts and with the given, they can try to know the *given* "through" pure concepts, and this is a different task. This task is what Kant calls metaphysics. Is it possible? Kant will remain faithful to his idea that there is no science—and in this case we cannot have metaphysics—unless something is actually given. And he tells us that what is given to me in sensibility, internal or external, can be reduced to its *minimum* in order to have something given without entering into the whole richness of the details of the given. If I were to enter into the richness of the details of the given, I would have through external sensibility the unfathomable richness of physics, and through internal sensibility the richness of the *I* and the whole of the psyche. But, if I take nothing more than the minimum strictly necessary and sufficient to have something given without any details, then we would have two facts: in the order of external sensibility, the *res corporea*, {217} and in the order of internal sensibility, the *res cogitans*. This is just the Cartesian way. Since corporeity and cogitation are given, it is possible to have a metaphysics, that is, a knowledge of nature and the human spirit through pure concepts because these concepts do nothing but determine something that is really and truly given. Because of this, Kant says that this metaphysics is, strictly speaking, an *immanent metaphysics* that by means of concepts constitutive of things gives us knowledge of them that does not force us exceed the domain of the given. Such knowledge rather manifests the given, and allow us to know it in a completely different metaphysical dimension that lies beyond the dimensions of physics or psychology.

Up to this point things are clear. But Kant says that human understanding has always had the desire to increase its knowledge beyond the given. (Later Kant will have to tell us why it has always been trying to do this). It does so in order to lead us, by means of reasoning and the system of concepts, to objects not given in experience, to transcendental objects. With this the "meta-" of metaphysics no longer simply means *trans* in a transcendental sense, it means "transcendent," that is, the supersensible.

Kant says these objects are the object of "metaphysics properly so-called" (*eigentliche Metaphysik*). This is the weighty inheritance of Leibniz. Regardless, that is what Kant says. How has human understanding managed to do this? It has done so in a manner that is not simple, but plausible.

No one has seen all the things that are in the universe, but I see some things, perceive some things, intellectually know some things that are conditioned, that depend on a particular condition, which in turn depends on another, etc. Then, because of my reason I rise to the consideration of everything that is conditioned, insofar as it {218} naturally depends on something absolutely unconditioned. This is just the idea of the world, the idea of an unconditioned totality.

Analogously (though the reasoning may be somewhat simpler), if I do the same with what refers to states of mind, I shall be led to the idea of a soul.

Finally, if I take the totality of these two unconditioned totalities—world and soul—into a single totality, I have the idea of God.

Metaphysics—classical philosophy—sought to deal with the world, the soul and God as entities without which what is given would not be possible. But precisely here is the locus of Kant's sharp and irrefutable critique.

In the first place, we speak of "what is given to us." But no one has received the conditioned totality of experience; we have been given fragments of experience. If someone had in front of his eyes the conditioned totality of everything that happens in the world, then that reasoning might be applicable, but we do not have this. Each person has an experience, more or less rich, more or less ample and voluminous, and can add all of his or her experiences to the experiences of others, but in no way, either individually or collectively or historically, is the totality of external experience something given. *A fortiori* the same happens with the totality of internal experience. That totality is never given. Humans have experience of internal states, but their totality is never given as a totality. Its existence may be something inferred by man, but it cannot be demonstrated.

In the second place, Kant says that the proof that these {219} empirical totalities are never total but fragmentary resides in the fact that any attempt to apply transcendental reasoning to them leads to inexorable "antinomies". Since they are well known, we shall only allude to them briefly. Whether reality is divisible or indivisible to the infinite, whether there is a first term in the series of these events, etc. There, we find reasoning with the same evidence for the thesis or for the antithesis. The reasoning is strictly antinomic because the totality (that would allow us to resolve the problem) is never given in experience.

In the third place, because the totality is not given in experience, humans have the subsidiary (and erroneous in Kant's view) impression that our system of concepts refers to things in themselves, whereas in reality concepts *cannot* transcend the order of objects and objectuality. From within this order of objects it is absolutely impossible to step to things outside the world of these objects; we are constrained to move only within that world of ob-

jects. These three ideas: world, soul, and God are indeed immanent, but immanent to what? Not to the given, because the totalities of experiences are not given; they are immanent to knowledge, and constitutive of knowledge. What they are useful for is to
make human knowledge more than a simple accumulation of iso-
lated truths, something that truly constitutes a system. They are
ideas *regulative* of reason; they are the ground for knowledge to
have the form of system. But they are not at all objects which we
attain as an inexorable conclusion from the totality of experience,
subjected to a system of categories. As regulative ideas they are,
Kant says, not constitutive of things, but regulative of knowledge
and immanent to it. {220}

This does not mean that for Kant these objects are in fact
possible—that is separate problem—only that they are at most
nothing more than possible. If these objects were to fulfill the
conditions for being something given, and that this something
given could actually render possible application of the categories,
then everything would be perfectly in order. But this never happens in speculative reason. Speculative theology, speculative
cosmology, and speculative psychology are for Kant the dreams of
reason. This is no metaphor. Kant wrote a pamphlet against Swedenborg,[20] a famous visionary, and the title was, *The Dreams of a
Visionary Explained by the Dreams of Metaphysics.*[21] Metaphysics,
thus understood, is for Kant the dream of reason. To pretend to
reach something that transcends this world of sensed objects by
the succession of experiential facts, internal or external, to attain
the reality of these three great ideas of God, soul and world, is
completely chimerical. That is purely and simply the dream of
reason. We shall never have science and true knowledge unless
concepts are based on and applied to something given, or these
concepts actually constitute some immanent moments of objects
and things; beyond this it is impossible to have knowledge. Kant
says that we can have "thought." Of course, we can think anything we wish, as long as we do not fall into contradiction; but
this does not mean that what we think is an object, an object
given in the world. To presume to reach a transcendent being,
God, the soul or the world by mere prolongation of the intellectual
and transcendental constitution of the order of experience {221} is
for Kant forever just a dream of reason (*der Traum der Vernunft*).

Why? Because the very experience upon which all of science
and this entire attempt to create transcendental metaphysics is
based is that which is given under the form of an empirical intuition, i.e., as something that appears to us in space and time.
Kant says that there is nothing that will allow us to step outside
these limits of space and time; and within these limits, the totality

of internal or external experience is never given—never mind the totality of the two totalities, which is God.

Before proceeding to another kind of given, we need to reflect for a moment about Kant's vigorous construction of immanent metaphysics and his critique of speculative metaphysics.

Kant starts his whole construction from the point that all human knowledge begins with experience. Kant has no doubt about this, because how else could our capacity for knowing be activated unless by the objects of the senses that impress us, that produce sensations? This is true and there is no need for the genius of Kant to affirm it. But, what does Kant understand here by "impression"? Do we understand by "impression" purely and simply what empiricism understood? After all, rationalism, when it criticized empiricist philosophy, was squarely opposed to this. Does it just mean that an impression is the mere affection of a subject? In that case, we would be lost, because in fact *any* impression, including the most trivial, just because it is an impression, causes some sort of appearance of that causing the impression before the subject. Clearly, there is something more: there is a moment of "otherness." {222}

Moreover this otherness in humans, in contrast to other animals, has a specific dimension of its own. In the impression a human being feels not only the sensitive contents, whatever they may be and with all their richness, but also something else: he or she feels their own characteristic of reality, feels the content with a special *formality* of its own, the impression of reality. And granting this, one's intellectual reflections will take a quite different direction from that followed byKantian metaphysics.

The first of these differences consists in Kant telling us in an evidently plausible and truthful way that human understanding has to make an object out of things in order to know what they are; this is quite clear. But the question always is, when I make an object out of something, even supposing that I make the objectuality of the object, do I know the *res objecta qua objecta* or *qua res*? Do I know it as object or as thing? The answer for Kant is clear: it could only be as object because (as Kant sees it) in impression *there is no moment of reality*. But if there were one, the anwer would be quite different.

In the second place, Kant demonstrates that the truth of understanding and reason is primarily and radically a *verum logicum*, a conformity of understanding with things that essentially depends on a *verum transcendentale*, that is, on the way in which a human being behaves with respect to its first impressions, i.e., though the synthesis operation Kant describes. But this assumes that transcendental truth (based on synthesis), in this sense, is the primary truth. But what if primary truth is not the primary truth? What if it is simply the naked presence of reality in the intellective act? What if the intellection of humans is sentient intellection? Then we would have a "real" truth. And if real truth exists, then *judgment* is not what determines the intelligibility of things; {223} actually *reality* is what determines the structure of knowing that enables judgment.[22]

Because of this, the Kantian meditation leads to other meditations. In addition, it leads to some questions that may appear as matters of detail, but that are actually are very important for Kant. For example, Kant insists that science would be impossible without synthetic *a priori* judgments (let us prescind from the question of whether they are synthetic), that is to say, without absolutely necessary universal truths; the immediate example Kant gives is causality. In his view, if we do not have a causal vision of the world, if objects do not have a causal connection, they would be unintelligible. Kant understands causality as "everything that is in time has an antecedent, which determines it in time." Is Kant's statement true? Is it true that a temporal antecedent intrinsically and necessarily determines everything that is in time? Present day physics, correctly or incorrectly having eliminated the idea of deterministic causality in the realm of elementary particles, and in having introduced a measure of indeterminism, accords poorly with Kant's ideas. However, I do not wish to pursue the issue further; that is something for the physicists to argue. The only thing I mean to say is that the idea of causality is not the same as the idea of temporal determination; it might or might not be true that everything that appears in time has a cause. And if it so, does this mean that the cause is an antecedent given in time? What if that were not so?[23]

So there are indeed clouds surrounding Kant's vigorous construction. And now Kant has {224} another question pending. Is empirical intuition, including its transcendental conditions of time and space, the only way something is given to human understanding? Kant will reply that there is another completely different way.

b) The moral fact

This second way in which the moral law is given to us is through moral conscience. Kant says that this is also a *factum*. But it is a *factum* that is not part of the order of time and space. On the contrary, as we shall see below, the moral law rules above and beyond the conditions of space and time; it is something absolute.

Then something opens up for Kant: not just the possibility, but the necessity of bringing to bear the interplay of the categories on this order, the order of moral conscience. With this it seems—and this opinion has been repeated in the majority of the books that deal with Kant—as if an enormous duality exists within the Kantian philosophy. On the one hand, there is its limitation to the sensible side, through which the human mind is incapable of elevating itself to a strictly transcendent order. On the other, there is a poor practical reason that can only lead humans to a more or less blind and irrational morality juxtaposed to science. However, this is completely erroneous. Kant has expressly said the opposite, viz. that it is not the case of a duality in knowledge, or of a duality in the intellectual conditions of the categories. We have alluded above to the paragraph in the *Critique of Pure Reason* where Kant tells us that the difference lies in the different ways in which the moral law and the phenomena of nature are given to us. Let us ignore, for the moment {225} everything we have just said about the phenomenal. And let us say that what is given has to fit one way or another into the categories, if it is going to belong to the transcendental order and constitute an *a priori* synthesis with these categories.

For Kant, reason determines the will, and this is what morality is. Therefore, Kant begins by telling us that morality is not a *sentiment* or *feeling* of duty, or a series of commands that are more or less extrinsic, but primarily and fundamentally *a determination of the will by reason*.

Precisely in the measure in which this will belongs to the domain of a *praxis*, that is to say, to something that has the finality or the end in itself, Kant says that reason acting in that way is a practical reason. "Practical" because it concerns the praxis, not because it refers to anything practical, in the common meaning of the term. Morality is not a sentiment, feeling, or inclination, but is the *objective dictate of reason to the will*. This objective dictate is just what we call "duty". The order of the moral for Kant is formally the order of duty.

Having determined what Kant understands by morality, we must now ask:

i. What is the character of this fact?

ii. What is the intelligibility proper to it?

i) Its absolute character. Transcendental freedom and the person.

What is the character of this fact? First we must say, with Kant, that this is a *fact*, not a {226} construction. Kant emphasizes the *factum* of the moral. Sometimes he calls it "experience," and at other times he says that it is not experience, but something greater than experience; the term does not matter. It is something precisely given (*etwas Gegebenes*). Actually, man finds himself, as he says at the end of the *Critique of Pure Reason*, not only with the starry heaven occupying his mind, but with the moral law in his conscience. For Kant this is a fact, a *factum*, the *factum* of morality. It is something rigorously given, as rigorously given as the colors of this room or the movement of the stars.

Secondly, this fact, though rigorously given, is not an *empirical* fact. What does Kant mean when he says that it is not an empirical fact? That this moral determination of the will, the "ought," is something that refers to humans, but not to humans as beings that appear in time and space, who had parents, who were born, who have a biography, and who will die. He refers to humans considered as absolutely subject to something that is unconditioned, to duty. Duty does not command in a biographical way, duty commands absolutely. It has to be done *because* it should be done; it has to be this way *because* it should be this way.

In the end, the *factum* of the moral is an unconditioned *factum*, absolutely unconditioned, and because of this, it is not empirical. Kant calls "empirical" what which appears in space and time. However, the moral law does not appear in space and time; as we shall see forthwith, it certainly ties in with what is in space and time, but it is a "categorical imperative" as Kant says in his terminology. As a fact, then, it is not an empirical fact, but an unconditioned fact, a categorical fact.

How does reason determine the will in {227} this categorical way? Thus far, and putting it negatively, reason does not rule because it is some sort of antecedent from which actions must follow. The content of the moral law does not consist at all in giving antecedents, from which each human being must draw some inferences. To be sure, human beings, in the performance of their actions in time and space must do that; but the formal characteristic of the moral law—duty—does not consist in imposing an antecedent. How does it impose, then, but in a positive way? We have just explained. The moral imperative of morality for Kant is a categorical imperative. This means that the will, considered as the faculty of ends, if ruled in an absolute way, is so because an *absolute finality* is imposed upon it.

But that the fact that a reality has a determination and an absolute finality in this sense means, for Kant, that it is an intelligible determination, not an empirical or sensible one. Absolute finality, precisely because it is absolute, determines the will at an intelligible level, never at a merely empirical level. Consequently, the fact we are considering here—morality—is the fact of something that is intelligible "in itself," not through the forms of space and time; it is a fact with respect to the human will considered as an entity that belongs to the intelligible world. In Kantian terminology this means that each human being, considered as a will, is a "thing-in-itself," not like a phenomenon that appears in space and time. As a thing-in-itself and because of its finality, this determination consists in being absolute; the will receives its characteristic of will and of organon of morality precisely because of that determination. In other words, the absolute determination, the absolute finality, is a determination that we can {228} consider as pure. It is what constitutes the moral will in itself *qua* moral. This is what Kant calls "autonomy." It does not mean that the will can dictate its own morality to itself—something that never occurred to Kant. Rather it means that from the standpoint of the morality of the will, it is that very morality that constitutes the will itself. For Kant, the will is not a psychological faculty, but primarily and formally the moral determination of man. Therefore, it is an absolute finality; it is a will that determines itself, considered as an absolute finality.

As a thing-in-itself, the will is, in this sense, something that belongs to the intelligible world. It is something that shows no resemblance to the determinations that appear in time, in which one thing is determined by others that have preceded it. Here, before anything happens, we encounter a will that at the level of the intelligible is determined in a rigorously intelligible way to be what it is by itself. That is, the will and the human being that has it are things-in-themselves, not phenomena.

Granting this, let us consider two things. First, consider that this is a *datum*, a fact; as such, it is perfectly legitimate—and not just legitimate, but necessary—to apply to it the categories we have mentioned, the concepts. These concepts were not useful to us speculatively to gain theoretical knowledge because they were not applicable to something given; applied to something given they were incapable of crossing the frontiers of temporal succession and spatial determination. But here we encounter a fact with a curious characteristic. It is a fact and in this sense not only *permits*, but *demands* the application of the categories with complete rigor. But, on the other hand, it is a fact not about a phenomenon, but about {229} a thing-in-itself; hence the transcendental synthesis in this dimension is going to lead along paths completely foreign to speculative reason.

In causality speculative reason found *temporal* determination; here we find something different: a determination in the *intelligible* world, but nonetheless a strict causality—except that it is in the intelligible world. Because of this, what for pure reason was a possibility, for practical reason is an objective reality. Why? Because practical reason has a fact completely absent in theoretical reason, i.e., the absolute fact of morality, the fact of the will. As a determination of the will in and by itself, this determination is duty for the sake of duty. Morality exists only when something is done because it should be done, independently of any other empirical consideration: duty for the sake of duty. Consequently the self-determination of the will, which involves the formula of duty for the sake of duty, consists purely and simply in freedom. In other words, freedom, for Kant, is not the decision to break or change some temporal succession, but of now being determined to myself and by myself in the intelligible order; it is a *transcendental freedom.*

Hence, Kant can give us a more rigorous definition of what he understands by "practical." Kant tells us that "practical" is everything that is possible through freedom. Freedom, Kant says, is a form of causality. It is the form of intelligible causality that is rigorously demonstrated by the pure concepts of understanding, supported by the incontrovertible fact that is the categorical imperative, which is constitutive of morality. Speculative reasoning does not lead us from the temporal succession of the will to some causes, without us knowing what they are. Something completely {230} different is in play. We are using, for example, the concept of causality (that belongs to the order of intelligibility as such) to know a fact that is not a fact of temporal succession, but the fact of the absolute determination of the moral will.

It is appropriate to make some observations before continuing.

There is no doubt that Kant understands that morality is duty; i.e., there is no morality unless there is duty. But this is rather problematic. Is it really true, strictly speaking? Is man moral *because* he has duties? Could it not be the reverse: that he is capable of having and actually has duties because *prior* to these duties he is a moral entity? If the moral is opposed to the physical, then what constitutes morality is not exactly that it doesn't take place in space and time, as Kant claims, but something else. It consists in the fact that the determinations that constitute human beings from this new point of view are determinations that do *not* proceed from a causal chain, determined in space and time, but from an act of appropriation by the will itself. No one has science or virtue through a chain of causes in space and time; they may be *conditions for*, but they are not *causes of* that science and that virtue. Humans have science and virtue when they really accept and make their own the possibilities of virtue and science. In the measure in which each human being has properties that belong to him or her really and effectively, physically, by virtue of an appropriation, in this sense we say that the person is moral. Who can fail to see, then, that duty is grounded on morality, and not morality on duty? Strictly speaking morality is not the domain of the *should-be*, but rather the domain of the *being-owed*, which is something different, though always within the realm of being. {231}

After these marginal observations let us return to Kant.

Kant understands that freedom, that is, that humans as entities determined intelligibly in the form of transcendental freedom with free causality (though only in the intelligible order), are *persons*. For Kant, the person is the transcendental dimension of each human being, as a thing-in-itself, as an absolute thing. Consequently, Kant substitutes for the Cartesian division of things into *res cogitans* and *res extensa* his own transcendental difference between *res* and person. For Kant, therefore, a human being as a thing-in-itself is a person.

But does this contradict in any way what he has told us with respect to pure reason about the inability of that reason to apply the categories to the order of reality? It would, if the concept of causality were applied to the will in such a way that we might say, "Here I have an object, which is the will, and here I have a category, which is the cause." But Kant says that the will is not an "object". That is the point. The will is not an object, but is purely and simply the order of duty, of what ought to be; it is never an object, something that is defined by the order of what "is." This is why we have no intuition of the will as organon. We have the *factum* of the imperative that rules us, but we have no intuition at all of the will as object. That is why the transcendental use of the categories is not only perfectly licit, but necessary in the order of freedom, of freedom understood as self-determination in the order of morality. But it would not be freedom at all were it to be considered as a physical property of a being and called "morality." It is, as Kant would say, a transcendental synthesis of the categories and morality within the confines of morality itself, {232} i.e., in the order of praxis, in the order of practical reason. On the other hand, speculative reason placed us in the order of theoretical reason, in the order of what is, not in the order of what ought to be.

The problem Kant poses is just this: what is the intelligibility proper to the order of transcendental freedom?

ii) Its intelligibility

What is the intelligibility proper to the fact of morality? We are not going to explain this point in detail since that would entail a complete summary of Kant's philosophy of Kant, well known to all. Therefore, we are only going to recall Kant's two main ideas

According to Kant, morality rules absolutely, categorically, with full rigor, over all conditions of space and time. But no one in space and time, regardless how moral he or she may be, can realize morality in all its fullness and in all its integrity. Consequently, the moral imperative would be impossible unless we had available an "infinite progression," and not simply the finite moral space in which each human life consists. In other words, the intelligibility proper to the moral order, which is what Kant calls "holiness" (*Heiligkeit*), demands immortality.

On the other hand, Kant tells us that one's achievement of morality is *eudaimonia*, happiness (*Glückseligkeit*). But in fact no one is happy in that way. Happiness consists in everything going smoothly between the intelligence and with the will; but no one is completely happy, no one realizes that supreme goodness. This is why it is necessary that the supreme goodness of the will have a cause that is intelligible and real, which is God. {233}

The immortality of the soul and the existence of God are the two conditions that cannot be demonstrated speculatively. The only thing that can be demonstrated is the existence of freedom. But those two truths are included in transcendental freedom itself; we shall see immediately in what way..

Indeed, let us ask first, what are these conditions of intelligibility? And second, what are the characteristics that these conditions have?

What are these conditions of intelligibility of transcendental freedom we have just enunciated, viz. immortality and God? As we mentioned, they are not propositions that can be demonstrated; in this sense, Kant calls them *postulates*. What does Kant understand by "postulates"? They are not postulates in the sense of Euclid's parallel postulate. For sure they are propositions that cannot be demonstrated by speculative reason, but are objectively included and required in that of which they are postulates, i.e., in the very intelligibility of freedom; they are objective exigencies of freedom. In a note found in the *Critique of Practical Reason* Kant refers to the "subtle and clear headed" Wizenmann,[24] who told him that with his argument he seeks "the right to argue from a want to the objective reality of its object, and illustrates the point by the example of a man in love, who having fooled himself into an idea of beauty, which is merely a chimera of his own brain, would fain conclude that such an object really exists somewhere."[25] Kant replied by saying that if he were referring to demands derived from an inclination (*Neigung*) then his critic would be correct, but that is not the case. The moral imperative is an *objective* imperative; for that reason what it demands is also included {234} in the objective world. It is not the case, therefore, of a postulate that gratifies some feelings, because morality is not a feeling, but an imperative of reason. And therefore, the objectivity of morality includes *by way of an intrinsic requirement of intelligi-*

bility—not by way of demonstration—God and the immortality of the soul. As Kant says, freedom is the "keystone" of the whole of metaphysics.

In the second place, what is the ultimate and radical character of this morality or of the conditions of intelligibility? Let us think about what we have just said. The immortality of the soul stems from the fact that morality, which is purely moral, could not be accomplished physically in the course of a finite life and needs an infinite life. It also stems from the fact that the happiness of which human being is capable would not be achieved perfectly if there were no cause outside of him. Why is this so? Here a conflict between nature and morality surfaces. What Kant tells us is that this conflict cannot exist. The postulates of practical reason, i.e., the conditions of intelligibility of the moral imperative, are the real and formal coincidence between the moral and the natural, between nature and morality. Immortality is something demanded by duty in the order of nature; God is something demanded for the achievement of happiness. Precisely because because morality is an objective imperative, these conditions of coincidence have to exist; you must, therefore you can (*Du sollst, also du kannst*). Otherwise, whence is a categorical imperative to come, if this imperative does not have an adequate objective, and one which is objectively imposed? Because of this, what pure reason has declared as merely possible—the transcendent—practical reason actually reaches; in this sense, at the hands of practical reason we have achieved a {235} transcendent metaphysics, which speculative reason by itself was radically incapable of achieving.

What characteristics does this metaphysics have? The first thing we must say is that, for Kant, it is basically an *immanent* metaphysics. The situation is similar to that of *res corporea* or *res cogitans*. It is "immanent" in the sense that what metaphysics discovers and attains is *in the given*. It is determined intelligibly by the understanding, but it is something immanent, as immanent as, from another point of view, the properties of extension or the *res cogitans* are in Descartes' metaphysics.[26]

It might be said that the parallelism is false, since the *res corporea* and the *res cogitans* are an immanent metaphysics, but here we have a transcendent metaphysics. How can we now affirm that Kant's metaphysics is immanent? For that, it is indispensable to recall what happens with the fact of morality. It is the "fact of a thing-in-itself," which is equivalent to saying that, in the end, the transcendent which practical reason achieves is something immanently given in it. Specifically, *the person is the immanent fact of something transcendent*; it is the fact of reality as a "thing-in-itself." It follows that this attainment of the transcendent by the human will is something that, strictly speaking, is immanent. In the end, the transcendent metaphysics of Kant is the transcendent metaphysics of something immanent. It is the transcendent metaphysics of the person.

In the second place, it is a metaphysics in which reason, by means of concepts, reaches the objective reality of the thing-in-itself, namely, immortality and God. Kant clearly affirms this.

Kant has also told us that the concepts are applied; but, {236} what are these concepts? The conceptual intelligibility of transcendental freedom is what compels human beings to affirm intellectually the immortality of the soul and the existence of God. In fact these two notions, viz. immortality (including freedom itself) and the existence of God, whose reality is assured objectively, in reality, and actually by practical reason—in the way we have just said—are not apprehended by representative concepts, but by constitutive ones. That is a separate question. Though they are not apprehended by representative concepts, as Kant says, they assure us of a reality, a reality of which we cannot make a concept (uns keinen Begriff machen können).[27]

Nevertheless, what is clear is what we have indicated above, that it is the case of an immanent metaphysics, understood as the metaphysics of something that is immanent and transcendent at the same time, as the person is. And in second place, it is an attainment of the transcendent order by mean of concepts. Therefore, regardless of the reshaping that these concepts may require, it is something rigorously known intellectually. The metaphysics of practical reason is anything but a blind irrational sentiment.

In the third place, why, indeed, are these concepts constitutive, but not comparable to those of speculative reason? Simply because here the fact is not an object, but something that ought to be; it is something in the practical order, not a fact of the representative order; that is why the concepts are not representative. As we said earlier, the transcendental synthesis depends on the type of the given; and here the given is not a subject, but a free determination; however, it is rigorously intelligible, which means that it has intellective predicates. {237}

In fact, Kant himself tells us in the Critique of Practical Reason that we have "a knowledge, but only in a practical aspect (eine Erkenntnis, aber nur im praktisher Beziehung)," by which he refers to the soul and God.[28] For example, if we try to think about what God could be by using concepts, Kant says that we shall be reduced to two predicates, viz. intelligence and will. Of these we must say that intelligence is an intelligence "that does not think, but intuits" (der nicht denkt, sondern anschaut), and that the will is directed to objects on whose existence that very will does not depend. Consequently Kant writes, "all these are properties about which we have no concepts," i.e., they cannot serve to represent their object to us. Indeed, who has a representation of the divine intelligence or the divine will? Of course, that question may seem to be a kind of lifesaver we throw at Kantian philosophy; however, we need to think, for example, of the tons of lifesavers that have been thrown at the exegesis of St. Thomas or Duns Scotus; apparently, this cannot be done with Kant. But, putting this aside, let us stay with the facts themselves of Kant's philosophy. Kant says that from the practical point of view, of these properties of reason and will, we are left only with a residue in the concept of "relationship," which determines practical law, and therefore, objective reality. However, Kant distinguishes here quite clearly between what a *representative* concept is and what *mere intellection* is. How could Kant possibly say that this relationship is unintelligible? It is indeed an act of intelligence, it is known intellectually; but it does not lead to a representation. {238} Where is the adequate representation of the divine will or the divine intelligence in any theology, beginning with the Old and New Testament? Nowhere at all. When Kant tells us that something is intellectual, something is intelligible, he wishes to say that we are left with just "the concept of a relationship."(*der Begriff eines Verhältnisses*).29 What has theology of any period ever been able to supply, except this? If Kant denies the cognitive characteristic, if Kant denies that we have concepts of it, he is referring only to the representative concepts, i.e., to theoretical and speculative knowledge. There is no doubt that on this point an enormous abuse against him has been committed. How can we possibly admit that all of the purely conceptual arguments constituting countless folios and filling so many libraries really pertain to theology itself? If Kant denies this, it is precisely to say that we do not have an adequate representation except of what is given in an intuition, in a phenomenon. Therefore, the only thing we have in this case is a kind of intellective residue, by virtue of which what the categorical imperative is cannot be intellectively understood objectively without considering the immortality of the soul and the existence of an intelligent and volitional God. Kant presents this as terminus of an intellective act.

III. *Unity of Kantian metaphysics*

We now take a third step. The first step was to determine the problem of Kantian philosophy. The second dealt {239} with the constitution of the transcendental order. This third step is going to cover the unity of Kantian metaphysics.

Is it a fact that Kant admits of two metaphysics: speculative metaphysics, referring to things that are, and another metaphysics, more or less amputated, the practical metaphysics of the intellective order? I have always thought this is not true; Kantian metaphysics has a strict, rigorous unity.

1. By its way of conceptualizing.
2. By its object.
3. By its principle.

1. By its way of conceptualizing

The concepts of metaphysics that refer to the philosophy we call "special," that is, the one that deals with the world of nature or the world of the spirit (the *res corporea* and the *res cogitans*) have three aspects, as we have pointed out. In the first place, they are *immanent* :they do not leave, at least they do not pretend to leave, the given object itself. In the second place, they are *constitutive*: they give us constitutive properties of these objects. In the third place, they are *representative*: they adequately represent that which is given in experience.

But the concepts of transcendental metaphysics are *not* representative, we have already seen why and in what measure they are not. The fact that they are not representative does not mean that they are devoid of any intelligibility, as we have pointed out, because these concepts are still immanent and constitutive. Kant clearly says this. Whilefrom the speculative point of view the ideas of God, soul, and world are nothing but regulative ideas of reason, in practical reason they are constitutive moments of the {240} intelligibility of the objects that make the moral imperative possible, viz. God and immortality. It is precisely in the use of immanent and constitutive concepts that we find, from the point of view of conceptualization, the conceptual unity of Kantian metaphysics as a whole. The fact that these concepts are adequately representative in one case, and not in another, is a difference that does not affect the unity of metaphysics. If it were to affect it, what would be left of traditional metaphysics? Here it is the case purely and simply that they are immanent and constitutive concepts. Insofar as the immanent metaphysics of nature and the immanent metaphysics of the spirit, like the metaphysics of practical reason, function *in* and *by* immanent and constitutive concepts, metaphysics is by its way of conceptualizing a perfectly unitary system.

2. By its object

In the second place, there is the unity of metaphysics by reason of its object. This may seem more problematic. It is, after all, where one always hopes to corner Kant. The object of metaphysics for Kant is always the objective reality of that which is known through concepts, and that objective reality is, therefore, based on intelligibility, on the *verum transcendentale*, which is something determined by the internal structure of reason itself. Let us put aside this determination and simply pay attention to intelligibility.

This intelligible (or at least *intelligenda*) reality appears to be double. On the one hand, we have the things that are, and on the other {241} hand, the good; a situation, in other words, correlative to both sides: to empirical intuition and human volition. And we ask, are these two termini, the reality of things, i.e., natural real things, and the good, irreducible for Kant? In the first place, for him the object of morality, i.e., that which makes morality intelligible, is not the highest good; were it so, on the one hand we would have the *bonum*, and on the other hand, *ens*, the *res*, but this is not true at all. What Kant demands from the existence of God as cause of the categorical imperative, i.e., as cause of the supreme good, is just to be *causa*. In other words, Kant requires not that God be good, but that the good be real. That is just what constitutes the lynchpin of the Kantian argumentation. Therefore, it is not the case of counterposing natural reality and the good, but of doing something completely different. It is the case of just showing that in the good there is a *res* at the bottom, a *res* about which Kant tells us that it is intelligent and volitional precisely because it has a causality provided with morality. It is indeed the creative *organon* of the teleology of the universe. In Kant's view, this *res* is necessary, because without it transcendental freedom would not be objectively intelligible. Ultimately, for me, the the transcendental of God is the intelligibility of God as objective reality; it is the divine *verum transcendentale*.

Therefore, for Kant the question of whether the good and things are irreducible melds into another one. Are the *verum transcendentale* of God and the *verum transcendentale* of things, two different dimensions or two different transcendental orders? Kant tells us in the *Critique of Practical Reason* that "God is a supreme nature, possessing causality in conformity with morality."[30] Precisely because of this, He can rule, {242} He can be the cause that makes the categorical moral imperative of transcendental freedom intelligible.

But Kant says something more, not in the *Critique of Practical Reason*, but in the *Critique of Pure Reason*. Indeed, after affirming that God is the systematic teleological unity of all things he adds, "And this unity, that (...) with respect to the sensible world can be called nature and with respect to freedom can be called the intelligible world, the moral, inevitably leads to... natural laws and moral laws, and therefore, unifies practical reason with speculative reason. The world has to be represented as emerging from an idea... by which the investigation of nature (...) is converted into a physico-theology... which brings the final ends of nature to grounds (*Gründe*) that *a priori* have to be found indissolubly tied (*unzertrennlich verknüpft*) to the internal possibility of things, that is, to a transcendental theology. Thus one adopts the ideal of the supreme ontological perfection as a principle of the systematic unity that entwines all things in accordance with necessary and universal natural laws, since all these same things proceed from a single primordial being (*Urwesen*)".[31]

For Kant, it is in the concept of God thus achieved that the maximum coincidence is realized, the transcendent coincidence between the order of nature and the moral order. Precisely because of this, for Kant there is a single object of metaphysics. The transcendental order referred to God is the same as the one referred to things. This order consists of the reality inscribed in the intelligibility, in the *verum*. Therefore, there is a strict unity. But, what kind of unity? {243}

For Descartes, it was the case of two orders unified by a free act of the will of God, by the divine veracity. For Leibniz, human reason was an image of the divine reason. For medieval metaphysics the being of God, when creating things, impressed them with certain entifying characteristics, which are the same that God in himself possesses in an eminent way.

Kant rebels against these interpretations. Against Descartes, it is obvious: it is not a case of veracity. Against Leibniz, because human reason is not an image of divine reason, as we saw, but essentially different from it. Against the medieval interpretation, because this whole transcendent way that leads to God is grounded on the intelligibility that morality has for me. But, "I" make the intelligibility, God does not make it; so it is just a characteristic of my reason.

But it is absurd to think that Kant intended to say that I am the creator of God. What Kant tells us is that I have created or have in me the conditions that make it possible for God to be something intelligible for me. I ask, where is the heterodoxy? I make the conditions that make God intelligible *for me*, this is clear, not *for Him*, because that would be another task. It is not, therefore, in the order of reality, but in the order of cognition, of intelligibility, where there is a strict unity.

However, there is a difference between the order of nature and the order of morality; but it is a difference that affects not the reality of things or the reality of God, but His capacity of being adequately represented by man, which is a different matter. The unity of truth does not mean a unity of intellectual comprehensibility. And conversely, the diversity of conceptual representability does not mean {244} a rupture of intelligibility. The unity of the *verum transcendentale* is always the unity of intelligibility, and this intelligibility is just made by the "I," the "I think."

Therefore, metaphysics has a strict unity by reason of its object, as long as we are told, in the end, what the unity of metaphysics is by virtue of its origin.

3. By its origin

For Kant, reason, the "I think" as rational thinking is what makes things intelligible for me. To this there are no exceptions, for stones or for God.

It is true that the ascent to the transcendental order for Kant follows a different path than the traditional one. Traditionally it has been thought that by considering things that appear in space and time by means of a series of connections and arguments based on succession, we reach a being at which we must arrive or risk the fate of making the world inexplicable. Kant follows a completely different way. Kant ascends to God not by way of the physical world, but by way of the moral world, as we have shown.

But once he has reached God, he descends to the physical world and makes us see that this physical world is a free creation of that God to whom he has arrived by way of morality. As Kant tells us, few people have believed in God and admit his existence through speculative reasoning; there are millions that have admitted it through moral reasoning. The way of Kant is different that the physical way, because the uniqueness of God as cause is a *second* step that follows a first step, which is the ascension to God by way of the will. In fact, for Kant, God is not a being that is necessary {245} so that reason can speculatively know things-in-themselves—reason could never achieve this—but a being absolutely necessary for reason to be reason.[32] Because of this, there is a radical and formal unity between what is called "practical reason" and "theoretical reason." Kant clearly says so: "They are one and the same reason" (*Sie sind eine und die selbe Vernunft*).[33]

Inasmuch as through its practical side reason reaches the transcendent, it has primacy over theoretical reason, but it does not have it in respect to theoretical knowledge. This is why we can now understand the paragraph quoted above in which Kant tells us, at the end of the *Critique of Pure Reason*,[34] that the *Critique* has demonstrated, first, that the pure concepts of understanding—the categories—do not have an empirical origin, but have their font and *a priori* source in pure reason. And second, that when applied by practical reason to something given, they lead to a particular way of thinking about the supersensible. Now we can see how these two ways, these two aspects, are for Kant purely and simply two facets of a single transcendental order, a transcendental order constituted by the dimension of intelligibility, determined *by my own reason* acting on *the condition of intelligibility*.

The true principle of intelligibility and the key to metaphysics is reason in its absolute characteristic; freedom is nothing but one manifestation of it.

When Leibniz, followed by Wolff, asserted that metaphysics is the science that contains the first principles of {246} human reason, Kant had no fundamental objection, provided that those principles were clarified for us. For Kant, it is the very structure of reason *qua* reason that determines *a priori*, transcendentally, the intelligibility of every possible object, whether an empirical object or a transcendent object.

The true entity, ground, and principle of all metaphysics is my reason. This is why the philosophy of Kant is not rationalism; it is something I have sometimes called "reasonism," which is something different. It is a "reasonism," in other words, that grounds all metaphysics on the crux of what reason is. That is why Kant is able to say at the end of *Critique of Pure Reason* that philosophy comprises three questions: What can I know? What should I do? What can I hope for? And these three questions, he tells us in another work,[35] are reduced to just one, what is man? Here he refers to man as reason, as seat of the absolute and of the absolute intelligibility of everything.

Nothing is intelligible except in the form in which its intelligibility is determined by reason. That is why the transcendental egology of Descartes eventually culminates in the philosophy of Kant. The philosophy of Kant is expressly and thematically transcendental philosophy, the anthropological version of first philosophy.

---

[1] KrV B 72.

[2] *Metaphysik. Vorlesungen* (Kowalewsky), p. 183.

[3] KrV A 841, B 869.

[4] KrV A 846, B 874.

[5] KrV A VII, translation of Norman Kemp Smith (1929), available at http://www.hkbu.edu.hk/~ppp/cpr/toc.html.

[6] KrV A VIII, translation of Norman Kemp Smith.

[7] KrV B VII, XV, XIX, X.

[8] [For the Spanish *pensabilidad*, possibility of being thought—trans.].

[9] [Luis de Molina, 1535-1600. Spanish Jesuit philosopher.—trans.]

[10] *Zubiri note*: If I do not distinguish terminologically throughout this exposition between "reason" and "understanding" it is due to my desire

for simplification. Therefore, as long as I do not indicate to the contrary, let us take them as synonymous.

[11] Cf. KrV A 77, B 103.

[12] KrV A 146, B 185 (Zubiri's quotation in this case is not literal).

[13] *Metaphysik, Vorlesungen* (Ed. Kowalewsky), p. 183.

[14] [For the Spanish *principialmente*, a Zubiri neologism from *principio*, principle, principially.—trans.].

[15] An Garve, *Briefe*, 110.

[16] An Markus Herz, *Briefe*, 96.

[17] An Markus Herz, *Briefe*, 48.

[18] KrV A 247, B 303.

[19] "Now then, the critique... demonstrated *primarily* that [the categories] are not of an empirical origin, but have their *a priori* source and fountain in the pure understanding; and in *second place* also, that, since they are referred to *objects in general*, independently of the intuition of the same, produce the *theoretical knowledge* only when they are applied to *empirical* objects; but, however, applied to a given object by practical reason, they are useful for the *particular thought of the supersensible*, although only insofar as that supersensible is determined again by the predicates, that necessarily belong to the pure *practical purpose*, given *a priori*, and the possibility of the same" (E. Kant, *Critique of Pure Reason*, tr. M. García Morente, Madrid, Espasa-Calpe, 3rd. ed., 1984, p. 196).

[20] [Emmanuel Swedenborg, 1688-1772, Swedish scientist, philosopher, and Christian mystic.—trans.].

[21] *Träume eines Geistersehers, erläuter durch Träume der Metaphysik*, a work published by Kant in 1776 (Königsberg, J. J. Kanter).

[22] [Zubiri here outlines, in a very sketchy fashion, his philosophy of human knowing. According to Zubiri's thought, human knowledge unfolds in three stages: primordial apprehension of reality, which puts us into direct contact with reality, logos, wherein we learn to name things, and last (not first) reason, the stage in which we seek to understand through philosophy, science, theology, literature, music, and so forth. This is important because it completely inverts Kant's scheme, and makes a certain level of direct contact with reality (which Kant deemed impossible) the foundation of all human knowing. The basic meaning of "truth" also appears at the first, not the third level; it is what Zubiri terms "real truth." For further discussion, the reader is referred to Zubiri's great work, *Sentient Intelligence*, English version, published by the Xavier Zubiri Foundation of North America, Washington, DC, 1999.—trans.]

[23] [For a further discussion by Zubiri of causality and modern physics, the reader is referred to his essay, "The Idea of Nature: The New Phys-

ics," in *Nature, History, God*, published by University Press of America, 1981. Text available at http://www.zubiri.org.

24 KpV, 143, note. (*Kritik der praktishen Vernunft.* The edition used by Zubiri is the one published by the well-known "Philosophishe Bibliotek," Ed. Meiner, Leipzig (now Hamburg) that issued numerous printings.

25 Translation of Thomas Kingsmill Abbott,
http://philosophy.eserver.org/kant/critique-of-practical-reaso.txt

26 [The orginal has "Leibniz," but this must be a typographical error on Zubiri's part, since the reference is clearly to Descartes.—trans.]

27 [Tr. note: probably from *Träume eines Geistersehers, erläuter durch Träume der Metaphysik*, 1776, mentioned above].

28 KpV, 137.

29 KpV, 138.

30 KpV, 125.

31 KrV, A 815-816, B 843-844.

32 KrV, A 816, B 844.

33 KpV 121.

34 KrV 141.

35 Zubiri refers here to the well-known text that appears at the "introduction" to the lectures edited under the title *Logik*, published in 1800 with little critical rigor by his disciple G. B. Jäsche.

CHAPTER 6
WESTERN PHILOSOPHY (5)
HEGEL

We shall treat Hegel in the same way as the previous philosophers. Initially Hegel shares the framework of Descartes, Leibniz
and Kant. Hegel explicitly says that he wishes to apprehend the
radical structure of things; and he detects that radical structure
in the fact that things are created, in the framework of creation.
After all, we must not forget that Hegel's principal intellectual
formation was theology, and that he was a theologian before he
became a pure philosopher. Theology, on the one hand, and the
philosophy of Kant on the other, weighed on his spirit in different
proportions, with an advantage always on the side of theology.

So Hegel therefore finds himself in the framework of creation.
From this vantage point we must inquire about the nature of the
problem that Hegel sought to resolve. Afterwards, we shall ask
how Hegel dealt with this problem.

§1

HEGEL'S PROBLEM.
THE FRAMEWORK OF NOTHINGNESS:
THE ABSOLUTE AND REASON

Within the framework of creation, the framework of nihility, medieval philosophy and theology emphasized the intrinsic finitude of being. But in Descartes we saw something different, viz. the uncertainty of the knowing subject. Somewhat later, Leibniz placed possibility ahead of reality. Kant places objectuality first, ahead of things-in-themselves.

Faced with this panoply of philosophical theories, which he knows quite well, Hegel determines that the whole way of dealing with things within the framework of nihility is completely inadequate. First, because in all these conceptualizations what draws our attention immediately is the moment of production of *things* since things are what was produced by divinity out of nothing. But the very *moment of production* is always forgotten, since things are already there. For Hegel this is improper, with respect to both things and God.

It is improper with respect to things because they are not just what they are. Hegel affirms straightaway that what belongs to things formally and intrinsically is their characteristic of being produced, the fact that they come from God. One might think that this is just a gratuitous affirmation on Hegel's part. But perhaps it is not so if we consider that traditional theology, which Hegel knew, had schools of thought that believed that in all created being the relation of creation pertains categorically to {249} the created entity as such. Regardless of whether he knew it or not, what is certain is that Hegel agrees with this line of thinking. Created things do not leave behind their aspect of production, but rather their having been created. Therefore, their producer belongs in one form or another to the very nature of the entity of things.

Hegel thinks the same way about God, which is something much more problematic. For Hegel, God is the beginning of things, and as such in one way or another the things of which He is the beginning belong to Him. We do not know God except as Creator, and as such He does not receive His concretion except with respect to the things He has created. Therefore, in a sense that at the same time is different and unitary, things belong to God just as much as having been produced by God belongs to them. So strictly speaking what Hegel sees in the framework of Creation is the unity of God and things. This is what Hegel calls the Absolute (*das Absolute*), and it is the framework of finitude that Hegel sees.

However, there is a difference. While for earlier philosophies the framework of nothingness revealed something to them—the intrinsic finitude of entity, uncertainty, etc.—the framework of Creation reveals nothing special to Hegel, except that the framework itself is, formally, the Absolute. With this, Hegel installs himself in this framework with a radicalism not equaled by the earlier philosophies, at least apparently.

Putting it in Hegelian terms, the Absolute is at one and the same time the beginning and the end following from it. Otherwise the beginning would be but a vague generality. Nothing is a beginning—and especially in the case of God—unless it so by virtue of being the concrete beginning of these particular things; anything else, as Hegel says, would be a vague generality similar to pretending to have written a zoology book {250} by saying "all animals." The Absolute is beginning as much as the resulting end, and therefore, this Absolute is the All (*das Ganze*).

In the second place, Hegel wants to apprehend that All in its truth. He expressly tells us that when confronting the Absolute philosophy must avoid the temptation of being edifying; philosophy has to be a *rational* and intellectual apprehension of the Absolute and the All. Truth is the All, and the All is truth.

Therefore, *a limine* Hegel is going to orient the problem of truth towards the *problem of reason*. While truth in Descartes was oriented towards evidence, in Leibniz towards unity, and in Kant towards objectuality, Hegel orients the problem of the truth of everything towards reason. Therefore, the Absolute falls back upon truth and the truth falls back upon reason. What Hegel wishes to apprehend is the All in its rational truth. That apprehension of the All in its rational truth constitutes the entire problem of his philosophy.

Of course, this is quite an obscure formula. To clarify it requires the development of Hegel's philosophy.

§2

HEGEL'S DEVELOPMENT OF THE PROBLEM

Hegel is compelled to explain several things to us:

1) What does he understand by reason, that towards which the very structure of the Absolute and the all point?
2) What is the internal structure of that reason?
3) How is reason in fact the beginning of things?

The first question is the subject of *Phenomenology of the Spirit*. The second is the subject of *The Science of Logic*. The third is treated in the *Encyclopedia of Philosophical Sciences*. Let us follow, then, Hegel's three steps, not in order to summarize his philosophy, but to search for the essential concepts of the matter in a very synthetic way.

I. *Discovery of reason. From consciousness to Absolute knowledge.*

What is reason? We have seen that the formula in which Hegel frames his problem is "everything in its rational truth." Therefore if Hegel wishes to tell us what truth is he must first clearly say what the truth of the Absolute is. In the second place, he must explain the reason that possesses that truth. And third, he must reveal how we reach that concept of truth.

Let us begin with the first issue.

In his *Phenomenology of the Spirit* Hegel tells us that the answer is, at first glance, quite simple. After all, it has been more or less the way traditional philosophy, including Kant's, has posed the problem of {252} knowledge. On the one hand, we have the known thing; on the other, the subject that knows it. In other words, on the one hand, we have an Absolute; on the other hand, an act of knowing—of whatever type—in which we know the truth of that which is Absolute. So on one hand, then, is the Absolute; on the other, reason.

But then, Hegel deems this to be completely false. It is so for a variety of reasons, which boil down to two. In the first place, it is false because of something general: no act of knowledge, according to Hegel, is structured by that dualism we have just described. In the act of knowledge those two factors are indeed always involved, viz. the thing and the knowledge (or the intellectual activity, regardless of how it is called). And depending on the preponderance we give to one or the other, we have an idealist philosophy or a realist one. For example, Hegel does not hesitate to characterize all Kantian philosophy as a grand idealism; and in his *Science of Logic* he repeats *ad nauseam* that Kantian philosophy moves in the realm of pure subjectivity (*Kantische Philosophie ist die reine Subjetivität*). The reason is because the thing-in-itself (*Ding an sich*), according to Hegel, is a phantasm (*ist eine Gespenst*). This phantasmagoric characteristic of the thing-in-itself is what Hegel wishes to overcome in the development of his whole philosophical enterprise. Truth not only involves the thing, but also my knowledge of it. It is not enough for a thing to be materially and brutally true. In addition, it is necessary that the understanding, which has understood something with truth, know that it is true. Therefore, truth involves, at one and the same time, things and the knowledge of them; and truth is *at one and the same time thing and knowledge*, but not because of an external coupling. This is something that concerns all knowledge, regardless of type. {253}

But the issue becomes more difficult if what we wish to know is the Absolute. Then Hegel must first reject two concepts about the knowledge of the Absolute.[1]

Above all, Hegel tells us there is a conception according to which anyone who thinks that he or she can know the Absolute, believes him- or herself to possess a mental *organon* with which to achieve knowledge of the Absolute. It is an *organon*, that is, an instrument (*Werkzeug*) by which we apprehend that which is there, viz. the Absolute. According to Hegel, this instrumentalist theory of reason is completely inadequate in the case of the Absolute, much more so than in the case of any other knowledge. Were it the case of an *organon* that captures the Absolute and extracts truth for the sake of reason, then reason would not have the Absolute, but only the elaboration of the Absolute by that instrument, which my reason is. Regardless of how many notes one cares to add, what is known will never be the Absolute; rather, it will be whatever aspect of the Absolute that reason, conceived as the instrument to know the Absolute, has elaborated .

There is another conception by virtue of which reason is not an *instrument*, but the *medium* by which a thing is known. It would analogous to a light by which one sees things and knows them; in this particular case, reason would be the light by which we know the Absolute. But Hegel replies that, in this case, we would not know the Absolute, but just that light; that is, it would no longer be the Absolute.

Regardless of the way we approach the question, we cannot start from separation of reason and the Absolute, whether we

{254} suggest an instrumentalist conception of reason or produce a conception where reason is considered as mediating. In neither case do we reach the Absolute. Hegel could have concluded that then we do not know the Absolute. But what he says is just the opposite: the fact is that there is no such dualism, that the Absolute is its own truth. Anything that is Absolute is true by being Absolute and inasmuch as it is Absolute; at the same time only the true is Absolute. Here we have a conversion, which is not the conversion of intelligibility with being or the conversion of truth with unity or otherness. It is something more: not conversion, but the simultaneous radical and unitary constitution of the thing with my knowledge about it. In other words, the result will be that my knowledge of the Absolute—truth—is not the truth about the Absolute, but is what is absolutely true, truth in its absolute characteristic.

This is fine, as long as Hegel tells us what "simultaneous" is. That is the second step.

What is "simultaneous"?

In order to answer this question, Hegel examines the problem with brevity and precision from two perspectives. On the one hand, he looks from the viewpoint of the thing, that is, the Absolute; on the other, from the viewpoint of what my certainties and my certain knowledge are with respect to that Absolute.

Let us take the question from the viewpoint of the certainties. When do we say that my certainty is true, i.e., that I have knowledge or a certainty that is authentic, true, and corresponds exactly to what it has to be as knowledge? The answer is clear: it is when that certainty in fact corresponds in its internal structure to the concept that we have of what true knowledge has to be.

Let us examine the question from the viewpoint of things. When {255} do we possess or say we possess the absolute truth with respect to something? It is when that thing is actually authentic in the sense that corresponds to its own essence. But then, the essence in this case is the concept.

Regardless of how we view the question we come to the same conclusion, viz. the intrinsic unity between certainty and reality. That is, the formal structure of truth as Absolute *is* the concept. The two moments are identical; in the concept there is an identity between certainty and truth (*zwishen Gewissheit und Wahrheit*), as Hegel says constantly in all his works. True certainty is true because it gives me what an object that manifests itself in its truth must give me. The object is true precisely because it corresponds to its concept. In both cases, the unitary identity of truth and certainty is the concept. Therefore to say that simultaneously their truth and their certainty belong to things is equivalent to saying that absolute truth is the concept. For Hegel, the concept is formally the *verum transcendentale*, transcendental truth. Precisely because of that transcendental characteristic, we have simultaneously the truth of my certainty and the truth of the thing. The concept is the identity of certainty and truth, and this identity in the concept is what, for Hegel, defines reason.

Reason is simultaneously reason for (explanation of) the identity of the thing and reason for (explanation of) my knowing it. It is not an *organon*, but the seat of conceptualization, of the concept. Consequently, for Hegel, reason is the absolute truth itself, the All itself in its truth. Here it is not the reason "of" the Absolute, but of "the" absolute reason, which is a different thing. As he says in his *Phenomenology of the Spirit*, the concept is the certainty {256} that reason is the whole reality.[2] This affirmation may seem somewhat extravagant, and though perhaps it is not, it still needs a clarification.

Hegel tells us, as we have just seen, that reason is the whole of reality, that is, it is simultaneously the concept of a thing and my certainty of its truth. Then Hegel must tell us what he understands by "concept." What concept is he talking about? Afterwards, he must explain what it means to say that the concept is the reality, not only of a thing, but also of my certainty.

After this, no one will find it strange that for Hegel a *concept is not a representation*. In all philosophy up to and including that of Kant, the idea that concepts are intellectual representations of things was still circulating. Clearly, a representation is a second presentation of a thing that was already present in a first presentation, and returns to be present in a second act. Thus the intelligible and intellectual re-presentation of something would be a concept. However, this has nothing to do with the Hegelian idea of concept, because for Hegel it is not the case of knowledge *about* the Absolute, but of absolute knowledge in itself. Again, therefore, what does Hegel understand by "concept"?

Let us orient ourselves in traditional philosophy. Traditional philosophy (primarily, but not exclusively medieval) always distinguished, in concepts, two distinct and perfectly separable aspects. On the one hand, we apply "concept," for example, to a circumference, and we say we have the *concept of circumference*. Here, "concept" means "objective concept," what the terminus of the intellectual act is whereby we conceive what a circumference is. Obviously, this {257} objective concept is identical in all men, in all that understand these words and agree about their thinking, so that all geometers of the planet essentially have the same concept of circumference. This is what a scholastic would call *conceptus objectivus*, but the term also has another sense in traditional philosophy. With respect to this second sense, a concept is the act of conceiving, hence it is no longer the case of an objective concept, but of the act by which my mind is conceiving the objective concept. This is what scholastics called the *formal concept*, which obviously is multiplied in each mind and each time a mind produces that same objective concept. So we have, then, two completely different things: one is the formal concept and the other the objective concept. The circumference is not part of me, but the act of conceiving it is definitely part of me. Therefore, is Hegel talking about *objective concepts* or *formal concepts*?

The truth is that he is not talking about either because he is talking about *both* of them simultaneously. Here is where the question may appear to be quite artificial but perhaps is not so. Suárez, who is not a Hegelian, when talking about the concept of being at the beginning of his metaphysics, distinguishes between the *formal concept* and the *objective concept*. He affirms that we do not know things except through objective concepts; and while some can be known through formal concepts—and by just one formal concept—knowing in that way is something exclusive to God.[3] Hence, this idea is going to provide unity to Hegel's thought. It is not a case of {258} taking the formal concept on one hand and the objective concept on the other; but the objective concept insofar as it emerges from the type and the act of the formal concept. This is what Hegel calls—at least this is the way I interpret his phrase—"conceiving thinking" or "conceiving thinking" (*das begreiffendes Denken*).[4] Conceiving thinking is formal thinking, not simply as act of my mind, but as producing the objective terminus, the objective emerging out of the formal. Conceiving thinking is, at the same time, what is going to draw us nearer to God. We are dealing with objective concepts, of what objects are, insofar as they emerge out of my conceiving activity. Because of this, for Hegel to conceive is not simply a formal act of the subject, nor a creation *ex nihilo* of things. "To conceive is the activity of the concept itself."[5] This is what we are talking about: not that a subject has the activity of conceiving, but that the concept, taken unitarily, is in itself a living thing, whose activity is precisely the conceiving (*das begreiffendes Denken*).

Concepts are, for Hegel, something provided with life, each one partially, but authentically. Hegel does not plunge into the depths of the great formal abstractions, the supreme abstractions; that is to observe Hegel's philosophy from the outside, the saddest thing that can happen to any philosophy. For Hegel, concepts are living units, moments of an organism that is molding itself precisely in its conceiving characteristic, in its characteristic of *begreiffende*. Hegel is the master who has given life to concepts, {259} who has seen concepts as life, as vital units.

The concept, in its unity, is just what Hegel understands by "reason." Reason is the life of the concept, a life that does not consist only in enunciating abstract characteristics of the apprehending act, but in something more radical and profound, what Hegel calls "the exertion of the concept" (*Die Anstrengung des Begriffes*). The concept has an inner "exertion," but in order to reach what?

This is the second moment of the question. Hegel must tell us not only what he understands by "concept," but also what he understands by *is* when we say that the concept "is" the Absolute and the reality. What does Hegel understand by "being"?

Classical logic says that a judgment has a clear structure. We have the basic scheme of judgment (prescinding from subtleties or complications), which is the used by Hegel, viz. S is P. Every judgment has a subject and a predicate; and their unity—regardless of the type of this unity—is affirmed precisely by the copula "is," A is B, S is P. Putting it this way, the P of the predicate (for example, "the dog is alive") represents a property that the subject has, and just by virtue of the subject having it, the understanding—which places itself outside the subject, outside the thing and makes concepts of it—predicates the content of this concept of the subject. Thus, life is a property (however profound and radical) of the dog, but still a property of his, the dog has it. This, Hegel says, is a logical proposition.

However, this is a truth that is only penultimate, because the ultimate truth is more profound. The ultimate truth is not that the dog is living, but just the reverse, that the living, *hic et nunc*, is this dog. This is what Hegel calls a "speculative proposition." Here the terms are inverted, because it is not the case {260} that the subject has a predicate, but that the subject is what it is thanks precisely to the fact that *the predicate determines the subject in its internal characteristics*. The subject is not something that externally receives some predicates together with the objective contents of the concepts, but something that is duly conformed by the predicate, which classical logic attributes to it from the outside. The speculative proposition, Hegel says, is strictly the reverse of the logical proposition. The logical proposition starts from a subject and attributes a predicate to it. On the other hand, the speculative proposition places itself fully in the predicate and tries to find out, by an internal motion of the predicate—the life of the concept—how it constitutes the subject, the dog I have right in front of me.

Some may think this is something very artificial. True, but those like us who are not philosophers in the Hegelian style and who are familiar with the history of philosophy recall, for example, that St. Thomas said that the transcendentals do not divide up into pieces in order to become part of things, but meld with the things. For Hegel, that is the case for every concept and not just for the transcendentals. In order for the object that I have in front of me to be in a particular way, there needs to be a melding of other concepts and other determinations.

Let us not think that philosophies are monstrosities. Philosophies are not made by individuals who make mistakes with their reasoning. Any mistakes occur at the point of departure, not in the stage where the ideas are worked out. For Hegel, in a logical proposition all the physical and transcendental properties of a subject are gathered in a predicate that is predicated with truth of that subject. But a speculative proposition has the meaning that what is called "subject" comprises something by virtue of its predicates. These predicates do not have the character of being property of a subject, but of {261} being the "conformed" life of the subject's reality. The transcendental order, which in St. Thomas appears as the order of the *magis communia*, of the most common characteristics of being *qua* created, in Kant acquires the character of *constituting* principle of the object for my intellection as such. But in Hegel it is something much more radical: the *conforming* order of things *qua* things. Therefore the subject is the result of the predicate. The subject is not *sub*-predicated, i.e., something beneath the predicate, but is constituted by the predicate itself.

From this point on, Hegel can tell us something that has always seemed like an exaggeration: "the truth of the concrete is always the general." Now we can understand it. The concrete is precisely constituted by the internal life of concepts, by their mutual syntheses, and the truth of what is concrete resides squarely in that which we call "general." So Hegel affirms definitively that truth is always what is general.

As we can see, reason is but the life of the concept, and the concept as *begreiffendes Denken* is that which simultaneously involves the reality and the certainty of things. This is reason, towards which Hegel orients the Absolute, in order to constitute therein transcendental truth. Reason is not something extrinsic to the Absolute, but on the contrary, is the radical and ultimate way in which the Absolute is such, i.e., is absolutely true.

With this we have somewhat expounded the goal of *Phenomenology of the Spirit*. But we still have to ask how Hegel arrives at this notion of reason. That is the third point.

As affirmed in the first line of *Phenomenology of the Spirit*, Hegel starts from consciousness. Man is aware of some things: he knows them, faces them, perceives them and {262} is aware (*ist*

bewust); he has a conciousness (*Bewust-sein*). Conciousness is
something each and every one of us has, and is the first thing
Hegel uses to investigate what reason is. Let us say, then, that
"consciousness" means more or less being aware of something,
i.e., it is knowing *qua* being aware. To be sure, this is not easy to
maintain, particularly in the case of Hegel, because he alone of all
philosophers since Descartes not only will not identify consciousness with reason, but also split them radically. However, we are
still going to attempt the way of consciousness and try to reach
reason.

The difference is going to be that reason, as seat or if you will
as expression of the truth of what a thing is, does not appear as
such in consciousness. It appears simply as a consciousness that
I as an individual have "of" the thing. And precisely because it is
not absolute knowledge, absolute reason, but only the way something appears to consciousness, Hegel just calls it a "phenomenon," the analysis of which is taken up in his *Phenomenology*.[6] It
is a phenomenon, a φαίνεσθαι, precisely because it appears in the
form of consciousness.[7] In order for this to be so, consciousness
must undergo an experience (*Erfahrung*), of which we have to ask
what is its *object*, what is the *form* in which this experience is realized, and what is the *process* of this experience. {263}

In the first place, there is the *object* of the experience, as we
have just indicated. In my consciousness I have knowledge "of"
things that are there in a dual form. My knowledge of what they
are appears there radically under the form of consciousness. But
the object Hegel searches for is not the form in which this absolute knowledge appears. Through the form in which it appears, he
is trying to arrive at the φαινόμενον, the φαίνεσθαι, at what absolute knowledge is itself as true absolute knowledge. This concerns
being and not the way absolute knowledge appears; it concerns
the knowledge of knowledge, the knowledge that not only involves
the unity of the thing and certainty as a concept, but also knows
itself in that unity.

In the second place, the way Hegel seeks to accomplish this is
to submit consciousness to a kind of progressive development of
what it is *qua* consciousness. This submission is what Hegel calls
the "dialectic of experience" (*Dialetik der Erfahrung*) because it is a
dialectic of how this absolute knowledge continues to appear in
the different forms of consciousness, until it reaches the point of
knowing itself as absolute knowledge. Needless to say, this dialectic is not what we find in the *Logic*, which is not a dialectic of how
knowledge appears, but the internal and constitutive dialectic of
reason itself and of knowledge as such. Putting it briefly, what
Hegel makes here is an experience, to enable us to understand

through experience the configuration that the whole of consciousness as such acquires as a manifestation of absolute
knowledge. This internal dialectic, this dialectic of experience, is
not a dialectic of different acts of consciousness, but the complete
development of consciousness as a *Gestalt*, in its total configuration, with analytic phases, and of how it is shaped into different
forms, with some necessarily emerging from others. In {264} each
form the entire consciousness is always present, but always with
different forms.[8]

In the third place, Hegel describes the process by which some
forms of consciousness emerge from others in six points.

a) Let us start from the most trivial, from consciousness. We
have "consciousness-of," for example, this glass of water. Here is
the glass of water; I am aware that this glass of water exists. I
have a series of perceived objects endowed with more or less rich
properties, duly organized, etc. Here is the object I have in front of
my consciousness, and my knowledge of it consists, so far, in being aware that it is actually there and has some particular properties.

b) But through an internal process that internal configuration
of consciousness can fall back upon itself; this is *reflection*
(*Sebstbewusstsein*). Then, consciousness discovers itself {265} as
self-consciousness. In self-consciousness things do not appear at
all, only my thoughts about them, that of which consciousness in
the previous phase became aware. Now I appear with my
thoughts, only I. That is the control of self-consciousness, the
control of the *I* in which philosophy, from Descartes to Kant, had
centered all philosophical knowledge. For Hegel, this is something
of the second or third order, because actually, in what does this *I*
consist? In having itself as object. I have my thoughts; I am an *I*
that has my thoughts, my certainties, my possible doubts. Then
the *I* appears as an object, indeed, but as an object of self-
consciousness, in the same way that this glass of water appears
as an object of the direct consciousness. This is precisely the "rei-
fication" of the *I*. What can we say about this *I*, constituted as
such an "object"? We can say everything that the philosophies
riding on apperception have said, for example those of Leibniz
and Kant, viz. that it is an *I* which accompanies all the representations and remains identical in all of them. Were we to remove
from that *I* all the concretion of the acts that are riding on it, what
would we have left? Purely and simply the radical and general
form of the identity of the object as such. That is the philosophy
of Fichte. As Hegel tells us, Fichte makes his whole philosophy
start from that identity, that *A* is *A*, the *I* is identical to itself. By
means of a very long process that fills many volumes of his work,

what Fichte wants is to obtain the whole world from this identity. But what is really happening is that in each of the divisions Fichte makes, the great partition is becoming wider without ever reconquering the unity postulated at the beginning, simply because that unity is vague and formal. It is a formalist vagueness, because we must not forget that from the very beginning *I* with my thoughts {266} not only have thoughts, which are mine, but with them I know the thing; and inasmuch as I know the thing they are of it, since I know it as truth. In my self-consciousness I discover that the certainty, that the *I*, not only consists in things being themselves and the *I* being one more thing itself, but also that in the measure in which things are known by the *I*, so they are for me.

c) Consciousness showed itself as self-consciousness; now it shows itself as unity of certainty and truth about things. This is the third stage, *Vernunft*. Reason is the way absolute knowledge appears within self-consciousness, or more properly, at the border of self-consciousness. Thought, reason, is not consciousness, rather consciousness is only a mode of manifestation of reason. Hegel tells us that this identity between certainty and truth is the essence of reason.

d) Nevertheless, this identity is not lifeless. It seems as if on one side we have the object—the thing, which is in itself—and on the other the *I*—which would be itself and for itself. And there will always be minds capable of creating a great abstract concept, which in one way or another would cover both. But that is not the case. For Hegel, it is a living unit, a real life in which the possible duality between certainty and truth emerges from the unitary nature of the concept and from its inner life. This is precisely what reason (*Vernunft*) is.

e) Reason, when it appears, allows a fifth step to take place because that reason is the inner life of the concept. Inasmuch as it is life, it is truly spirit (*Geist*). This is the next step. Self-consciousness emerges from consciousness, or rather in self-consciousness we are shown knowledge in a fuller way. Out of self-consciousness knowledge has been manifested {267} to us as something that belongs to reason; now reason appears as spirit. Spirit is something whose being is only activity of the self (*ist nur Selbsttätigkeit*); its being is "actuosity"[9] and because of this its being is an absolute process.[10] Being is actuosity, and precisely because of it reason in its ultimate essence is spirit.

f) But, in what does that actuosity of spirit consist? It consists not only in going through the stages we have just recalled here, but in the fact that at the end of these stages the spirit discovers itself in the form of absolute knowledge, and appears in the vari-

ous forms of consciousness. Yet a moment arrives in which reason and spirit somehow have to transcend these forms of appearance and face what the spirit is in reality, viz. absolute knowledge;
they must cross over from the order of phenomena to the order of
being. This is the stage when spirit is the concept of itself (*das
Begreiffen seiner Selbst*). Here it is not the case that absolute
knowledge is already *appearing* in my consciousness, but that
this *is* the knowledge, the truth that we might call "cognizant" (*die
wissende Wahrheit*). For Hegel then, truth is the Absolute; the
Absolute is the {268} concept and the concept is the living spirit
itself. The Absolute, in the end, is spirit.

But what kind of spirit and what kind of reason are we talking
about? This is what Hegel must tell us in the third part; for the
moment, let us not pose this problem. The Absolute is the All (*das
Wahre ist das Ganze*) and this All is in the process of self-
conforming. It does so first in the form of phenomena in various
manifestations within consciousness, which afterwards leads the
All to be discovered in something that formally consists in its own
internal conceptualization.

Consequently, for Hegel the transcendental order is first and
formally a system of concepts; and second, is a principled order.
Except that the principle of the transcendental order is neither
truth (for example, in the sense of Leibniz) nor the "I think" (in the
sense of Kant), but something different, namely, the very life of
the spirit. Such is the principle of the transcendental order. The
conceiving reason is the very essence, the internal structure of
the transcendental order; and the reason that knows itself to be
this is absolute knowledge. We can now understand that reason
is not knowledge of the Absolute, but the very form of the Absolute, the absolute form of the Absolute.

Thus Hegel, reaching the end of this path, of the *Phenomenology of the Spirit*, i.e., reaching the concept of reason, can set forth
a few expressions that taken in isolation may seem dreadful, but
should be understood in context. Hegel tells us, for example, that
being is thinking, i.e., that being means being thought, being
conceived. No thing is more than the way in which it realizes a
concept that, as such, is an act of conceiving thinking. Therefore,
Hegel affirms that the concept as such is being in itself and by
itself. There is no difference at all {269} between *concept* and *being*.
But here we do not refer to an abstract concept, only to that moment or that act of conceiving thinking, a thinking that is conceptually determining the subject, which is properly the object with
which the understanding is concerned.[11] Consequently, Hegel affirms, "In reality, the forms of the concept are the living spirit of
the real",[12] and the real is only that which is true by virtue of

these forms. That is, the real is only that which is conceived this way, because the rest would merely be chaos, not something real. Consequently, emphasizing this point, Hegel says that "logical reason is the substantial or the real".[13] It is the case then, of a vision of being and reality taken simply from the conceiving thinking, from that which conceives being and reality and in which the real is that which is conceived by reason.

Once we have reached this level, and have attained this concept of reason, we have also discovered that the true problem is not in how reason appears in the forms of consciousness. The problem is in something more profound, in the structure of this absolute thinking, and Hegel must now answer the question, what is the internal structure of this order of reason? It will be the second step in the development of Hegel's thought.

II. *Internal structure of reason*

The first step was *Phenomenology of the Spirit*, which led us to the notion of absolute reason. The second step {270} must determine the internal structure of reason and is the subject of *The Science of Logic.*

Here we must repeat some things. The first of the four that I am going to select for my analysis is, from my perspective, the internal structure of reason for Hegel.

The first is what we have just covered, viz. that reason is the unity of the objective and the subjective. It is a unity that, as Hegel has shown us, is not dead but alive. It is not the case that they continue being two (the thing and the subject) and that a more or less universal concept can be elaborated encompassing the thing as well as the subject. That is not the point; rather, we have a living unity because the contrary—this is how Hegel opposes Schelling—would be the philosophy of identity. That would consist in saying that in a radical way nature is the same as spirit, understanding by that sameness that it is something indifferent to nature and spirit. Out of this, Hegel says, nothing can ever result since that is like the night wherein all cats are black. It is not the case of an empty and vacant identity, but of a living unity (*eine lebendig Einheit*), and in that unity the two moments are inseparable. They may be different, but they are inseparable, because in the abstract unity each element continues to be what it is and they are equal (in fact they are different), but their unity and their difference is the internal product of the unity itself. Therefore, that difference is not abolished, but contained within the unity. The unity itself is the one that contains their difference, and their essence precisely consists in differing.

Next we must ask Hegel in what the life of the concept consists. Hegel says that the life of the concept is logos, by which he intends to follow {271} the Greek tradition. Hegel recalls that Aristotle told us (see the chapter on Aristotle) that in the act of true knowledge, in the ἐπιστήμε, from the beginning the thing and the knower are ταυτόν, the same, the logos. The ἐπιστήμε and the ἐπιστητόν, are ταυτόν. What did Aristotle understand by this ταυτόν? Aristotle understood that the perfect actuality of the act of knowledge (ἐντελέχεια) is the presence of the actuality itself in which the thing consists in act. It is a ταυτόν in that order, not a ταυτόν of the reality of the intelligence and of the reality of things. On the contrary, Aristotle expressly says that the εἶναι of what is heard, the εἶναι of the eyes, the εἶναι of the νοῦς is different than what the εἶναι of a bell ringing is. When I listen to a bell ringing, I have an act whose actual ἐντελέχεια on my part is precisely the same as the ἐντελέχεια in which the pure sonority of the thing emitting the sound consists. But Hegel goes much further.

Hegel quickly understands that this Greek ταυτόν means the total unity of the λέγειν and the ὄν, and therefore, Aristotle's logic is a logic of the ὄν, and conversely, Aristotle's ὄν has to necessarily adopt the form of a logos. Aristotle plays some part in Hegel's conception, since we already saw that the transcendental order, the order of being, is not viewed from the logos as something external. Rather, the structure of the λέγειν belongs in one way or another to the structure of the ὄν. It is here, in Hegel, where this idea yields one of its last fruits, by virtue of which Hegel is given the possibility, on the one hand, and is forced, on the other, to incorporate into ontology the doctrine of the ὄν, the moment of the λόγος. Because of this it constitutes for Hegel the very life of the concept, the very structure of absolute reason. {272}

We next proceed to the third moment. This life of reason, this living unity in which the logos consists is a becoming (eine Bewegung) for Hegel. Why and in what does this movement of the logos consist? From a speculative point of view, for Hegel what is conceived is what determines the subject, but never adequately. That is the problem. Hence, the result of the fullest conceptualization of something is always inadequate and insufficient for the constitution of that thing. Consequently, the logos will also have to go back in order to rectify its first positions in one way or another, and to acquire new ones. Is this a doing or an undoing? Hegel will say that it is neither. In all this movement of the logos there is something that remains identical. What is it? Hegel appeals to a comparison: I take an acorn, the acorn is the oak tree, but in a form different from the tree; it is the oak tree, but in a germinal form. Out of the acorn a small shrub begins to grow and flourishes. It is the same as the acorn, but now with another form, and in that way it becomes the oak tree. At first glance it does not resemble the acorn, however, it is the same acorn in another form. It is not the case that now it is and was not before, and the whole process cannot be ignored when we say "oak tree," because the truth *is* the whole. Precisely that which is the same in its apparently different and opposed phases is what the unity and sameness of the logos is. This sameness of the logos is what concerns Hegel the most; it is the internal movement of the concept, which is always an unsustainable movement. What is the reason for this unsustainability, and above all, why does this unsustainability constitute in a positive way the life of the concept and reason?

This is the fourth point. That motion is dialectical. What does Hegel understand by "dialectical"? And {273} what reason are we dealing with? Who has that reason? Is it mine or is it an absolute reason, the divine reason? In fact Hegel says that it is both things at the same time, though not for the reason Leibniz claimed, viz. that human reason is an image of the divine. Rather, it so because ultimately we are not dealing with an image, since substantially human reason *is* divine reason and divine reason *is* human reason. In a certain way, it is clear that divine reason is more than human reason, because it is infinite while human reason is finite. But, in what does the finitude of something consist for Hegel? That is the question.

Hegel tells us thematically in an obscure text—Hegel always says the most important things in obscure texts—of his *Science of Logic*, "Finite things are finite insofar as they do not have in themselves the full reality of their concept," but need other concepts. Hence, for Hegel, the finitude of human reason consists in not being the fullness of that which is involved in the concept of reason. But inasmuch as human reason is a realization, though fragmentary, of that concept, it is the same as divine reason.

For Hegel, there is another profound difference between human reason and divine reason. Human reason is characterized by something that divine reason lacks because it does not need it, namely, consciousness. Divine reason is not conscious; it is absolute reason that knows itself, a thing that in Hegel is always something much more than consciousness. Consciousness is the manifestation of absolute reason, and in this sense human reason, insofar as it manifests itself in its own consciousness, is definitely the manifestation of divine reason. Consequently, it is the case of the same reason, but one that has, so to speak, two moments, one is the absolute {274} of divine reason, and another, the non-absolute of human reason. We shall have to ask in another context what it is that Hegel understands by this non-absolute. Nevertheless, let it be clearly understood that insofar as human reason is reason, any investigation about reason is really and truly an investigation that connects with what absolute reason is, the divine reason.

That is what Hegel understood by reason. Now Hegel must tell us what the internal structure of reason is, in order to explain afterwards how with that internal structure of reason he does not see things simply as something conceived by acts of reason, but finds things in fact real.

This deals with the internal structure of reason. Since this reason, according to what Hegel tells us, is a living reason, the answer will have to center on two points. First, Hegel will have to say in what the formal structure of reason as such consists. Second, he must say in what the internal life consists, i.e., the structure of the internal life of reason.

1. Formal characteristics of reason

Of course, Hegel does not tell us everything in one place, and it will be necessary to review the different levels of his thought, something particularly indispensable since Hegel maintains that in him the Absolute Spirit acquired its first formulation in all of history. Consequently, we have the right to carefully analyze what Hegel understands by reason and what its internal structure is. {275}

A) Living unity

The first characteristic that this reason has is unity, the unity of the objective and the subjective. Otherwise there would be a split between truths on one side, and certainties on the other. Indeed, we are told that this unity is not a dead unity (ist keine tote Einheit), but a living unity (eine lebendige Einheit). Hegel understands by "dead unity" the unity of two terms that, while remaining distinct from each other, can be subsumed by an act of abstraction into a single more or less general concept. For example, with regard to different men we can elaborate the general concept of man; with regard to the diverse living beings, we can elaborate the general concept of living, and so on. This, Hegel says, is a dead unity because it is the subsumption of unities that are separated from each other under a common concept. Viewed from this standpoint, the unity would be the unity so dear to Schelling, the unity of indifference; it would amount to saying that spirit and nature are one, that they are an undifferentiated unity. But Hegel maintains that the objective and the subjective are precisely differentiated and that it is insofar as they are differentiated that they are one.

The living unity consists in the fact that the unity, by its own internal nature, makes the linked terms differ from itself, those terms by which it is distinct and different. This way the unity is not an abstract concept that hovers over each of the separate terms, but just the opposite: it is the unity of the terms, which will never be separated, but are different with a distinction achieved by movement internal to the very unity from which they proceed and in which they are constituted. {276}

But then we shall have to ask Hegel in what this unity consists. That is, from my perspective, the second characteristic of reason.

B) Logicality

Hegel clearly tells us that this unity is the logos. For his contemporaries, the logos was alien to the contents, and logic, considered as the science of the logos, was merely a formal science. Hegel thought that modern logic (in a certain way he was right) was concerned with the forms of the logos, with logical forms regardless of their contents. For example, I say that *A* is *B*, for any *A* and for any *B*. I say that it is universal or particular, regardless of the type of this universality and particularity.

However, for Hegel this is chimerical and incorrect. In the Greek world the logos was not empty of content, but just the opposite. Hegel considers that in one way or another the logos (for example, of Plato or Aristotle) forms part of reality. In Greece logos was the reason for and explanation of the thing. No doubt this is true, except that in Greek there is no term *reason* different from *logos*. Nonetheless let us accept, in this case as in many others, the Hegelian version of the Greek concepts. After all, the philosophy of the nineteenth and twentieth centuries is rich with translations of Greek texts keyed to particular philosophies. Hegel, therefore, tells us that reason is the logos of things, and actually, that "*of*" did have a formal expression in Parmenides and Aristotle, the ταυτόν. In the act of knowing, the actuality of knowing, inasmuch as I know this object, and the actuality of this object insofar {277} as it is an object known by my reason, are just the same, they are ταυτόν, and in that sameness clearly consists its ἀλήθεια, its truth. Of course, Aristotle says that it is a ταυτόν that refers to the ἐντελέχεια of the act of knowing and the ἐντελέχεια of the known *qua* known, and therefore it is outside of ταυτόν as reality properly so-called, the εἶναι of the particular logos and of the particular thing. But then Hegel inverts the terms of the question. He starts from that ταυτόν that the logic and metaphysics of Aristotle established. He sees both terms—the *logos* insofar as it is something that would belong to me, and *the thing* insofar as it has its own reality independently from me—as two moments whose unity is just the ταυτόν. And the ταυτόν is that sameness they possess when reason knows a thing, exhaustively in the case of Hegel, or fragmentarily in the case of Aristotle. Hence, instead of going from things and the logos to their ταυτόν in which the content of the truth would be, Hegel starts from the ταυτόν, and ἀλήθεια. He does this to see how the internal development of this ἀλήθεια and of this reason constitutes the differences between the logos and things. Consequently, Logic as science of the logos belongs formally to Metaphysics. It is logos τοῦ ὄντος and now we understand why: because they are ταυτόν inasmuch as there is truth. If there is no truth, there is nothing that can be done, either with the logos or with the ὄν since they would not belong to each other mutually in a ταυτόν.

Hence, logic is not just a philosophical discipline conjoined with the others, but a structural moment of reality itself. It is the structural moment of the concept, involving therein these two dimensions: subjective reason, and objective reality. Logic is simultaneously logic of the thing and logic of my own reason, of my own logos. This {278} is clearly the truth, it is the ταυτόν. The living unity of reason is, for Hegel, truth as concept, as ταυτόν.

C) Movement

We can still prod Hegel in order to ask him in what movement consists, not just as a living unity, but as a living experience. Since we are dealing with thought that is quite central to the whole of his metaphysics, Hegel's expressions multiply. The life of the logos does not consist in being a combination of λόγοι; it does not consist in reasoning. Quite properly he warns against the excesses of reasoning. The life of the logos is something different. As we have seen in the speculative proposition, which for Hegel is the conceiving thinking (*begreiffendes Denken*), we are trying to see how the activity of the concept, which we express with a predicate, is really that which in an active way constitutes the subject. In the case of a dog, life taken in the abstract (with the predicates we would need to add) constitutes that canine reality which I have in front of my eyes.

We can see that the life of the logos is a movement, but not the movement of combining reasoning processes, but the internal movement of constituting and conforming reality, starting from determinations that, insofar as as they are in the predicate, are in some way prior to its reality. Because of that, the movement Hegel speaks about is the one that constitutes the proper and formal life of the logos.

Whose motion is it? Is it a motion of my thinking as different from the object or of the object as different from thinking? {279} No, it is a motion of the concept, and therefore, is simultaneously a motion of the object and of the logos itself. It is a motion of the conceiving thinking.

Continuing along this line we can ask Hegel why there is such a movement. Is it simply a postulate, something arbitrary? Hegel will tell us that if I enunciate a predicate of a subject in our everyday logic, it turns out that this predicate is not enough to constitute the subject. To say that the living thing *hic et nunc* is a dog is true provided that this "to say" has millions of predicates between living thing and the particular dog I have in front of me. Therefore Hegel would be quite ready to say that, in the end, every judgment, from this point of view, involves a contradiction. Because on one hand I affirm that the living thing *hic et nunc* is a dog, but on the other, that the dog is many other things, which a mere living thing is not. In a certain way this would negate what the dog is as a living dog. Can we then concur with what has been said many times, that what constitutes the internal motor of thinking, of the conceiving thinking, is contradiction? I have never shared that opinion, but not because Hegel did not say it many times and in widely quoted texts. Indeed this makes us think seriously about it and also to consider that in Hegel's philosophy, thematically, above all in the concepts, there is something like the principle of contradiction. But then, Hegel would never admit this; every concept necessarily involves movement, self-movement if you will, by its very reason of conceptualization, insofar as it is concept. Why and how, if it is not contradiction?

The truth is that underlying contradiction and prior to it, there is a moment of the logos, of the movement of the logos, which is the one that constitutes the motive power, the internal movement of the logos. The fact is that, in the end, the logos is constitutively {280} restless, the restlessness (*ist die Unruhe*) of reason. Why is the concept restless? Simply because it does not fully realize that which is; in other words, no system of predicates can adequately and totally constitute the reality of the subject from the point of view of the speculative proposition. Hence reason is in constant motion because it is the thought of conceiving thinking, which never reaches the final terminus of what is conceived and its conceptualization.

So when Hegel says that the life of reason is movement, he is not talking about the multitude of concepts, about each by itself and each as an example of a concept. That is not Hegel's thought. Hegel's thought is that the multitude of concepts does not represent anything but aspects of just one thing which is conceiving, *the* concept (in the singular). This is the motive force. In what measure and in what form can this involve a contradiction?

It involves a contradiction the moment we consider this movement as finished, fixed, reaching a state of repose. In that case, we would have something alive—let us say a dog—that would be nothing but something alive, which is a contradiction because there are many living things (as well as non-living things) that are not dogs. It ceases to be a contradiction in the measure in which movement continues, because the contradiction is the abstraction that a movement makes of itself in order to fix in static terms that which it intrinsically is: the dynamic unity through which the concept conceives its own subject as conceiving thinking. The reality of conceiving is a movement that constitutes a process and in that process there is an internal unity. Let us consider an example; we referred above to the acorn and the oak tree. Hegel will say—and this is an idea firmly established in his thought—that the {281} oak tree "refutes" the acorn, for example. There is the form of acorn, there is the form of flower, there is the form of oak, there is the form of tree, and it is true that each one "refutes" the previous one. But ultimately there is only one thing, which to clarify Hegel's thought I have called the "oakhood process."[14] And this process is the same one that produces the acorn, the flower, and the tree. In that dynamic unity there is no refutation whatsoever and what is true is the whole, in particular, its process. Its conceiving thinking (*begreiffendes Denken*) consists in just that. Indeed, the terms in which there is an apparent contradiction only arise when they are considered as separate products and cleaved from the movement in which they exist, and with respect to which they would only be abstractions, as we shall immediately see.

Nevertheless, we may still consider this is not enough and ask Hegel in what the entire structure of this movement consists.

D) Dialectic

It is not enough to say there is a conceiving thinking that conceives things. How does it conceive them?

Let us start with an example, the example with which Hegel's *Science of Logic* begins, and we shall see what we must say about it; this will allow us to make a less arduous presentation. Hegel says that I think with my logos, with my reason, and I have the concept of being; if I think what being is I find out it is not this, not that; that it is not heavy, not hot, not red, not sonorous, not triangular, not good, not bad..., so what is it? It is absolute indetermination; {282} in other words, to think about being is really equivalent to think of nothing. Because of this, Hegel says that being and nothingness are the same. However, this is impossible, which means that the concept wherein I have conceived being has to reassume (or absorb), in one form or another, the moment we call "nothing." The "result" of this resumption—let us use the term "result" at this point in order not to complicate matters—is becoming. This movement is what Hegel calls "dialectic." The structure of conceiving movement is just dialectic.

Hegel now must say precisely what is understood by that dialectic. The life of the logos is dialectic. What does "dialectic" mean here?

Clearly, dialectics is not what it was, for example, during the medieval period or even prior to Kant. Dialectics was a kind of discussion of the reasons (δια-λέγειν) through which everyone expressed his own point of view, his own reasons, and one side would maintain the "pro" while the other the "contra." It is said that Abelard was the first one to introduce dialectic in this sense—ut sic et non—within the traditional philosophy of the Middle Ages. But in Hegel dialectic is not contraposition of reasons, it is not contraposition of being and nothingness because in every contraposition of reasons there is always the possibility—assuming that there is a sufficiently powerful reason or explanation—to show that only one of the positions is the truth. The intention of classical dialectics presupposes that one of the possibilities is true and the other is not, and it is a case of *eliminating* the latter. However, this is not what happens in Hegel's dialectic.

A second concept of dialectic is the one Hegel inherited with all the weight of Kant's philosophy behind it. We saw that in Kantian philosophy the intent of speculative transcendental metaphysics proceeds not by practical reason, but as {283} Kant says, by speculative curiosity, and leads to insoluble antinomies. For example, one can argue *ad infinitum* about whether the world is finite or infinite, whether it had a beginning in time, and whether matter is infinitely divisible. This is dialectic, and for Kant dialectics is formally antinomic. However, this is not the concept Hegel has of dialectic. In the earlier and merely formal example of dialectic, we had the underlying idea that one of the terms is false and has to be eliminated in favor of the other one that is true. In that case, the purpose of dialectic would be to do something to get rid of the contraposition of reasons. On the other hand, the Kantian dialectic is a kind of intellectual attitude confronting the outcome of the logos, confronting the outcome of reason by pure concepts leading to a contradiction, which leads to an antinomy that cannot be resolved. The antinomy is something in which one remains trapped.

But Hegel neither eliminates nor remains in the antinomy and precisely here is the origin of the Hegelian dialectic. He does not remain in it, but rather in a certain way he steps out of its terms. Steps out, towards what? We shall soon discover. That "stepping out" or "leaving" is what Hegel expresses with his term *Aufhebung*. The contradiction is *aufgehoben*. What does the Hegelian *Aufheben* mean here? In order to answer it will be necessary to ask the following three questions:

(1) What is the beginning of that stepping out?

(2) What are the moments of that stepping out?

(3) What is the internal structure of that stepping out?

In the first place, *what is the beginning of that stepping out?* Is contradiction the beginning of that stepping out? Yes and no, as we have just seen. Contradiction is the expression of the unsustainable in the determinations of reason, and it is unsustainability by inadequacy. Here the moment of non-being intervenes, the μὴ ὄν {284} as Plato would call it; that negativity of the real, as Hegel calls it, which forces reason to continue its conceptive process. It is a negativity that consists in reality not being adequately conceived by the predicates of reason; and Hegel calls this "the enormous power of the negative" (*Die ungeheurige Macht des Negative*). Contradiction is nothing but the radical expression of that restlessness, but it is not what formally constitutes the movement of conceiving thinking, as we have seen. Contradiction only appears when the steps become static moments, and therefore appear as sufficient realities each one in itself. Let us recall that this is somewhat similar to what happened with the paradoxes of Zeno. Zeno thinks that we cannot go from here to there in a continuum because first I have to pass through the middle point. Being a continuum, before passing through the middle point I must pass through another middle point between this point and the initial point, and so on. Since the continuum is divisible *ad infinitum* I would never be able to take the first step. This is true if we assume the continuum is a series of pillars and assume we take a first step from here to there; the second from there to the next, and so on. But the continuum is not that, it is precisely the opposite; we just go through without stopping on the middle point, which is clearly passed over. Zeno's paradox appears when the continuity of the motion is converted into an addition of each of the points that constitute that trajectory. Indeed, the same thing happens here, the contradiction only appears the moment I consider as quiescent and static endpoints those things that are only but aspects and moments of the movement.

After this is understood we have a question: *what are the internal and structural moments of this stepping out from the restlessness or the* {285} *contradiction?* We can use the term "contradiction" in order to simplify the problem, because after what we have just said there will be no confusion. All history of philosophy texts say that Hegel "put" as components the *thesis*, the *antithesis* and the *synthesis*; in accordance with this, there is a thesis, afterwards we have something contrary to it, viz. an antithesis, and there is a third moment, which is the synthesis. It is at the synthesis that Hegel actually aims with the term *aufheben*, "stepping out of." Now we must make this term more precise because it does not have a only one meaning in German, and here the difficulty resides.[15] In the first place, there is a meaning according to which *aufheben* consists in eliminating or removing whatever is in the way. This is what happens in the logical dialectic; if there are two postures, the thesis and the antithesis, it is assumed that the one with the right reason removes the other, and in that sense *aufheben* means *tollere*, to remove. But, as we have seen, this is not what Hegel intends in his dialectic.

Aufheben has a second meaning. If, for example, there is incompatibility between two functions, *aufheben* would consist in suppressing the incompatibility, and with this the two terms would be preserved in the new situation. In this case *aufheben* does not mean *tollere*; rather it would mean *conservare*. But this is still not the full sense of the Hegelian dialectic, which goes beyond that.

The third meaning of *aufheben* is to raise, to lift up, *heben auf*. It is precisely *elevare*, the sense of "elevating," and here is where the "surmounting" resides. This is the moment of the Hegelian dialectic, *aufheben* as "to surmount." The two terms, the thesis and the antithesis, {286} are not eliminated in the sense of *tollere*, nor are they preserved purely and simply in the sense of the Kantian quiescent antinomy; instead they remain after having been surmounted. Where? Precisely in the synthesis. *Aufheben* is to surmount; we step out of the antithesis with respect to the synthesis by surmounting.

Then the third question appears. It is necessary for Hegel to tell us *what he understands by that synthesis*. It is not so simple to explain what a synthesis is. Probably this idea came to Hegel from Kantian philosophy. Against Leibniz' position, Kant has used *ad nauseam* the idea that reason is essentially and constitutively synthetic. But what does Hegel understand by "synthesis" and what did Kant understand by it?

Independently of Kant—we shall immediately return to this point—one thing is clear, viz. that Hegel's synthesis is not a deduction. It is not the case of establishing two premises, a thesis and a synthesis, and then drawing a conclusion from them, whatever it may be. That would not be *aufheben*, but to deduce, and the Hegelian dialectic is not a deductive synthesis, rather in a certain way it is just the opposite.

The opposite has been part of philosophy since the time of Plato. When Plato talked about the knowledge of ideas he understood that ideas separated from things can be studied intellectually in two ways. One way is to take ideas as the suppositions on which the real world rests. Then one tries to see—here the deduction appears—by means of a διανοεῖν, and by a kind of review of knowledge through these ideas, what the structure of real things in the world is, the structure of the world that can be known through the senses. Here the ideas are precisely ὑπόθεσις, that is, hypothesis, not in the logical sense of scientific hypothesis, but as primary suppositions through which {287} the real world is understood. However, internal problems of the Platonic metaphysics—this is not the place to consider them—force Plato to move to a second point of view. After all, ideas are many, although Plato is unable to say how many or which ones, but certainly many. Then, we can think about things, not by taking ideas as points of departure in order to understand them, but just the opposite: to think about multiple ideas as problematic terms of the ideal constitution of things. In this case, we are not descending from ideas to things, but of returning or ascending from ideas to that which constitutes the supreme reason for the ideas, to something that will be absolute. In the *Republic* of Plato there is the idea of τοῦ ἀγαθοῦ, the idea of the good. In some other dialogs the question is handled differently—it makes no difference—, but it is always ascending from ideas to that which constitutes the ultimate reason for that absolute characteristic they possess. This is what Plato called dialectic, διαλέγειν; it is not a dialectic that descends from ideas to things, but the difficult process that, starting with some ideas, leads us through these ideas to that which is absolute, to that which constitutes their primary and radical unity. The dialectic here is ascensional and not descendent.

We might think that this is the Hegelian dialectic. Yes, but only as long as Kant's synthetic reason does not interfere. Indeed, Kant not only would not deny what we have just said, but explicitly hints at it in the last part of *The Critique of Pure Reason*. However, Kant's synthesis, for the most part, especially with respect to what concerns us here, is exactly what the term "synthesis" means, viz. a reunification; in other words, the unity of synthesis is the result of the reunification of the synthesized things. Nevertheless, the Hegelian ascent does not share that characteristic. It is not {288} a synthesis by association or by reunification, but a regression with a completely different characteristic. This is because it is not a synthesis that *results from* the terms that it synthesizes, but the germinal and *prior* unity that has expanded naturally into two terms, which are the terms that quiescently appear to us as antithetical. It is an *originative and originating* synthesis. This is the reason why Hegel's synthesis is not a synthesis that results from anything, but an originative and starting synthesis. We are not dealing with a kind of trick by which this

unity is hidden under the terms, but that these terms are absolutely necessary. For what? So that the originative synthetic unity
can formally exist as such a synthetic and originative unity. In
other words, dialectical thinking is "circular thinking," and here
Hegel would repeat what he told us at the beginning of his philosophy: the Absolute is at the same time beginning and resulting
end. The synthesis is the primary principle of the diversity of the
terms, thesis and antithesis. It is through the thesis and antithesis that the synthesis returns. Returns to what? To result in a
synthesis that did not exist before? No, to be more fully *what it
was before*, to be precisely *a result of itself*. Consequently, the
synthesis, a dialectical movement of Hegelian thought consisting
in being the beginning and the resulting end, is an idea that, although not formulated precisely in this way, really constitutes the
quintessence of Hegel's whole metaphysics and whole philosophy.
The dialectical movement is an self-conformation, a kind of enormous self-morphism in which a form is self-conforming itself.
Therefore it is not the result of those terms in which it conforms
itself; but without them it would not have the fullness of what it
actually is.

That is why Hegel applies here the Aristotelian concept of
ἐντελέχεια; it is the τέλος, but a τέλος that was already included in
the ἀρχή. Therefore, the dialectical movement only {289} explicates
and exposes the "entelechial" characteristic, the characteristic of
ἐντελέχεια, which has the fullness of the origin of synthesis. Thus
Hegel's conceiving thinking is not linear, but essentially circular,
cyclic thinking; and in this resides the self-morphic characteristic
of everything that his thinking contains.

Because of this, the essence of dialectic is the type of movement that characterizes absolute reason. We must understand
what this movement of absolute reason is. It is just that constant
position of the different terms, which by differentiation of the
unity—here the first characteristic arises—begin appearing as
thesis and antithesis yet remain *aufgehoben*, that is, remain
surmounted. Surmounted in what? In that from which they never
separated, that is, in the primary and original unity from which
they proceeded. This is why Hegel tells us that being and nothingness are two abstractions; the only thing that is concrete is the
occurrence. Movement itself is the movement in which the Absolute consists.

All this is rather monotonous, but I believe it necessary in order to understand what this man attempted, one of the few in history capable of living with the experience of conceiving thinking.
Hegel must have lived a life of pure continuous joy, because at
every moment he must have had the intimate, unquestionable

fruit of intellective knowing; that he made some errors is a different question.

Having said in what the structural characteristic of reason consists, we now must ask Hegel about the structural characteristic of the dialectic movement. {290}

2. The process character of reason. From being to idea.

Hegel tells us that the structural development of reason is logic, which for him is not a philosophical discipline alongside the others, but the very essence of the logos, the essence of reason *qua* absolute reason. Because of this, logic is not a *science of* the Absolute, but *is* the absolutely Absolute, the absolute form of the Absolute. The Absolute, as we shall see, can assume very diverse forms; but the Absolute will always be the Absolute, which does not mean that logic always knows it. To know the Absolute as Absolute is not to have before my logos a thing that is the Absolute, but that the Absolute acquires that full form of identity with itself which absolute "knowledge" is. That is why Hegel says that logic is nothing but exposition of the spirit of God.

Therefore when we ask what the Absolute is, for Hegel there is only one way to reply: to expound logic *per longum et latum*. Logic *is* the exposition, the answer to the question of what the Absolute is. Of course, this logic has to address the fact that it has a beginning, a development, and a final point.

In what does the beginning (*Anfang*) consist? The beginning can be extrinsic to a thing; but Hegel tells us that something cannot be expounded in the usual way when we are forced to assume a starting point that perhaps is extrinsic to what we are talking about. On the contrary, Hegel understands by "beginning" that particular start corresponding to the principial and intrinsic characteristic. We should *start* from that, which is the very *beginning* of things. This is more complicated than the former. It presupposes a search for the very beginning of thinking, of the {291} conceiving thinking (*des begreiffenden Denkens*). Since the logical is something that belongs to this conceptual thinking we can say that it is pure knowing (*ein reines Wissen*).[16] Then, it will be necessary to ask what it is. In what does that first step of pure thinking consist?

Hegel expounds this question from different angles. For example, the first step, which is the one he is concerned with, consists in saying that reason (*Vernunft*), conceiving thinking, conceives something that is. This is just being. We have already seen how this eventually leads to saying that being is the same as nothingness. This is not because they are formally identical (Hegel never said this), but because they are the two motives that remain surmounted (*aufgehoben*) or were surmounted precisely in their concretion, which is becoming. Being and nothingness are contradictories taken as separated terms, something that never happens in the logos because there they are only moments of something superior and primary, which is the becoming. And in fact, Hegel tells us that it is sufficient to think that being is not yet a determination, and in that sense it is nothingness. We could also begin with nothingness; however, it would not then be the nothingness that is simply nothing, but the nothingness of Creation, a nothingness out of which something is going to emerge, out of which being is going to emerge—in other words, a nothingness ordered towards being. In the end, regardless how we take the question we find that being and nothingness are the two concrete moments of something unique, which is the becoming, "the becoming is the first concrete thought, and therefore, the first concept with respect to which being and nothingness are empty abstractions".[17] Hegel {292} remains, therefore, in the dialectic of being and non-being, in the internal and dialectical concretion of becoming. By this same procedure he is going to bring out out of this dialectic everything that has been called "metaphysics," "ontology," and "classical metaphysics," for which Hegel uses the Kantian expression "the metaphysics of the objective concept," although applied to a different object. Here metaphysics strictly speaking is not Kant's transcendent metaphysics, but ontology. Through a route that we shall not cover here, we get to a point in which the whole world, viz. being, essence, reflection, the set of objective forms and the set of objective concepts, appear in a subjective way in the form of subjective concept. Only formal logic has taken this up as something different from reality.

From the viewpoint of the dialectic, what does Hegel understand by the appearing of the subjective world? Hegel is very clear and very thematic, and never starts from a dualism, but follows the dialectical movement; and if the subjective concept appears it is because of an internal and dialectical movement of the objective concept. This internal and dialectical motion is something very precise and particular; it is interiorization, the concept is interiorized. The process of "interiorization" is called *Er-innerung*, which has the general meaning of "remembrance," but for Hegel it does not have that meaning. For him it has the etymological sense of interiorization. In that interiorization there is a moment of remembrance, and here Hegel might appeal to the Platonic ἀνάμνεσις, that to know is to remember. He might do this because in that interiorization the subjective concept manifests itself as remembrance, in other words, as something that it originally {293} was, though the subjective concept does not yet apprehend it in its totality. Because of this, it must continue the dialectical movement until this concept reaches its final terminus.

This final *terminus* is just the concept, which knows itself adequately and is not only identity of truth and certainty, but also knows adequately that it *is* that identity. The concept that knows itself in that manner is what Hegel calls "idea." Having reached this point, let us think about what we mentioned above when referring to the difference between the formal concept and the objective concept, the explanation of which we postponed. Suárez—if I remember correctly repeating Fonseca[18]—says that to know all possible and real things by only one formal concept is exclusive to the divinity.[19] This is exactly the Absolute reason of Hegel. Hegel's idea is *reason that knows itself as formal conceiving act of its own reality and that of things.*[20] From this point of view, Hegel's metaphysics certainly involves an aspect of identity of human reason with divine reason, but also an aspect of diversity. The finitude of human reason resides in the fact that it is not yet the idea. It reaches the idea painfully in an intellective act, and in addition, this reason has a manifestation in the form of consciousness. Absolute thinking is not consciousness, but the full and absolute reality of conceiving thinking. In such fashion, general metaphysics—*die eigentliche Metaphysik* as Hegel says—is the metaphysics that involves the ultimate and radical structure of being and reason in its absolute unity, {294} which is what constitutes the concept. This is exactly general metaphysics, which has always attempted to constitute itself as absolute science and has always been in *aporía*, in difficulty (*Verlegenheit*), so that once again the Aristotelian idea of *aporía* reappears, as it did in Kant. Hegel has the presumption, coming so soon after Kant, that his logic *is* absolute knowledge. In a more modest way Kant had attempted something similar when he wrote *Prolegomena to Any Future Metaphysics That Will Be Able to Come Forward As Science.* Hegel thinks that this was in fact realized with his version of absolute knowledge.

Furthermore, Hegel bases his conception of metaphysics on the whole of history. He begins with Thales of Miletus and goes through the entire history of philosophy. After all, Hegel is the first philosopher to formulate a history of philosophy, and he has made the history of philosophy a part of his own system. Hegel tells us that philosophy began with the spirit in Thales, and that in the end (this *in the end* is his own philosophy) the Absolute spirit has reached the point of knowing itself. It has cost the Absolute spirit twenty five hundred years of labor because, *Tantae molis erat se ipsam cognoscere mentem.*[21]

Nevertheless, the rigorous science that Hegel tells us about is not a *science* of the Absolute, but *is* the absolute form of the Absolute itself; it is its own internal occurrence. Hence, as Hegel tells us explicitly, the transcendental order "is nothing but the very spirit of God, in its eternal essence, before the creation of nature and any finite spirit."[22] Logic is purely and simply {295} metaphysics, and together with it, it is theology, primary and radical theology, that theology in which the transcendental order itself is constituted. In the second place this transcendental order is a system of concepts; in fact it is the concept as system. In the third place, this transcendental order as a conceptual system is formally in movement, and its movement consists in dialectic. In the fourth place, because it is the order of the Absolute, the transcendental order is something prior to particular things. In the fifth place, these particular things are nothing but things made in conformace with this absolute order, which is primary and antecedent.

While for St. Thomas the transcendental order only *expressed the most common or most universal characteristics* created things have as created, for Kant it was something more, it *constituted* the object as such object. But in Hegel it appears as something even more profound and also much more problematic. The transcendental order appears as internal *conformer* of reality. Again we encounter the presence of the idea that the entire order of being and reality is a self-conformation; this is an enormous self-morphism and this self-morphism consists in the reality of the idea, the reality of Absolute spirit.

It is necessary, of course, for Hegel to analyze not only this idea, but also the two things he just mentioned, viz. creation of nature and finite spirit. What is the transcendental order as conformer of these two great zones of reality? Are nature and spirit really "two" zones of reality or are they simply stages of a singular process? Perhaps nature is not only {296} prior to spirit but also necessarily leads to spirit?

The answer to this emerges in the path he has followed in his *Encyclopedia of the Philosophical Sciences*.

III. *The realization of reason*

Hegel himself tells us that the determination of the idea can follow three different paths. First is the one we have just explained, viz. to describe what an idea, Absolute spirit, is: the spirit that is identical, and furthermore knows in its identity that it is both reality and subjectivity. So it is logic that is *becoming*. In the second place, the idea can be manifested as a becoming *directed towards concretion*, which is just creation. And in the third

place, this becoming has a dialectical structure by which the production of things, which are but possibles in that Absolute spirit,
reverts in their reality to the very structure of that spirit, which is
what we shall have to discover.

Therefore, we have two problems.

In the first place, what is the formal structure of creation for
Hegel?

In the second place, what is the concrete progression of creation?

1. Reason as thinking activity. Reason and creation.

In order to apprehend this difficult Hegelian thought, which is
his whole metaphysics, we must never loose sight of the fact that
for Hegel creation is not {297} strictly speaking *production*, and we
shall presently see why. In general terms, for Hegel to create is
not to produce, but something different, something that no doubt
has some relationship with production, but is (to reuse terminology that originated with Kant and Fichte) *position*, creation is position. We shall see below in what this position consists and what
its relationship with production is, but for the moment we set this
aside.

Let us start from the idea, the Absolute spirit, just as we
found it at the end of the Logic. What does it put forth? This is
the second concept, which we must keep in mind in order to
comprehend what Hegel understands by "creation."

What is put forth is something "outside of itself." In this sense,
creation is exteriorization (*Entäusserung*), but exteriorization with
a peculiar characteristic. Indeed, up to now the term "position"
has been vague and confusing. But terms have been used vaguely
and confusedly when talking about creation, even by the most
famous theologians. Does not St. Thomas say that creation is
emanatio entis? And yet, St. Thomas is no emanationist even
though the term *emanatio* is still appropriate and we all know
what it means. The term "position" is not at this moment a term
that causes serious difficulties, though later complications will set
in. We are speaking of placing something outside God in one form
or another, which does not appear to be improper. The difficulty
arises from the fact that for Hegel this exteriorization is not a
simple otherness. The exteriorization, then, means that something–i.e., Absolute spirit—puts forth or issues "outside itself,"
not ceasing to be what it is itself when doing so. Since this Absolute spirit and {298} Absolute reason—which that position that
creation is—is so *of* reason and *from* reason, it means that for
Hegel this exteriorization is definitely not simply *otherness*. Absolute and rigorous otherness could never be in any theology of

WESTERN PHILOSOPHY (5): HEGEL

creation. It could not possibly be claimed, even in the most transcendent of theologies, that God and the world can be two nu-
merically. This would be absurd, since the fact they are not identical does not mean they are "two." Here the concept of number
has no strict application.

Up to now Hegel appears to say nothing particularly momen-
tous or difficult beyond the obvious internal difficulties of the
problem. But in fact he does say something more, viz. that when
we have this term "position," apparently other and in many
senses really other, it is because it is put forth by the Absolute
spirit, a kind of realization of the Absolute spirit. I believe that
this is also traditional in the theology of creation, in which there
are many real things, many additional "entities," but there is no
more "being," since God is the *Ipsum esse subsistens*. But Hegel
says something more, he says that in that "de-position" of the Absolute spirit, which this Absolute spirit puts forth outside of itself,
in this action, it *converts itself by this act of position into another*
opposite itself. This is the sense of "ex-teriorization", which is not
simply to stand outside, but something more strict and rigorous,
a thoroughgoing *alienation*. That which constitutes the very essence of Absolute spirit is alienated into that which it puts forth;
therefore, creation is above all position; secondly, it is *Entäusserung* in the sense of alienation.

But with this exteriorization, how does the Absolute spirit
continue to be truly and definitely Absolute, given the conceptualization of it that he has provided to us in his metaphysics?
Hegel will tell us that certainly there is alienation, but it is not the
case that the Absolute spirit is left behind {299}; rather, it is an
action that the Absolute spirit performs in order to be able to enter into itself and be itself to itself. The essence of alienation is
mediation (*Vermittlung*). This is the third concept. Creation is first
of all position; secondly, alienation; and thirdly, mediation.

"Mediation" in Hegel does not mean "intermediacy." For example, the emanations of Plotinus [204-270] are an old idea in
the history of philosophy, revived (more or less) by Al-Farabi [872-
951] at the beginning of Islamic philosophy. But in Hegel it is not
the case of "intermediacy" inside the emanation, but of "mediation." But for what purpose does the Absolute spirit have this
mediation? Precisely to enter into itself. Absolute spirit, in its
concretion, is mediated with respect to itself; the way Absolute
spirit becomes Absolute *in its concretion* is mediation, when passing through the mediation of the other, of the alienated. Thus, we
have the fact that creation is *dialectic of position*, and dialectic of
position in the end is *dialectic of alienation*, which in turn is essentially *dialectic of mediation*. The result is that Absolute spirit

with respect to creation just enters into itself. It cannot enter into itself except from outside itself; and since there is nothing but itself, it means that the "other" is mediation issued by itself in order to be itself, something it could not be, Hegel says, if it had not created.

It is in coming to be itself that its own infinity consists. Creation is definitely the dialectic of the infinitude of Absolute spirit. Of course, infinitude is initial; if the idea were not Absolute, there would be no place for this process. Nonetheless, creation does contribute something: it makes the Absolute spirit enter into itself. Hegel would mention here what he said in the "Preface" to {300} *Phenomenology of the Spirit*. The beginning, *qua* beginning, is the end, the outcome; and in this cyclical character is the becoming in which the very being of Absolute spirit consists. The dialectic of infinitude is the very life of the idea; it is the very life of the Absolute spirit. If from the point of view of logic Hegel's entire metaphysics is centered on the concept of *idealism*, in the sense that the ultimate reality is idea, the process of creation comes together in the single term of *pantheism*, a term that must be explained. The identity between idealism and pantheism will be the key to Hegel's metaphysics.

2. The stages of thinking activity

In what does the dialectical progression of the idea in its creative act consist? It consists in a creation that, by virtue of being mediation for the Absolute spirit, is not free at all, because without that mediating creation, the Absolute spirit would not be Absolute, would not enter into itself. Therefore, we now ask, what is the concrete structure of this dialectic of idea or Absolute spirit in Hegel?

He clearly tells us, "The idea shows itself to itself as a thought that is simply identical to itself and is, at the same time, an activity according to which, in order to be for itself, it needs to be counterposed by placing something that confronts it, and in that other confronting it, to enter into itself".[23] With this, aside from the Logic that constitutes the first part of this explanation, the process of creation {301} is constituted by incorporating two distinct elements. These are the constitution of nature, which is just to be the other (*Andersein*), and the entry from that other into itself, which is the philosophy of spirit. It is necessary for us to learn in two steps what Hegel understands by "nature," what he understands by "finite spirit," and then finally how much of this ends up back in the Absolute spirit.

A) Reason realized "outside of itself". Nature.

We shall repeat many things, but Hegel is the essence of repetition. Nature is the idea in its being *other*; a wall, of course, is not formally divine reason or my reason, but Hegel will say that it is the idea, Absolute spirit made into an *other*, converted into an other (*Anders-sein*). This means that everything we call "exteriority" or "nature" is dominated and constituted within the realm of a *télos* that is nothing but Absolute spirit, of which nature is an internal position. Its being other is just to be another within the télos and therefore, nature is built over this télos, which the Absolute spirit is, insofar as being another is in one form or another alienation and mediation.

But we must press Hegel to explain to us what he understands by "nature," to avoid thinking that these vague statements constitute a deduction of what nature is. Unfortunately, Hegel does not tell us much more, and we shall have to squeeze his thought to extract what we seek. That "being another" must be clarified along two lines.

Hegel tells us, "The idea that is for itself, considered in this unity with itself that produces the other, is to intuit (*Anschauen*). The intuiting idea (*die anschauende Idee*) is nature.[24] {302} This may seem somewhat strange. What does intuition have to do with everything we have been saying up to now? Hegel does not limit himself to this, but says that this being *other*, which now is the terminus of an intuition, formally consists in exteriority (*Äusserlichkeit*). Hegel must explain what he means here by "intuition" and "exteriority."

In the first place, consider intuition. It may seem quite strange that Hegel here uses the term "intuition," but it will not seem so if we remember that he labors under the weight of theological tradition. In God classical theology always distinguished two types of science, or as the theologians say, two types of intellection. One is called *simple intelligence*: when knowing himself, God knows the infinitude of all things that might have had existence and which are possible in the divine mind. But of the things God has wished to create theology says that, at least from the point of view of the terminus of his activity, they are the object of a different science, what theologians call the *science of vision*. This is precisely Hegel's *intuition*; it is a *videre*; so saying that nature is an intuiting idea (*anschauende Idee*) is to say, in a phrase with idealist resonances, the same that classical theology has been saying with respect to creation, that it is terminus of *scientia visionis*. But this is not enough.

Someone may argue that every intuition presupposes an intuited object, and this would appear to somewhat unravel everything Hegel has said up to now, which up to a certain point is true. Hegel now makes the concept of nature more precise and says, "Nature is not only something relative to the idea of Absolute spirit, but is also in itself an exteriority (*Äusserlichkeit*). And to be this is what constitutes the {303} determination according to which what we call 'nature' is nature."[25] We now ask what this exteriority is and what it has to do with intuition; or is Hegel just manipulating concepts in a trivial manner? No; Hegel is a rigorous man and his conceiving thinking never stops being such. To understand what this exteriority means we should recall what was said about intuition: it is an intuition in the sense that it is idea, Absolute spirit, the absolute reason of God seeing. Seeing what? An object he has made? Definitely not—and here is where the problem begins. Nonetheless, the object of intuition has some type of being and that being is what Hegel calls "exteriority." How is that exteriority conformed to the idea that it is a science that is *a priori* in the divine mind?

Here Hegel shows the influence of Kant's philosophy, which gave us an initial answer to this question. When Kant asks how we intuit things in the sensible world, he tells us that every intuition has a moment in which we are given something, which is not from the person who receives it.[26] But in order for this to occur, so that the intuition can take place, it is necessary for the intuiting structure of the human spirit to constitute *a priori* the form of time and space, i.e., to have a component he calls "pure intuition." However, inasmuch as space (putting time aside for the moment) is space, it involves an exteriority of the object with respect to the subject and of the parts of space among themselves. Inasmuch as it is *a priori*, the spirit "puts forth" its unity. Space is a kind of intelligible matter placed *a priori* by the spirit itself; this is {304} Hegel's exteriority. Hegel, familiar with the Kantian concepts, understands that from itself intuition places the real multiplicity in which exteriority consists. With this, Hegel reassumes the totality of the facts of intuition—not only space—in this structural moment of the spirit by which the intuiting reason places multiplicity, places matter as something outside of the spirit. This is just what Nature is.

This is why he tells us that nature can be considered from three viewpoints. First, purely and simply insofar as it has this moment of exteriority of parts with respect to others (*Auseinander*). In this sense nature is isolation (*Vereinzelung*), it is a system of these individuations, of these *singuli*. Second, each one of these elements has an internal and special peculiarity, which is something more than mere singularity; it is individuality (*Individualität*), which for Hegel is the object of physics, just as the first is the object of mechanics. Third, we can consider isolation and the whole of determination as an activity that falls back upon itself and is nature as organism, the object of organic physics.[27] We are not interested now in analyzing the process by which nature is structured; what is important is how this concept of nature has gained precision in Hegel's mind.

Throughout history nature has always been constrasted with something that is not natural. For example, in the Greek world nature is the substance provided with internal capabilities in order to have a mobility of its own; it is a φύσις, and in this sense, beings that have it are {305} φύσει ὄντα, natural beings. But the naturalness of these beings is at least extrinsically defined by their contrast with τέχνε, with beings man produces that do not enjoy that condition. For a Greek, what will become a house or any type of artificial object is the realization of an idea that is not in matter itself, but in the mind of the craftsman. Therefore while this may be a reality, it is not φύσει ὄν, but τέχνε ὄν, it is artificial. The natural is that which is not artificial, that which is born and sprouts from itself. Is this what Hegel understands by nature? Obviously not.

Centuries later, more or less since the time of Galileo, and culminating in Kant's idea, "nature" has been understood as a system of laws with a definite meaning. That meaning is simple: given certain antecedents, one can determine what the consequences will be. Hence they are natural laws, the *leges naturae*. In this sense, nature is no longer contrasted with what is artificial, but with chance, with what is fortuitous. Is this the case with Hegel? Clearly not.

Hegel does not contrast nature with the fortuitous, since he says that, actually, the fortuitous may occur. He then tells us that it is necessity (*Notwendigkeit*), and in this he is an heir to Greek thought, because these chance occurrences that exist in the world are termini of ἀνάγκε, a kind of *fatum* that necessarily falls on things. At any rate, the Hegelian concept of nature is not determined from laws, but by something different.

There has been a third concept of nature, older than the one from laws but later than that of the Greeks, by virtue of which nature has been understood as the sum total of the world's activity, that by which all natural things are being produced. It is nature in the sense of *natura naturans*, different from the set of beings that would be *natura naturata*. In {306} this sense, nature in a certain way sits opposite to God, unless through a more complex theological reasoning process God is turned into *natura naturans*. Nevertheless, there will be some difference between God and *natura naturans*, even though it may only be that God is not *natura naturans* unless he wants to be such. The concept of nature in Hegel is also not opposed to God; especially since in a certain way it is God himself; Spinoza had already said *Deus sive natura*. But Hegel is very much opposed to Spinoza and this complicates matters.

To what is the concept of nature in Hegel opposed? Hegel insists that nature is just exteriority, it is ex-teriority as such; here it is opposed to spirit, which is interiority whereby nature is formally conceived through and as opposition to spirit, and that opposition is exteriority. It seems, then, there is a certain contradiction between this opposition to spirit and the thesis that there is no other reality except Absolute spirit; but actually there is no opposition at all because that is the cyclic characteristic of reality in Hegelian thought. The resulting end is the beginning and the beginning is the resulting end, because that real opposition to spirit is precisely the source from which spirit enters into itself. Exteriority is the mere alienation of spirit.

B) Reason "returning to itself". Spirit (from finite spirit to Absolute spirit).

What does Hegel understand by "spirit"? First of all, it is to be there in itself (*bei sich selbst sein*). This is what Hegel calls "freedom," freedom in the sense of possessing itself {307} and being there within itself. The fact that finite spirit can emerge is strictly a problem of mediation; in other words, this freedom in which the spirit exists is not something that is there *next* to nature, but something that exists precisely *through* nature itself—not in the sense that spirit is a product of nature, but in the sense that nature is the mediation whereby spirit can exist. Spirit exists primarily as liberation and as liberation from nature, from exteriority; and with it the entering into itself as interiority immediately appears. Freedom is mediated there by nature, and the entry of the spirit into itself is also mediated there by nature. But it is necessary for Hegel to tell us with some degree of precision what this that he so vaguely calls "spirit" really is.

Hegel says the evolution of spirit is given in three stages:

1. In the form of a relationship with itself, which is called *subjective spirit.*
2. In the form of reality, which spirit has in the world, and therefore, something different and superior to subjective spirit; it is *objective spirit.*
3. In the identity in and by itself of the spirit that has actually entered into itself and eternally exists with itself; this is *Absolute spirit.*[28]

For the moment let us put aside Absolute spirit and ask about the finite spirit, which is both subjective spirit and objective spirit. What type of being do they have for Hegel?

We shall be quite brief about subjective spirit since what we mentioned above concerning the *Phenomenology of Spirit* is the answer to the idea of subjective spirit. Hegel tells us that subjective spirit begins to emerge in the bosom of nature as liberation from it. This is what is {308} called "soul" (*Seele*). The soul is so characterized because in its supreme function it is aware of what is not itself; its own reality and the reality of things appear in what we call "consciousness" (*Bewusstsein*). That is what subjective spirit is.

But the great creation of Hegel is objective spirit, with respect to which we have to ask three things. In the first place, what is it? In the second place, what is its internal and structural dialectic? And in third place, what is its relationship with subjective spirit?

In the first place, what is objective spirit? Hegel never says that that objective spirit is any kind of social consciousness or public consciousness, not at all; "consciousness" is something that only individuals have. Objective spirit is not a form of consciousness, but has a much greater reality: it has objective reality. But consciousness is the domain of the subjective, and it is not the case that in objective spirit there is *no* consciousness. There is a consciousness of objective spirit, but it belongs to each of the individuals that comprise it or are in it, not to the objective spirit itself. To be sure, objective spirit is not independent of these individuals, not only because of consciousness, but for several reasons, because of all its other dimensions. This means—Hegel affirms this specifically—that individuals are the support of objective spirit. However, objective spirit is not determined by the complexity of the individuals that comprise it, but just the opposite. Objective spirit, Hegel tells us, is the Absolute idea; in other words, it is an idea from which has been subtracted, in some way, the moment of "for itself." Absolute spirit in the full sense is in itself *and* for itself; recall that Absolute spirit that has not yet entered its dimension {309} of "for itself," and is only existing "in itself," is manifested as objective spirit. Objective spirit is not outside individuals, nor yet does it emerge from them, rather they dialectically make what the objective spirit is appear *ad extra.* Consequently, the individuals that comprise objective spirit as its support are merely the accidents of objective spirit, which is the only thing that is substantial.

This may sound terrible, but it is the lynchpin of Hegel's entire philosophy of spirit. Individuals are the *accidents* of the objective spirit. It is true that great historical individuals exist, but these individuals are great and belong to history insofar as they incarnate the objective spirit, not insofar as they are provided with personal greatness.

Objective spirit thus understood is purely and simply the manifestation—if you will, by alienation and mediation—of the Absolute spirit in which God consists. It is the universal spirit (*Weltgeist*). Objective spirit is the objective concept God has of himself. Insofar as that universal spirit undergoes different geographic and temporal determinations it gives rise to what Hegel calls the "spirit of the people" (*Volkgeist*); these are determinations of objective spirit, of the universal spirit, which are different and multiple in accordance to the regions and moments of time.

In the second place, if this is objective spirit, we must ask Hegel in what the internal dialectic of objective spirit consists. Is it and simply that Absolute spirit acquires an objective form in order to bestow it upon individuals? That is not the dialectic of Hegel's objective spirit. Objective spirit is not the individuals, but neither is it the result of individuals. Here we see something mentioned above in connection with synthesis, viz. that we are dealing with an originating synthesis. {310} Objective spirit, insofar as it is realized *ad extra* in each individual, causes that the objective form of spirit to spring forth in each of them. This dialectic is the one that for Hegel formally constitutes history.

The dialectic structure of objective spirit is history. What does Hegel understand here by "history" (*Geschichte*)? To be sure, it is the temporal process of objective spirit; that much is clear. But this temporal spirit, this temporal dialectic flows into three great categories.

In the first place, we have the category of "variation" (*Veränderung*). The objective spirit is in continuous disquietude (*Unruhe*); if it were in constant quiescence it would not be objective spirit, but simply dead nature.

But, in the second place, that variation to which it is subject is not arbitrary. It is not simply that the forms of objective spirit, the spirit of peoples, can be of a certain type and after some time become corrupted, perfected, or enriched and turn into something different. Hegel understands that if we *pursue*—we shall immediately see what this means—the heart of the matter, something completely different happens. In all these variations the objective spirit that appears to die is reborn from itself in a process of "rejuvenation" (*Verjüngung*). Hegel then asks in what the natural death of the spirit of a people consists. His answer is summarized in two words, its political nullity (*politische Nulität*). But, like the Phoenix, it is reborn from its ashes, and history continues its steady progression, although in another place. Not only can it continue in another place, but Hegel explicitly says that it is impossible for the same people to constitute two different eras of history; if they have done it once, they will not be able to do it a second time. {311}

But, in the third place, there is another category, which is the one most important for Hegel, the category of "reason" (*Vernunft*). Historical dialectic is reason in time, as Hegel has conceived it, as conceptivizing thinking. Reason is Absolute spirit that in the form of universal spirit dialectically constitutes itself, on the one hand from itself and on the other, from individuals and objective spirits. Inasmuch as this reason is, for Hegel, objectivizing thinking, it is obvious that reason in history is not a reason that "from the outside" governs the deepest ground of history. Reason, of course, "dominates" history, but it is not domination from the outside, it is reason that is internal and intrinsic to history itself. It is reason itself converted into history, into the objective form of history. Thus we are dealing with the internal history of reason realizing itself in time. For this concept of reason in history Hegel has made use of two very important traditions.

One is the idea of providence: there is providential reason; this Hegel learned from classical theology. The other is the idea of teleology. The course of human events has a final goal; it is directed towards something. Hegel says that it is directed towards the greater glory of God and, that in fact, this is the authentic goal of objective spirit. We shall leave that aside for now. For Hegel the idea of providence and the idea of universal teleology constitute the font for his notion of reason in history, provided that we rethink these concepts in a Hegelian way.

Providence is reason governing the world, which is evident from a certain point of view. But if we limit ourselves to expressing it this way, it would be subjective reason. It would be the reason God—the "subject" called God—has for having made the world and directed men to be in a certain way. This is not what Hegel intends; what he is attempting to do is to regard that type of {312} reason, which classical theology frequently designates as "providence," as something that molds itself objectively. This is what is important for Hegel: the objective molding of the reason that governs the world, because in this fashion it is not just any reason that governs the world, but a reason inscribed in the very bosom of the world. That reason is its *télos*, by reason of which the dialectic of its history will be the way to εντελέχεια, which is just Absolute spirit. Hegel takes subjective reason and objective reason simultaneously, just as he did in logic, as conceptivizing thinking. Here we now have historical reason, which is at the same time subjective reason and objective reason because it is the reason of the concept of objective spirit set on its steady progression through time.

At this juncture Hegel must tell us what the formal structure of that history, of that historical dialectic, really is. He provides us with a precise answer, viz. that this history is evolution (*Entwicklung*). It starts from a germinal nucleus and it consists in evolving. Of course, Hegel is not appealing here to evolution in the biological sense of the term. This was of great interest to Hegel at the time it began to agitate Europe; but he was more interested in something different, namely, *the idea that this evolution is the work of reason*. However, although this may be the work of reason, it is still evolution, though an evolution of reason and of reason dialectically constituted. With this, ultimately, all great creations of history are for Hegel pre-included in the germ from which they dialectically emerge. In this sense, no radical innovations are ever produced in history: "In the first stirrings of spirit, all history is contained *virtualiter*."[29] Does this mean that history is the dialectic of virtuality? {313} This is an important problem we should present to Hegel. What if history is not a dialectic of virtuality, and therefore, of realities, but a system of creation and closing of possibilities? Then history would be something different; it would clearly produce possibility prior to reality, and this would make it a quasi-creation. However, we shall leave this issue aside.

So Hegel presents a very precise idea of what he understands by "history." That idea is the reality, the nucleus, and the germ, just as in nature the seed is of the tree. That is why the first stirrings of spirit already contain *virtualiter* the totality of history. We may then pose a question: was the whole of history virtually contained in Adam?

The third question we have to ask Hegel with respect to objective spirit is the relationship between subjective spirit and objective spirit. Hegel has no doubts about two affirmations that would shake anyone given to reflection. He affirms that when the objective spirit is put into movement the subjective spirit has nothing to do; individuals are preserved simply as memories in history, but history is not made by individuals themselves, but individuals carried by history, by the objective spirit. They are, as we mentioned above, accidents; and now we can understand the radical meaning of that contingency. Hegel tells us that the whole of history could be written without mentioning one single personal name, which up to a certain point is true. But this makes us ask whether is it true that individuals are preserved in the objective spirit only as memories of what they were, and whether their only reality is the contribution they provided, which still lives in the objective spirit under the form of memory. Hegel would not say that individuals have nothing to do in history; but he is going to {314} give an answer that consists in making cleverness an intrinsic moment of the objective spirit; this is what Hegel calls the trick, the slyness of reason (*Die List der Vernunft*). This slyness consists in the fact that certainly history cannot be made except with individuals and by individuals, but it makes these individuals believe that they are working for their own individual self-interest when in reality they are working for the objective spirit. That is what happens with the act of individual reproduction, which can be undertaken for a wide variety of subjective reasons; but in reality nature works towards a different goal, namely, the preservation of the species. This is the slyness of reason. Everything individuals may perform is subjectively quite good for them, but the trick consists in making these apparently subjective and individual things useful to accomplish something that surpasses individuality; this is the course of events of the objective spirit. Individuals are preserved as memories, thanks precisely to this kind of internal trickery of reason. This excludes *a limine*[30] the possibility that one may be able to have in his hands both the concept of objective spirit and the *télos* of history. Because of this, philosophy of history cannot be turned into prophecy. "The philosopher has nothing to do with prophesying. From the point of view of history its concern is about things that have occurred, and about what is occurring now at this point in time. On the other hand, philosophy is not concerned with things that have had existence in the past or with those things that at some time have reached existence, but with that which exists now and will exist eternally, with reason. This provides us with plenty to do."[31] Whether true or not, this is a grandiose view of history. In this concept of history, nothing really passes away and everything is preserved; history concerns itself with {315} whatever "is" in the sense of absolute present. "In the idea, that which appears as something that has occurred remains eternally as something that has not been lost. The idea is always present. The spirit is immortal".[32]

Perhaps someone will ask what all this is about. Do we have to think that there is some kind of remembrance by which whatever individuals do is present in absolute reason? Rather we are dealing with something much more profound and radical. Let us not forget that this process is dialectic, and as happens in all dialectics, the second term is surmounted (*aufgehoben*) in the originative synthesis, of which the thesis and antithesis are nothing but abstractions. Because of that, in the Absolute spirit the individual is preserved, but only as "surmounted" (*aufgehoben*), i.e., having contributed in one form or another to the concrete determinations of the Absolute spirit. Hence, "the spirit is the concept that the spirit has now made of itself. It is the one that rationally maintains and regulates the world, and is the result of the efforts of six thousand years, the labor of the Absolute spirit in history"[33] in order to produce that history, and from it, to enter into itself. The consciousness of this characteristic of the Absolute spirit is first the philosophy of history, and afterwards access to the Absolute spirit itself.

The Absolute spirit in Hegel is just the idea in itself and through itself. But now that Absolute spirit is the idea whose concretion is mediated by alienation in the whole of creation. Because of this, Hegel can tell us that the philosophy of history—he disagrees with Leibniz on this—is the authentic theodicy. Indeed, if theodicy tries to justify evil, there is only one way to do so: we have to understand it. This is what theodicy is, viz. the philosophy of history. What is the relationship among {316} this Absolute spirit and each of the individuals and the objective spirit? With all these dialectic moves we keep going from one thing to another, and we lose track of the idea of unity, which, however, is what matters most to Hegel. The truth is the whole.

With respect to God and each man, Hegel tells us, "Inasmuch as God is present everywhere, He is present in each man, He appears in the conscience of each, and this is the universal spirit."[34] "If the essence of God were not the essence of man and of nature, it would just be an essence that is nothing".[35] Clearly, this is a most emphatic affirmation of *pantheism*. We need to clarify this concept, and we shall do so immediately. Nevertheless, it is clear that for Hegel, since the subjective spirit consists in consciousness, to say that God is the manifestation of his own Absolute spirit in the consciousness of each person amounts to saying that the consciousness of humans is the consciousness that God has of himself. God is not consciousness, He is Absolute reason; that this Absolute reason can have a consciousness of himself is the work of humans because they are the consciousness of God.

The same question, addressed to the objective spirit, will elicit a similar response. "The process that enables the spirit to enter into itself, into its own concept, is history".[36] The result of this progression is that the spirit, when objectifying itself "outside" and thinking about its own being, achieves its own concrete and internal determination. Further on Hegel says, "Universal history is the representation of the divine Absolute process of the spirit in its supreme configurations, in those gradations by which it certainly acquires its own truth about {317} itself".[37] This is a most resounding affirmation of *pantheism*. However, what does "pantheism" mean here?

Spinoza, for example, was a pantheist. He said *Deus sive natura*, that God is the only substance with two fundamental modes, that of extension and that of thought; and from that substance the entire complex of the *res extensa* and the *res cogitans* of Descartes is developed. Is that the pantheism of Hegel? Not quite; Hegel's case is different because the *substratum*, that which constitutes the radical reality is not a substance, but purely and simply a spirit, the Absolute spirit. Hence, the Absolute spirit, as Hegel tells us, is pure actuosity, pure process, pure activity. Therefore, we are not dealing with a pantheism that consists in being a substance that has different determinations as its properties, but with an activity. What kind of activity? A rational activity. In what does that rational activity consist? Does it consist in a purely subjective activity? Right from the beginning Hegel says it does not; it consists in *begreiffendes Denken*, in putting into that subjective activity something objective, which, however, has no other reality except by virtue of the position of subject. Inasmuch as we only consider its objective aspect, the philosophy of Hegel is not pantheist. Inasmuch as we only consider the subjective aspect, the philosophy of Hegel strictly speaking would also not be pantheist. It is pantheist inasmuch as we can see that the objective is precisely a rational product of subjective thinking. The pantheism of Hegel consists in that: it is the pantheism of rational activity. That rational activity is precisely God; because of this, God is *fieri* and that *fieri* of God is an *autofieri*. That it is "rational" is what defines {318} Hegel's idealism. That it is the whole of reality, what defines Hegel's pantheism. The identity between idealism and pantheism is what the Absolute is in Hegel. The whole of history is a self-conformation.

Recapitulating:

1. The transcendental order is the very spirit of God in His eternal essence, before the creation of nature and of any finite spirit.
2. The transcendental order is the concept itself as system.
3. This system is fundamentally and formally dialectical.
4. It is something prior to any particular thing.
5. It is the dialectical conformation of each thing.
6. The being of each thing is the mediated conformation of the concretion of Absolute spirit.
7. The Absolute spirit is self-conformation.
8. That self-conformation consists in the dialectical self-conformation of the infinitude of reason.
9. Thus it can be seen concretely that the beginning *is* the resulting end, and that this *is* is clearly the Absolute.

The beginning *is* the resulting end, and in that *is* we find the quintessence of the Absolute, i.e., the transcendental order. In the framework of nothingness, Hegel's Absolute, which is what he sees before his eyes, is purely and simply the self-process of reason, the self-conformation of reason. The way of not being nothing is to be Absolute, to be conceiving self-conformation. That is why thirty-five years ago I wrote:

> We are left with the impression that while he did not reach the point of absorbing all things into his philosophy, he nevertheless went through all of them as if they were incidents suffered by someone else. 'He' was what his philosophy was. And his life was the history of his philosophy. Everything else was his counter-life. {319} Nothing had a personal meaning for him which was not acquired through being relived philosophically. The *Phenomenology* was and is his awakening to philosophy. And philosophy itself was the intellectual revivification of his existence as a manifestation of what he called the "Absolute spirit." The human side of Hegel, on the one hand so quiet and far from being philosophical, acquires on the other a philosophical rank when it is elevated to the supreme publicity of what he has conceived. And conversely, the conceptivizing thinking apprehends in the individual that Hegel was, with the force conferred upon it by the absolute essence of the spirit and intellectual sediment of the whole of history. Therefore, Hegel is in a certain sense the maturity of Europe.

> Regardless of our ultimate position with respect to him, any present-day initiation into philosophy has to consist, in large measure, of an "experience," of an inquiry into the situation left for us by Hegel."[38]

The foregoing, which I wrote thirty-five years ago [1931], I would literally repeat today.

---

[1] G. W. F. Hegel, *Phänomenologie des Geistes*, Hrg. G. Lasson, 2nd. Ed., Leipzig, Meiner, 1921, pp. 52 ff. (Sp. tr. by X. Zubiri, Hegel, *Fenomenología del espíritu: Prólogo e Introducción. Saber absoluto*, Madrid, Rev. de Occidente, 1935, p. 104).

[2] "Die Vernunft ist die Gewissheit des Bewusstseins", G. W. F. Hegel, *Phänomenologie des Geistes*, ed. cit. p. 156.

[3] F. Suárez, *Sobre el concepto de ente* (On the concept of entity), tr. by X. Zubiri, Madrid, Rev. de Occidente, 1935, pp. 17 ff.

[4] Cf. G. W. F. Hegel, *Wissenschaft der Logik* (Philosophy of Logic), Hrg. G. Lasson. Erster Teil, Leipzig, Meiner, 1923, "Einleitung," p.23.

5 "Hier ist begreiffen, die Tätigkeit des Begriffs selbst", G. W. F. Hegel, *Die Vernunft in der Geschichte. Einleitung in diePhilosophie der Weltgeschichte*, Hrg. G. Lasson, 3 Aufl., Leipzig, Meiner, 1930, p. 3.

6 *Note by Zubiri*: I cannot forget that forty five years ago, when I competed as a simple beginner for my ill-fated Chair of the History of Philosophy [1925], one of the subjects I would have been required to write for four hours, if I had drawn the subject by lot, simply asked this, "What does Hegel understand by 'phenomenon'?"

7 *Zubiri note on the margin*: Appears, who? This is what has to be investigated. Anticipating, phenomenon is the manifestation of Reason in consciousness.

8 "Diese dialektische Bewegung, welche das Bewusstsein an ihm selbst, sowhol an seinem Wissen, als an reinem Gegenstande ansübt, insofer ihm der neue wahre Gegenstand daraus entspringt, ist eigentlich desjenige, was Erfahrung genaunt wird. Es ist in dieser Beziehung an dem soeben erwähnten, wadurch sich über die wissenschaftliche Seite der folgenden Darstellung ein neues Licht verbeiten wird", G. W. F. Hegel, *Phänomenologie des Geistes, op. cit.* p. 61. *Zubiri's 1969 translation of this passage is*: "The dialectical movement, which consciousness undertakes in itself, as much for what concerns its knowing as for what concerns its object, with respect to conscience shows it is from here that it quickly surges to the new true object, and that is what is properly called 'experience'." *Zubiri's earlier translation (1935)*: "This dialectic movement that conscience operates in itself, inasmuch in its knowledge as in its object, is properly what is called *experience*, inasmuch as from this movement there springs for consciousness the new true object" (*Fenomenología del espíritu* [Phenomenology of Spirit], tr. X. Zubiri, *op. cit.*, p. 118). It is experience: first, because in each stage a new *Wissen* is reached, which now brings a new object, and second, because each step is *"die ganze Felde der Gestalten des Bewusstsein."*

9 "Sein Sein ist Aktuosität", *Die Vernunft in der Geschichte, ibid.*, p. 52. [To translate *Aktuosität* Zubiri revives the old Spanish term *actuosidad* not commonly used today, meaning "an activity with diligence and care,", and applies it to make this distinction.—trans.].

10 In consciousness the certainty of being the whole of reality has not yet been realized. "Reason is spirit by being elevated to Truth, which is the certainty of being the whole of reality, by being aware in consciousness that Reason itself is the world, and that the world belongs to it." ("Die Vernunft ist Geist, indem die Gewissheit, alle Realität zu sein, zur Wahrheit erhoben und sie sich ihrer selbst als ihrer Welt und der Welt als ihrer selbst bewusst ist", G. W. F. Hegel, *Phänomenologie des Geistes*, Ed. cit., p. 284). "The entity in itself and by itself, which at the same time is real as consciousness and represents itself, is the Spirit" ("Das an— und fürsichselende als Bewusstsein wirklich und sich selbst vorstellt, is die Geist", *ibid.*, p. 285).

11 *Wissenchaft der Logik, ibid.*, "Einleitung", p. 31.

12 *Enzyklopädie,* § 162. (*Enzylopädie der philosophischen Wissenschaften im Grundrisse*. The edition Zubiri uses is the one published by G. Lasson, Meiner, Leipzig, 1905).

13 "Die logische Vernunft selbst ist das Substantielle oder Reelle", *Wissenschaft der Logik*, ibid., "Einleitung", p. 29.

14 [Sp. *"proceso encinil"*, Zubiri neologism from *encina*, oak.—trans.].

15 Cf. *Wissenschaft der Logik*, op. cit., (Erstes Buch, Erstes Kapitel, Anmerkung "Aufheben"), pp. 93-95.

16 Cf. G. W. F. Hegel, *Wissensachft der Logik*, op. cit., (Erstes Buch, "Die Lehre von Sein"), p. 53.

17 Zubiri translates quite freely the following passage in Hegel, "Das Werden ist die Ungetreuntheit des Seins und Nichts, nicht die Einheit, welche von Sein und Nichts abstrahiert", *Wissenschaft der Logik* (Erstes Buch, Erster Anschnitt, Erstes Kapitel, C. Werden, 2. Momente des Werdens. Enstehn und Vergehen), p. 92.

18 [Pedro da Fonseca, S.J. (1528-1599), brilliant Portuguese Jesuit philosopher and theologian.—trans.].

19 Cf. F. Suárez, *Sobre el concepto de ente* (On the concept of entity), tr. Xavier Zubiri, Madrid, Rev. de Occidente, 1935, p.24.

20 "Die Idee ist der adäquate Begriff, das objektive Wahre oder das Wahre als solches", G. W. F. Hegel, *Wissenchaft der Logik*, op. cit. (Drittes Buch, Dritter Abschnitt, "Die Idee"), II, p. 407.

21 [Hegel's adaptation of Virgil's text from *Aeneid* I, 33, *Tantae molis erat Romanam condere gentem.*—trans.].

22 "Dieses reich ist die Wahrheit, wie sie ohne Hülle an und für sich selbst ist, Man kann sich deswegen aus drücken, dass dieser Inhalt die Darstellung Gottes ist, wie er seinem ewigen Wessen vor der Erschaffung der Natur und eines endlichen Geistes ist", *Wissenschaft der Logik*, op. cit., I, p. 31.

23 *Enzyklopädie* § 18 (This is a somewhat free translation by Zubiri).

24 *Enzyklopädie* § 244.

25 *Enzyklopädie* § 247.

26 [The Spanish reads *"que no es el que lo recibe,"* "which is not the one that receives it". Since this makes no sense in the context, the Spanish text has been emended to *"que no es del que lo recibe,"* which does fit the context.—trans.]

27 Cf. *Enzyclopädie* § 252.

28 Cf. *Enzyklopädie* § 385.

29 *Die Vernunft in der Geschichte*, p.39.

30 [Latin *a limine*, from the very threshold, from the very beginning, prior to any argumentation.—trans.].

31 *Die Vernunft in der Geschichte*, p. 200.

32 *Die Vernunft in der Geschichte*, p. 165.

33 *Ibid.*

34 *Die Vernunft in der Geschichgte*, p. 37.

35 *Die Vernunft in der Geschichgte*, p. 38.

36 *Die Vernunft in der Geschichgte*, p. 49.

37 *Die Vernunft in der Geschichgte*, p. 52.

38 *Naturaleza, Historia, Dios* (Nature, History, God), 6th ed., (Madrid, Alianza, 1974), p. 145. [Please refer to http://www.zubiri.org for the Spanish and English versions of the book.—trans.].

CONCLUSION
THE FUNDAMENTAL PROBLEM:
THE PROBLEM OF KNOWING[1]

In this Conclusion we are going to revisit the problem proposed in the Introduction.

§1

KNOWING AS A PROBLEM

In the Introduction we referred to the fundamental problems of Western metaphysics and noted that the first thing we had to do was to reach an agreement about what metaphysics is, because metaphysics *is* the real definition of philosophy. If by "philosophy" we understand the search for the radical ultimateness of things, that ultimateness is what, from the point of view of its content, has been called "metaphysics," provided that we are able to reach an agreement as to the meaning of the *metá* in "metaphysics." We observed that, strictly speaking, it is a "trans," i.e., something such that each existing thing is what it is, but transcends all of its particular determinations. Therefore, philosophy, and in particular, Western metaphysics, is a philosophy of the transcendental.

But we elected not to deal with the internal problems of that aspect of the transcendental; instead we chose to deal with something different. We sought to reveal that the transcendental order in itself has an intrinsically problematic nature. And from that problematic nature the problems that the transcendental order has within itself emerge. The transcendental order is an intrinsic problem within its own internal context. In order to see this, we appealed to the history of metaphysics, which is what we dealt with in the preceding chapters.

In that history we were not only trying to inform ourselves about what certain philosophers had thought—we chose six, which will always seem somewhat arbitrary to some—but also through them to unravel the {323} intrinsic fabric of the transcendental order. Appeal to the history of metaphysics also had as a goal to reveal the internal structure of each philosopher's respective metaphysical position. Through such great personalities we indeed discovered that underlying what they say about metaphysics there is an internal fabric, which is what we were interested in discovering.

We began first with Aristotle, in some respects the predecessor of Western metaphysics, and with his idea of *being* (ὄν). Afterwards, we saw that in Western metaphysics the transcendental order was built on different structures; one such is the *intrinsic finitude of being* in St. Thomas. We next encountered the importance that *doubt and reason* acquire with respect to the truth of things in Descartes. In Leibniz, the whole transcendental order rests on the idea of the *possible*. In Kant, it is the idea of the *objectual*. Finally, in Hegel it is *absolute reason*.

Reflection upon these philosophies allows us to discover not only the internal problems of the transcendental order as such, but something else, viz. that at the bottom of all those metaphysics there is a *profound unity*.

We cannot say that this unity consists in the mere succession of philosophers since, after all, each tried to start from zero, and that is insufficient. Can we say that it is an internal and objective dialectic of reason in its progression towards the transcendental order? This—Hegel's thesis—would go too far. We find ourselves confronting something rather different, a unity that, as we can detect in the history of metaphysics itself, is real and something like the incorporation of philosophical thinking into the transcendental order, an order that, as we have repeated, is intrinsically problematic. {324}

Therefore, instead of confronting all the problems that this transcendental order exhibits, we shall concentrate our attention on just one of them, which can act as a summary. We choose one that certainly is radical and primary, in fact, because it underlies all of the metaphysics we have covered up to now. Indeed, if we review everything metaphysics has said to us from Aristotle to Hegel, we find that it began with Aristotle telling us about the νοῦς, intelligence, and in particular conceptualizing intelligence, if we wish to recall St. Thomas. For Leibniz metaphysics is the order of reason, and for Hegel it is absolute reason. Ultimately what underlies all these metaphysics is a certain structure of "philosophical thinking." But in addition, it is a matter *of law* (so to speak) because as we shall see, the internal unity of philosophical thinking is not only that way as a matter of fact, but constitutes the very root of our conceptualization of the transcendental order.[2]

I. *Ratio, intellectus concipiens, noûs*

Ratio, intellectus, noûs: these undoubtedly constitute the primary and radical unity from which all the difficulties and all the conceptualization involved with the transcendental order emerge. But the problem is to discover how Western metaphysics has understood that unity, or rather how it has understood the radical unity of philosophical thinking. Let us begin with the latter.

Hegel tells us that philosophical thinking is the work of reason, understanding by "reason" just conceiving or conceptualizing thinking (*das begreiffendes Denken*). On that point he draws on most of Kant's legacy, for whom metaphysics is a consideration of objects by means of the concepts of reason. Hence, reason—in Kant and in Hegel, but above all {325} in Hegel—is mounted upon itself. Then one might ask whether this is acceptable, viz. for reason to thus bootstrap itself?

Let us consider, in the first place, what Hegel is claiming about dialectical generation through concepts; is it about an object? But the object is not right there. If the object were there in front of him, the problem would be completely different. Without the object in front of him, what is it that provides direction, progression, and adequacy (or lack thereof) to the internal dialectical movement of thinking in the elaboration of its concepts? If we have a dog right in front of us, we can make a dialectic from anything we wish, for example, of living substances, and so have conceiving or conceptualizing thinking (*begreiffendes Denken*) of the dog. But, if we do not have the dog, where does the terminus of the dialectical movement come from, that in which, Hegel says, is the supreme concretion, and with respect to which all the other moments are abstracted? From this point of view Hegel's theory is not acceptable.

The same thing happened with Plato. What was Plato trying to reach with his dialectic of separated ideas, by means of divisions and subdivisions? He was not able to reach beyond the last species, the ἄτομον εἶδος; but from that point to the individual there is much ground to cover because, as Aristotle would say, the individual cannot be captured by means of ideas; it is right there in front of me. Then it is a question of asking whether the dialectical method is adequate given Plato's assumptions. Moreover, while Plato had an object, for Hegel there is no prior object for dialectics, and therefore dialectics would remain essentially suspended from itself, i.e., with no anchor.

But this is not enough, because reason consists in conceiving the object insofar as it can be conceived. In Hegel what reason confronts directly is the understanding (*Verstand*). Let us accept {326} that opposition; then it is clear that in Hegel reason produces internal movement by itself through a kind of unrest; however, we have already seen that this is not possible if there is no object present right in front of me. What could be the source for that internal movement of reason, that unrest that leads it to overcome the dialectical stages of its progressive determinations? With his understanding man is here-and-now present among things, he is understanding just as much as he is seeing with his eyes and hearing with his ears. Reason is something different, it is something that *goes towards*; it is a going, progression. Kant had clearly perceived something of this problem when he said that we would have to determine what was the interest that motivated reason to transcend understanding. Whether this is an interest or not—we shall refer to it further on—what is certain is that reason is engaged in a progression towards an object. This is not simply something in which one *is*, but something in which one *moves* by oneself "towards" (for the moment, we put aside the question of what objective reason is). Hence, reason is essentially, intrinsically, and constitutively a *quaerens* thinking, a thinking that searches; reason is not a conceptualizing thinking (*begreiffendes Denken*), but a *seeking* intelligence.[3] This means that reason does not rest upon itself, and the least that can be said is that it rests upon intelligence.

This brings us to the second determination, *intellectus*. What is the *intellectus*?

Classical philosophy always understood that it was an *intellectus concipiens*, something that conceives ideas. The senses give us things and the intelligence (knowing) elaborates, builds or conceives ideas about them. Although that may be correct, it seems insufficient to me, for at least two reasons. {327}

In the first place, it assumes that conceiving is something like passing the intelligence like a mirror before reality, and then some concepts are obtained, analogous to the way the eyes perceive some colors or the ears perceive some sounds. But that is not the case. Concepts, even the most rudimentary, are something that man has searched for and continues to conquer; in other words, they are the precipitate and the sediment of that "seeking" reason, of that "seeking" intelligence in its own *intellectus*. The concept is not something primary, some sort of gift given for intellective knowing,[4] but one of the means that reason has to discover things. We can definitely say that mankind has always used concepts, even without knowing it. However, it is a long way from what a concept was in the era of Hammurabi to our confidence in rational concepts and the continual progression therein that has predominated in the world since the Greek era. In other words, conceptualization is one of the ways which reason cleverly devises to search for things with its "seeking" function.

Secondly, we could say that at the very least there is one concept not forged by reason, viz. the concept of being, the concept *quid est*. But this is a great problem. Since Aristotle's time being has become problematic; it needed the operation of νοῦς, it was necessary to capture in some way what being *is*, since it is not something immediately given and upon which we can easily build a philosophical speculation. This forces us to reconsider the problem of *intellectus* and refer it to the problem of νοῦς.

Reason does not rest upon itself, but upon a conceptualizing intelligence; therefore, upon an *intelligence*. Intelligence, *qua* conceptualizing, rests upon an intelligence that does not have to be necessarily conceptualizing, but {328} as Aristotle would say, is simply the apprehension of entity by νοῦς; and the essential part of νοῦς, as Aristotle tells us, is the λόγος, which tells us what is being apprehended. Reason essentially remits to conceptualization, which in turn, remits to intelligence.

II. *Sensibility*

Though it might appear that we have succeeded in revealing the problem, in reality we have only begun to do so. If objects were not in front of us, nothing that happens within the process of reason would be able to take place. But from where do objects come in order to be present before us? We are told that it is from the senses, which are what give us things, and afterwards, the *intellectus* starts running its *conceptio*, its *ratio*. That is the picture. So the moment that intelligence becomes a problem, *eo ipso* and congenerically sensibility also becomes a problem, since it is that through which things are given. Therefore it will be necessary to start from this convergence between sensibility and intelligence in order to see in what the radical problem consists, the problem that in my opinion underlies the whole of metaphysics.

§2

THE IDEA OF SENTIENT INTELLIGENCE

Let us start by recalling that things are given to us in sensibility. This is a theory that permeates the history of philosophy at
least since Plato's time (perhaps before) until Hegel. According to
this theory, things are "given" to us in sensibility and what intelligence does is to "conceive" them. Hegel would say that what intelligence does is to engender them conceptually. From my own
point of view I would prefer to say that what intelligence does is to
search for them. At any rate, whatever intelligence does requires
that things first be given to it. There can be no objection to this as
long as we are told what sensing is and what is given in that
sensing. That is the question.

I. *Sensing and that which is given in sensing*

The idea of sensing, the function of sensing, has been sub-
sumed throughout the history of philosophy under two concepts.
One or the other has tended to dominate throughout that history.
These two concepts are *intuition* and *impression*.

On one hand, sensing is said to be an intuition, the first and
elemental intuition with which things are given to us; this is *intueri*, to see. It is undeniable that we have this in sensation, understanding by it the act of αἴσθησις, the act of sensing, and not
the psychological meaning that *intueri* also has. Though indubi-
tably {330} this moment of intuition exists, is it useful to characterize what we want to say, viz. that things are given to us in
sensing, in sensibility? Not at all. We are quite ignoring what is
essential to the question, which is what I am here-and-now seeing, what I am here-and-now seeing sensibly. In what does sensing consist? By constant reference to sensible perception as an
intuition, we end up considering it as some kind of diminutive
knowledge, with respect to which intelligence contains the whole
concept. So this view presents full intellection as riding on top of
that sensation. Is that true? Is sensing a kind of lower degree of
intellection? I do not refer here to what Leibniz had in mind when
he saw in sensibility a confused intellection, but to something
much more trivial and radical. If sensation were to contain nothing more than intuition, it would not be of much concern to phi-

losophy. Instead it would be the most modest and trivial type of knowledge, and would be placed among the many types of knowledge. However, just to perceive is by itself not the same as to know, nor is it the same as to know intellectually.

Next we can ponder what Kant would say, viz. that this intuition gives us something, which is precisely the impression, the affection (*Eindruck*). This is the second concept, provided that we are told what that "impression" is. Can we characterize sensibility by saying it is purely and simply intuition as impressed? It all depends on what is meant by "impression." Is it true that impression is what the empiricists said, which Kant repeats, taking it as the starting point for his whole philosophy of *Transcendental Aesthetics*, namely, that impression is something that affects the subject? If it were so, we could well ask how Kant manages to arrange them in order to put together the whole set of categories such that some affections, which are no more than affections in an impression, are able to constitute the world of objects with {331} which man lives in his daily life and upon which science itself is built. This would be rather difficult to explain. Because impression is not only to be affected, but also to be affected in such a way that in it the terminus (that which affects me) becomes present to me, i.e., the "otherness" becomes present to me. With the sensation of heat I also have present, in the form of a thermal affection, the heat of the object that affects me. There is, therefore, this second moment, the moment of otherness, by virtue of which the impression is not just to be affected, but is also to be affected or presented with something other. Only when this being affected by presenting the otherness assumes intuitive form can we talk about sensing. And this requires that we reach an agreement about what the otherness that impression presents to us is.

Here begins the major difficulty of the problem. Undoubtedly, what is presented to me is something like this table, this microphone, this glass of water; in other words, that which is presented is a content. This is undeniably true; but with all the psychological and physiological differences proper to the case, a dog would also be able to see this table more or less the way I see it. Is my perception of the table the same as that of the dog? From the point of view of content, it might be (at any rate, let us not get into that problem). What occurs, however, is that no content is present in sensibility unless it is present in a previous mode of confronting the thing. In the animal always, and in man in ninety-nine percent of the cases, the living being is confronting the otherness present in its impressions in a very concrete way, as *stimulation*, i.e., in the form of stimulation.[5] Pure sensing, both for animals and for humans insofar as they share that condition, apprehends the *otherness* that the stimulus is in an impression. The dog apprehends the stick of his owner, the face of his owner, but apprehends them as one {332} more stimulus, as an objective sign of the reactions he can have.

Is this the case with human sensibility? We said that in ninety-nine percent of the cases it is evidently so. A human being has millions of cells in its organism, all of which are stimulated. If a human had to perform a function such as the one we are going to describe below concerning the synaptic transmission of a neuron in the human body, the human species would not have been able to appear on Earth. Nonetheless, in some minuscule zone proper to some dimensions of the sensory receptors, it is not the case that the human being apprehends the stimuli as *stimuli*, but apprehends them as stimulating *realities*. Thus, stimulation and reality are two *formalities* through which things are apprehended. And because each human obviously can perceive a stimulus in this way, it is perceived as a *real* stimulus—something that does not happen with the animals that purely and simply are affected by the stimulation and react to it.

To this moment of otherness, which is proper and specific to humans, I have given the name *impression of reality*. I have spoken of *impression of reality*, not to indicate that there are two impressions (one for content and another for reality), but to denominate *a potiori* the totality of the impression of otherness, which is presented to us in a sensible impression. In that otherness, not only are color, sound, temperature, etc., present to us, but so are the colored reality, the sonorous reality, and the thermal reality.

This is the common deficiency of both empiricist philosophy and Kant's philosophy. By talking to us only about being affected, empiricist philosophy sought to critique what substance and causality are; and if we {333} refer exclusively to what sensible impressions give us *qua* affectations of the subject, that criticism might be justified. But the truth of the matter is that sensible impressions present *otherness* to us in the form of reality. And this totally changes the problem. Then it is not true what Kant says when he affirms that sensibility primarily gives us a multiplicity destined to be unified by the "I think." On the contrary, the truth of the matter is that *the first thing that sensibility gives us is reality.* "Reality" does not mean here thing-in-itself as opposed to "phenomenon," as Kant claimed, but an intrinsic and elementary characteristic of all sensible perceptions.

Nevertheless, this makes it necessary to ask an unavoidable question, namely, what is intelligence? Does it really perform the act of intellection on the objects given this way?

II. *The nature of intellection*

Starting with Aristotle philosophy has always understood that to know intellectively is, formally, to conceive and to judge. It is not false to say that intelligence conceives and judges, or even to say that *only* intelligence conceives and judges. But the question we are asking is different: *is to know intellectively, though our intelligence, formally to conceive and judge?* This is more than problematic, because—I will mention it here in a somewhat dogmatic way in order not to plunge into a detailed discussion—the formal and radical function of intelligence consists in *apprehending things as realities*, in the form of reality.

Indeed, to apprehend reality is the *elementary* act of intellection. We conceive and judge how things are in reality; but to apprehend them as reality, to deal with them as reality, is just what is proper to intelligence, {334} its *elementary* act. In addition, it is an *exclusive* act of intelligence. Sensibility moves in the order of stimuli; regardless of how complicated these stimuli may be, they can never produce one whit of what we call "reality." But also, this is the *radical* act of intelligence. By a process of which brevity here precludes a full analysis, intelligence begins to function when a human being has to suspend its autonomous reactions in the order of pure stimulations. That is the moment when the function I call "to become aware of reality" begins to act, which is the dawn of intelligence. Intelligence intervenes with its radical act, its elementary and exclusive act, by way of apprehending reality as reality.

What is proper to intelligence is not to conceive and judge, but to deal with things as reality, to apprehend them as reality. Only then it can also lead to conceiving and to judging

III. *Sentient intelligence*[6]

The difficulty is based squarely on the fact that here something ambiguous and obscure appears. When I mentioned sensibility, I affirmed that the sensibility of humans senses things in the form of reality, which is true. We not only sense heat, temperature, colors or humidity, but also sense their own characteristic of reality. From my perspective, it is absolutely essential to underline this fact in the phenomenon of sensing. A human being does not simply sense real *things*, but also formally senses their *character of reality*. Indeed, we have just seen that this is the very thing that intelligence does. What happens here is that pure sensing senses pure stimulations {335} (such is the case in the animal and nearly all the time with the human organism); but in certain zones of the human receptors the human being senses the reality, senses the characteristic of reality of things. Therefore, this can only mean that intelligence is not something separated and cut off from sensing; and in turn, human sensing is not separated and cut off from intelligence. There is only one act, the act of *sentient intellection*. What is sentient intelligence?

1. Its essential structure

Sentient intellection does not consist in the fact, quite trivial since the time of Aristotle, that intelligence and the senses have the same object. This is because Aristotle and his followers claimed that with respect to this object there are *two* acts, one of sensing and the other of intelligence or knowing. To me this appears rather problematic. Is it true that two acts exist, one of sensing and the other of intelligence or knowing?

We might recall that Kant just touched lightly on this problem when he discussed the problem of the synthesis of the categorial and the phenomenal. But Kant's synthesis is an objective synthesis of the categorial and the phenomenal. That is not the case with my concept of sentient intelligence. It is not an objective synthesis, a synthesis with respect to objective truth. It is not really *any* type of "synthesis". It is a *unity in the act itself*. There is only one act of sentient intelligence, and therefore, we do not have one complete act of sensing plus another complete act of intelligence, but only a single unified act. Because of this, the dualism that has dominated the history of philosophy since Plato needs to be overcome—not because there is no {336} duality between the senses and intelligence, but because that duality refers to the specific *contents* of intelligence and of sensing, which is quite a different matter. Moreover, in order to apprehend reality, there are not two acts, but only one act, an act that is uniquely and exclusively the act of impression of reality.

This act of impression of reality considered as *impression* is sensible; considered as being *of reality* it is intellective. In this unitary act there are two characteristics we must set forth.

Husserl's philosophy was grounded upon the idea of intentionality. But sentient intellection is not primarily intentional; it does not consist in addressing things intentionally. Intelligence taken *simpliciter*, merely as sentient intelligence—and not even sentient—is purely and simply "actualization" of what has been intellectualized.

What do we understand here by "actualization"? One might think that this is what Aristotle said when he affirmed that ἐπιστήμε and ἐπιστητόν are ταυτόν (the same) in the act of knowing. I will not say that this is false, but it is not that to which I am referring. This is because in that sameness Aristotle understands the ἐντελέχεια as an act, the act of a potency, the potency of man to know intellectively or to sense, and if you will, the capacity of things to be known. When talking about actuality I do not refer to the "act" of potency, but simply to "actuality," as when we say that the news of a story has great actuality in a society or at a particular moment. This is not the case with the act of potency, but rather of that characteristic by virtue of which we say of something that it has actuality, that it is in everyone's mind. The essence of the intellective act {337} is purely and simply actualization. The invocation of all of the other characteristics, whether ἐντελέχεια or anything else, is an explanation of that primary characteristic of elemental actuality, without which all the others would be left without solid foundation.

There is a question that immediately arises: can we say, for example, that the apprehension of heat is a pure actualization? After all, how can it be denied that the temperature I perceive depends in great measure on my conditions, on the temperature of my own body and many other circumstances? Two persons that touch or feel the same object can sense it in a different thermal form; so how can that be pure actualization? This is a critical point, because often it is claimed that secondary qualities are not real. What this means is that if I leave the room, things probably have no color, but do have a stream of photons or electromagnetic waves of a certain amplitude emanating from them. Probably this is true, but it is a separate question.

To resolve the question at hand, note that to know an object and the reality known in it is not simply to know what a thing is when it is not present to me, but what it is while it is here-and-now present to me. In other words, there are different "levels" of reality. Here we insist that in the apparently most subjective and most physiologically conditioned act, as sensation can be, in the measure that the sensation is produced, and precisely *at that level of sensation*, what becomes present to me is real. To pass from the reality of color or temperature to that which is the reality of thermal bodies or colored bodies, when they fall outside the level of perception, is, among other things, the level of science. And though it may seem {338} scandalous—and that scandal for me is a real scandal in philosophy—we must emphasize that *in the order of perception that which is perceived has reality immediately, but only with respect to the act I am performing.* This book has this color, *qua* color, precisely when I perceive it. One might argue that there can be illusions; but these illusions always refer to something real. A complete scientific theory will have to explain how illusions are produced; but illusion does not consist in having *no* object, but that the object appears to me in a different way than to someone else, and above all, different from the condition of the object when it is not present in any perception. But that is a different matter.

When Schopenhauer happily told us that if we had green eyeglasses we would see the whole world as green, he was right. But that is a real phenomenon: the green color of some eyeglasses and the chromatic conditions of that perception are perfectly real. The error would consist in affirming that they are real *independently of the eyeglasses and the eyes*—something I do not claim at all. The characteristic of reality is an intrinsic formality of what is perceived, and to pass from the level of immediate reality in the perceptive act to deeper levels—what things would be when man has no perception of them—demands the long and arduous road of science.

Therefore, sentient intellection is pure and simple actualization. Regardless of the type of processes that may be involved in the production of a perception, they are mechanisms required for us to have an actualization, to have an act of sentient intellection.

Nevertheless, in that actualization the object does not acquire something in the sense of acquiring a new property. It only acquires {339} actuality. One thing that is very actual—for example, man's trip to the Moon—does not acquire any new properties by the mere fact of being actual. But there is a certain dualism between what a thing really is and the dimension of actuality it has when it is before the mind that intellectively knows it, and insofar as that mind intellectively knows it sentiently. That duality is what makes us say that in the act of sentient intellection it is not purely and simply naked reality there.

Insofar as reality is actualized, that actualization constitutes its radical, formal and original truth. Truth is not primarily the conformity of thought with things, nor is it an ontological truth in the sense of conformity of things with the understanding, for example, with the divine intellect. It is not even, as Heidegger claimed, a mere unveiling. The truth is primarily the presentation of reality, the actualization of a reality precisely in its formal and constitutive dimension of reality. This is *real truth*, "real" because it refers to the thing *qua* real, and that is the way through which truth will have to enter, one way or another, into the transcendental order. It will never do it through conceptual means.

This is a unitary act. And that means that we can describe it using two facets, the sensible and the intellective. With respect to the sensible we have to say that every sensibility, every sensible perception, in one form or another, is intellective since in it *reality* is sensed. Conversely, we will have to say that any intellective act that apprehends reality *apprehends* something, i.e., apprehends it in a sentient way. By the first way, the act of sentient intellection

unveils to us sensing as intellective sensing. By the second, it unveils to us intellection as sentient intellection. Let us reflect, if
only {340} for a moment, on the two facets, in order to clarify the
unity of the constitutive act.

Consider intellective sensing. The sense of touch, for example,
involves the naked presence of a thing; touch is not simply to
sense the roughness or smoothness of a surface, but rather touch
gives us in a way that is, if you will, unrepresentative, without
any idea, without εἶδος, the naked reality of a thing. St. John of
the Cross pointed out long ago that God is present in the soul in
a kind of call, without manifesting what that call is in itself. That
is the naked presence of reality. But inasmuch as it is the presence of *reality* we are dealing with intellective sensing.

There is another way, which has fared better in the history of
philosophy. It is the way that something can be present to us as
reality in its own and internal figure, what a Greek would call the
intrinsic and constitutive εἶδος of it. Through vision things themselves are present by their εἶδος.

Through hearing we have something different. Obviously,
there is an immediate presence connected with sound. But it is
always present to us (at least, in a very small psychological elaboration) as sonority of something, something that is not present in
the sound itself; and this is precisely the feature that distinguishes it from sight. In vision I have the figure, and by it I have
the very thing with its figure, but in hearing I perceive something
that belongs to the thing itself, that is real, but the thing is not
present in hearing since it only notifies me that it is there. That is
precisely reality *by announcement* (or *notification*).

Synesthesia[7] is the form of apprehending reality by intimacy,
of apprehending it intimately.

Of course, there are other senses, for example, the sense of
orientation and equilibrium, kinesthesia. We are going to take
them all together. In these senses reality is present to me {341} in
several different forms; it is present to me in an act of "going towards" something, in "tension-towards." Definitely, this is essential for our problem. One of the great prejudices weighing on philosophy has been to think that what is essential to a perception is
to have the object "right in front" of me. Yet, there are perceptions
that exist *as towards*, as pure direction, and in which the object
is not right there in front of me. It is not that I can arbitrarily perform an act of going "towards" something, but that reality itself is
reality in its form of "towards." And if I proceed towards it, it is
because reality as such takes me "towards" its deeper dimensions. I do not go towards reality, but sense "reality-as-towards."

Therefore, we have naked presence, figure, announcement, interiority, and towards, which are the ways or modes of intellective sensing because they are modes of how reality is sensed in each of these types of sensing.

We reach the same conclusion if we approach the problem with respect to the process of knowing, which I have described as *sentient intelligence*. Intelligence apprehends reality, not in a conceptive manner, but in a sentient manner. In the case of touch, intelligence is *groping*. In the case of sight it is usually assumed that intelligence apprehends things as something that is right in front of me, what has been called *representation*; but it is completely wrong that *to intellectualize* is *to represent*, although human beings may legitimately have representations. When I intellectualize in the mode of hearing, I perceive real things as announcement, i.e., as *manifestation*. Something similar can be said in the case of interiorization proper to the act of synesthesia, that to intellectualize is to apprehend something intimately, and above all in the manner of "towards." It is absolutely false that the primary form in which intelligence {342} has and searches for things is by having them right in front of it (*re-praesentare*); the majority of times reality is present to me in the form of direction, in the form of "towards". And this is essential for our problem.

These modes of reality are not simply juxtaposed. Sentient intelligence and intellective sensing are, with all their multiplicity, manifestations of a single phenomenon, namely, the mode of apprehension of reality. This is why the multiplicity of senses and the multiplicity of modes in which the real becomes present to us are not—as Kant claims—a base upon which we synthetically realize the operation of the "I think" by which we conceive, intellectualize and judge. There is no such synthesis. It is just the opposite: the senses are present to us as *analyzers* of that primary unity in which our turning to reality as such consists. As a consequence of this the different modes intrinsically overlap among themselves. We are not going to review each of the modes, but will refer to just one of them, which is essential for us, the "towards." Reality in the mode of "towards" overlaps with reality in all the other modes of presence. The consequences of this are important since nothing is perceived purely and simply as something that is right in front of me, even in the case of sight, but rather as something perceived "as towards." In this case the "towards" is just intellection "towards" what is in the interior of what is seen, towards its interior. Also, there is nothing that can be perceived as mere sound, since sound, as something "open" through the "towards," takes us towards the sonorous thing. We always encounter this turning of the intelligence towards something that is beyond what is immediately present, not as something added to the presentation of the real, but as something constitutive of the very way in which reality is present. Nothing is present to us in its pure presentability, {343} but everything is present to us in a dimension of and bordered with reality "as towards".

2. Intelligence and reason

And thus, intelligence situated as "towards" is just our reason. From this it follows that sentient intelligence is the dawn of reason. It is the dawn of reason because reason is search; it is to go towards. Intelligence does not go towards things because it decides to search for them; just the opposite: intelligence decides to search for them because it is driven by reality in the mode of "towards." That is why Kant says that in contrast to the speculative interest that moves reason, he needs to search for an interest founded on practical reason, a practical or pragmatic interest. For this he always starts from the supposition that we are dealing with an "interest," With something, therefore, that is so to speak "injected" into intelligence and reason. This is not true. It is the mode of presentation of reality that inexorably carries with it the fact that intelligence not only apprehends the content of what is immediately given, but goes to what is present in the form of reality. And it may also go "towards" whatever there is in the depth of all that reality. Intelligence does not go "towards" something because of any interest on its part, but rather that the intellectualized reality, by its very mode of presentation, places intelligence here-and-now in a situation for searching.

In this going "towards" the object, in this "searching," in this *intellectus quaerens* that goes towards the object, reason does many things; it actually conceives how things are constituted, it has devised the procedure of the abstract concepts whose efficacy cannot be denied, etc. But this is not the only thing it does because, when all is said and done, intelligence needs {344} to confront everything it has searched for with the reality that is immediately and primarily present. At that moment things confirm our reasoning or refute it.

Here is where objective reason appears. Reason, our reasoning, which until now has not been presented except as a searching, is now presented to us as a candidate for things to approve or reject. Contrary what Hegel claims, the primary character of reason is not objective reason, but just the opposite. Objective reason depends on things in order to be accepted or rejected. Objective reason is not Hegel's *concept*; it is *things confirming our reasoning*.

Thus, truth acquires a new and appreciably different character. It is not simply *real truth*, i.e., the immediate presence of a reality merely actualized in the intellective act, but something like the truth of an "encounter." Here is where we will be able to say if this encounter is *conformitas intellectus cum re* or *conformitas rei cum intellectu divino*; but the first thing is that encounter. Intellectual fruition is the satisfaction of that truthful encounter with things *in* their already-presented reality, that of real truth.

IV. Transcendental reason and the problem of metaphysics

When, within this structure, reason takes us by way of the impression of reality—and not simply by way of the specific contents that this reality offers to us—then sentient intelligence constitutes the dawn, not only of reason in general, but of a very concrete form of reason, viz. speculative reason or transcendental reason. {345}

The transcendental is purely and simply the character of reality. The moment of impression of reality, proper to every sensation and perception, is transcendental, *a)* because it is above or transcends the specific content in which it is presented to us; *b)* in addition, because the moment of "towards," which envelops every sensible perception, takes us not only to other *things*, but also to other *dimensions* of reality itself. And just because of that character of reality, at least in principle it makes it possible for reason to be able to take in all other things. That is transcendental reason. I say "transcendental" because it is something that affects the impression of reality, and also because it takes us to the unitary and primary totality of the real. Due to this, the transcendental order is not a problem of concepts, subjective or objective, but is a physical moment of reality, as "formal" as anyone may wish, but actually real in them.

Along these lines of the transcendental, *questing* reason is as problematic as the character of reality itself. This "problem" should be explained, but here I only intended to introduce it and put it in context. We sought to show that, as a primary and radical problem, the history of metaphysics leads us to the problem of what intellection is. And in my view, this problem is about sentient intellection. It is in sentient intellection that philosophical thinking should be *anchored*, where the characteristics of the transcendental order should be *expounded*, and where the concepts that constitute the system of metaphysics should be *measured*. Because of this, sentient intelligence is the primary element in which transcendental consideration of the world and reality is to be found.

---

[1] [We have translated Zubiri's term *inteligencia* here as "knowing," since the literal translation "intelligence" would be a bit misleading due to its

connotative meaning of Intelligence Quotient (IQ). Zubiri is referring to the entire process of human knowing, which involves more than what is usually understood by "epistemology" in English. In *Sentient Intelligence*, Zubiri's term for that process is translated as "intellective knowing" to make clear its components of knowing and intelligence. In particular, for Zubiri, the process of knowing and the object of knowing are inseparable. Zubiri's philosophy of human knowing (and related metaphysics) is sketched in this chapter, in connection with the philosophical problems and the theme of the transcendental discussed in the book. The reader should bear in mind that "knowing" is embedded in that broader context.—trans.].

2 [The mean of Zubiri's expression *de derecho*, "by right" or "by law" in this context is unclear.—trans.].

3 [Zubiri Spanish neologism *"quaerente"* from Lt. *quaerens*, equivalent to *questing*.—trans.].

4 [The expression "intellective knowing" is the best rendering of the Spanish *inteligir*, from the Latin *inteligere*, which cannot be translated as "to intelligence" in English since we do not use "intelligence" as a verb.—trans.].

5 [Zubiri neologism from *estímulo*, stimulus.—trans.].

6 [Zubiri here briefly outlines his philosophy of sentient intelligence, which he developed at great length in his three volume magnum opus, *Inteligencia sentiente* (Madrid: 1980-82), published as one volume in English, Sentient Intelligence, tr. by Thomas Fowler, Washington, Xavier Zubiri Foundation of North America, 1999.—trans.].

7 [Spanish *cenesthesia*, general sensation of the body caused by the functioning of the internal organs.—trans.].

Index

Plato, 9, 25, 30, 32-37, 39, 44,
   55, 60, 79, 185, 190-192,
   220, 223, 227.
Possible, 12-13, 21, 32, 57, 61,
   72, 88, 95, 117, 119-120,
   122, 131, 133-134, 136-139,
   144, 146-148, 154, 157, 160,
   162, 164, 178-179, 196, 201,
   219-220, 233.
Potency, 108, 227-228.
Pre-Socratic, 28.
Proclus, 67.
Prime matter, 22, 40.
Protagoras, 35.
Psychology, 118, 126, 146, 148.

Q

quaerens, 232.
Quiddity, 60, 62, 75, 120.
quidditas, 61.

R

Rational, 30, 37, 73, 110, 112,
   113, 118, 121, 126, 127, 137,
   163, 169, 170, 211, 221.
Rationalism, 97, 111, 119, 149,
   164.
Reality, 9, 11, 22, 28-33, 36-45,
   47, 49-51, 54-55, 59-60, 66-
   70, 72, 76, 78-79, 83, 89-91,
   94-97, 106-109, 113, 115,
   120-121, 128, 131, 133, 137,
   143, 147-162, 168, 172-176,
   180-190, 195-200, 203-205,
   208-209, 211, 221, 225-233.
Reason, 14, 16, 63, 67, 69, 73,
   94-97, 99, 110-114, 117-123,
   125-133, 135-137, 140-144,
   147-164, 168-198, 201-204,
   207-212, 219-222, 232-233.

S

Sartre, Jean-Paul, 22.
Scheler, Max, 59.
Schelling,   Friedrich   Wilhelm

Joseph, 181, 184.
Scholastic, 57, 63.
Schopenhauer,
Science, 13, 18-19, 41, 52-53,
   55-56, 69, 84-86, 94, 109,
   116, 118-119.
Sentient Intelligence, 80n, 150,
   165n, 223-233.
Soul, 14, 78, 147-148, 156-160,
   205, 230.
Space, 32, 116, 144-145, 148,
   150, 152-156, 163, 202.
Species, 22, 57-58, 61, 126,
   209, 220, 225.
Spinoza, Baruch, 204, 211.
Suárez, Francisco, 75, 106-108,
   118, 122, 137, 174, 196.
Substance, 39-42, 47-48, 51,
   53-58, 64,
Summum Ens, 83.

T

Thales, 196.
Theophrastus, 35.
Tielhard de Chardin, 117.
Transubstantiation, 117.
Truth, 16-17, 29, 35-37, 43-44,
   61-62, 67, 70, 77-79, 85-99,
   103-104, 110-113, 117-119,
   121-122, 133-134, 137-138,
   140, 148-150, 156, 162, 169-
   180, 183-187, 189, 196, 210,
   227, 229, 232-233.

V

Victorinus, 70.

W

Wolff, Christian, 118, 125-126,
   134, 164.

Z

Zeno, 190.